Pissarides, Christopher A.

Labour market adjustment

DATE DUE

Labour market adjustment

Labour market adjustment

Microeconomic foundations of short-run neoclassical and Keynesian dynamics

CHRISTOPHER A. PISSARIDES
LONDON SCHOOL OF ECONOMICS

CAMBRIDGE UNIVERSITY PRESS
CAMBRIDGE
LONDON · NEW YORK · MELBOURNE

Published by the Syndics of the Cambridge University Press
The Pitt Building, Trumpington Street, Cambridge CB2 1RP
Bentley House, 200 Euston Road, London NW1 2DB
32 East 57th Street, New York, NY 10022, USA
296 Beaconsfield Parade, Middle Park, Melbourne 3206, Australia

Library of Congress catalogue card number: 75-21035

ISBN 0 521 21064 X

First published 1976

Photoset and printed in Malta by Interprint (Malta) Ltd

To my Parents

Contents

Preface

The body of economic theory which deals with the problems of disequilibrium trading in general, and those of inflation, unemployment and monetary exchange in particular, has witnessed a revolution in the last decade or so. Superficially the 'revolutionary' idea appears to be the relaxation of the assumption of perfect information which runs through the work of neoclassical economists – hardly a revolution if one reminds oneself of work done in the 1930s by Knight, Hicks, Robbins, Hayek, Keynes and many others. However, it is only when we carry the implications of the relaxation of this assumption one step further that we really get to the heart of a revolution, a step which in the 1930s appeared to elude economists. Ironically it was none other than the confusion and controversy brought about by the work of one of the greatest believers in the problems of uncertainty, John Maynard Keynes, that obscured the issues and led economists away from the problems raised by the existence of imperfect knowledge and into the world of complete certainty.

Today, after four decades of controversy, the natural step to take appears obvious. Stated briefly, imperfect information implies exchange at disequilibrium prices, and exchange at disequilibrium prices implies that *ex post* the system is never the same as *ex ante*. Expectations are formed and revised as the system reveals additional information and outdates that already known. The door to the theory of disequilibrium trading sequences, the existence of money as a medium that people *want* to hold, and the simultaneous existence of inflation, unemployment and diverse views about the future is open. The implications for modern macroeconomic theory in the first instance, but also for micro and general equilibrium theory, are still being hotly debated.

If we go back to the 1930s we shall probably find shy steps in this direction, with the names of Keynes and Hicks particularly outstanding. But for the recent systematic work in the area we are more indebted to a younger generation of economists, whose most prominent members are Stigler, Alchian, Phelps, Clower and Leijonhufvud. It is with the problems raised by this group of economists that this book deals, but it tries to avoid as far as possible controversies about the approaches of different schools of thought, and mathematical arguments about the existence and stability of static or dynamic solutions. Its main objective is to develop a general framework based on individual optimization, within which it is possible to analyse the interaction of markets in disequilibrium. As a first step towards this end it considers optimal firm and household behaviour in a sequence of labour and commodity markets when the former is out of Walrasian equilibrium. Commodity markets are always assumed to be in Hicksian temporary equilibrium.

The problems we attempt to analyse lie at the very heart of economics, the central question running through the book being: how does the market co-ordinate its activities and operate over time when households and firms engage in trading on the basis of expectations formed on incomplete knowledge? The framework developed in the main part of the book is shown to be suitable for the analysis of problems related to disequilibrium trading, expectations, inflation, unemployment and other more traditional problems of macroeconomics in general and labour economics in particular. Most of the traditional results concerning individual behaviour are shown to hold within the framework of the model, whereas other questions, about which the traditional model was very silent, come to the forefront.

My interest in the problems of imperfect information and disequilibrium trading date back to the days when as a student at the University of Essex I came under the influence of the theories that were being discussed by visiting economists at the time, in particular Professors R. W. Clower, F. P. R. Brechling, D. T. Mortensen and others in their environment. However, the central ideas of this book were written at the London School of Economics as a PhD thesis, entitled *Individual Behaviour in Markets with Imperfect Information*. The supervisor of studies during that period was Professor M. Morishima, who helped me shape my initial thoughts on the subject and very skilfully demonstrated the powers and limitations of the neoclassical model, enabling me in this way to develop the new ideas by paying due respect to the continuity of the subject. I am very grateful for his assistance and also for discussions with Professor J. Black, Dr D. Metcalf and Dr J. M. Ostroy. Professor Black has read the entire final draft of the book and corrected numerous errors. Any remaining errors are, of course, my own.

Finally, I am very indebted to my wife, not only for her encouragement during the writing of the book, but also for her valuable assistance in the preparation of the final draft of the book.

C. A. P.

I
Introduction

The adjustment problem

Economics studies the behaviour of systems which consist of individuals whose desires cannot be satiated by available resources. Systematic work on specific problems of economics began very early, but it was not until the second half of the nineteenth century that the extensions, modifications, and changes in emphasis brought to the original doctrines produced the first elements of an 'economic science'. The turning point in the early development of economics, which marked the transition from classical to neoclassical economics, appears to be the independent discovery by Menger, Jevons and Walras that the most important concepts of classical economics could be expressed in terms of the theory of 'incremental values'. Once it was realized that what mattered for economic decisions was 'incremental' values, and not 'total' magnitudes, the theory of the calculus and the methods of mechanics were there to be used – in precisely the same form as they had been used for centuries by physicists. The potential significance of this discovery was beyond even some of the best-known neoclassics.[1] Nevertheless, economics in the latter part of the nineteenth century put forward claims for a place in the junior ranks of the world of science – with undisputed success.

If one tries to single out a principle which underlies all major work in economics from early times to the present, one is likely to work one's way through to the neoclassics probably undecided, but pause there and pick up the principle. One would then discover that it was implicit in the classics, but explicit since the neoclassics; that it brings the analysis of the classics, the neoclassics, the Marxists and the Keynesians under one umbrella; and that it distinguishes economics

[1] Marshall is the best-known sceptic. See the preface to the first edition of the *Principles*, pp. viii–ix. Smolinski (1973) has recently argued that Marx was much more sympathetic to the use of mathematical methods in economics than commonly believed.

from the other sciences. To quote Marshall (1920, p. 21), '*economists study the actions of individuals, but study them in relation to social rather than individual life*' [my italic].

Thus the economist is primarily interested in the conduct of a group of people, and the behaviour of the markets which consist of such groups. This group may be the whole world; it may be an open economy; a closed economy; a district; or even an industrial group. It is the level to which a theory refers in this scale that distinguishes what appears to be the greatest division in our subject, that between micro- and macroeconomics. But one level which never interests us for its own sake is the level of the individual. To quote Marshall again, economists 'concern themselves but little with personal peculiarities of temper and character' (p. 21). For this reason we usually examine the behaviour of a 'typical', or an 'average', individual with a view to examining the behaviour of a group and/or a market which consists of such 'typical' individuals.

In our study of the typical individual we usually take great pains to explain his behaviour. In principle the method by which we explain individual behaviour is simple: we normally impose some standards of consistency which must be satisfied by the actions of an individual, and then examine his behaviour given these standards of consistency and the environment within which he operates. The standards of consistency we usually impose are that the typical individual seeks always to maximize his own well-being. He observes external events and the actions of others via their influence on variables which affect his own well-being, and reacts to them in such a way as to maximize his utility given those values of the variables which he observes.

The neoclassics, who first formulated this idea precisely, believed firmly that all the actions of an individual which had relevance to economic life were motivated by self-interest. Economic forces, in their turn, were considered of primary importance in shaping the course of society over time; so the belief of early economists – those of the last generation included more often than not – was that the study of economics based on the assumption of the pursuit of self-interest could provide the clue to an understanding of the future of industrial society. Marshall makes the point on the opening page of his *Principles*, and attributes competition and collective ownership alike to the 'free choice by each individual of that line of conduct which after careful deliberation seems to him the best suited for attaining his ends' (p. 5). The optimism that runs through the *Principles* as to the ultimate elimination of poverty is typical of neoclassical economics. It is in sharp contrast to Marxian and Keynesian doctrine, the former claiming that nothing can stop the destruction of a society which consists of such self-interested individuals, whereas the latter claims that with help from the central authority capitalism could be saved, and the neoclassical equilibrium state attained. The foundation, however, is common to all: individuals always choose that course of action which they think promotes their own well-being, given external events and the actions of others.

There is only one major exception to this general underlying principle. The literature which deals with the *adjustment* to an equilibrium position does not discuss the process of individual decision-making out of equilibrium, and so it does not obtain the dynamic process that individual optimization would imply for the system as a whole.[2] Instead, it takes a final equilibrium position – in most cases the neoclassical equilibrium – and obtains sufficient conditions on excess demand functions for the stability of that equilibrium. The sufficient conditions known to-date are mathematical restrictions on the set of excess demand functions, and bear little or no relation to *economic* restrictions. In other words, no known, reasonable economic behaviour by optimizing individuals has been shown to lead to the restrictions needed for the stability of neoclassical equilibrium – and given the state of the arts such demonstration does not appear to be tenable. Hicks's fears that this 'mechanical' approach to adjustment may not refer back to the economic problem, as formulated by Marshall and his contemporaries, appears to be justified, and the need for an *economic* theory of adjustment, which does depend on the actions of optimizing individuals, is as great as ever. It is to this problem that we shall address ourselves in this volume.[3]

[2] The authors commonly cited as pioneering observers of this fact are Koopmans (1957, pp. 178–83) and Arrow (1959). However, Hicks noted this fact and expressed some unease as long ago as 1946, soon after the modern formulation of the 'mechanical' adjustment theory by Samuelson. On the closing page of the 2nd edition of *Value and Capital* he noted: 'But for the understanding of the economic system we need something more, something which does refer back, in the last resort, to the behaviour of people and the motives of their conduct.' For a more extensive discussion of this and other methodological issues see, in addition to the above, the first part of Hicks (1965).

[3] The pioneer of the 'mechanical' approach to adjustment is Samuelson (1947, ch. 9) who extended Walras's idea of a tatonnement. (Note that Walras was at points willing to defend tatonnement as a realistic method of adjustment in some markets, something which neo-Walrasians have given up.) The literature is surveyed by Negishi (1962) and Arrow and Hahn (1971, chs. 11–13) and considered critically by Hahn (1970). Recently some authors have reconsidered the adjustment problem along individual-behaviour lines and some promising work is being done. The most notable attempts are those of Fisher (1970, 1972, 1973), Diamond (1971) and Winter (1971). Most of the recent literature is surveyed in Rothschild (1973).

Let us begin by considering the adjustment of an abstract economy where resources, technology, and tastes are fixed. In this economy each individual observes the values taken by a number of variables which affect his utility (or profit if he is a producer) and responds to any changes in these variables by changing his planned action so that his utility is always at a maximum. Changes in the values of the relevant variables may be caused by the actions of others, or by external events (nature). The cause of the change is irrelevant from the point of view of the individual. If the value of a given variable changes from *a* to *b*, he will respond in precisely the same manner whether the cause was nature or the actions of others. We refer to such an individual as an 'atomistic' individual, and to the market consisting of these individuals also as atomistic.

Suppose that at a point of time *t* each individual in an atomistic market plans to take the action that maximizes his utility, given the values of some relevant variables in the current period and his expectations for the future. We then say that the market is in *individual* equilibrium at time *t*. Let now each individual attempt to realize his plan. If expectations are not consistent there will be some individuals whose attempts are frustrated: in the aggregate the system will be in disequilibrium.

At period $t + 1$ the plans of those that failed will be revised on the basis of their experience at *t*, so at $t + 1$ there will be a new individual equilibrium. Individuals are again thrown into the market and there is a new attempt to realize their plans. Some of them may succeed but some may not – in any case the *ex post* situation at $t + 1$ will be different from that at *t*, since the individual (*ex ante*) equilibrium is different. Aggregate equilibrium exists in the system when every individual succeeds in realizing his plan to the full. In that case expectations are fulfilled, so no individual will revise his plan from one period to the next, and (in a static economy) the same equilibrium position will be repeated over time.[4]

If tastes, resources and technology are fixed, and there is a divergence between successive *ex post* situations, we say that the economic system is *adjusting*. If the discrepancy gets smaller over time we say that the system is stable and tending towards some equilibrium; but if the discrepancy does not show signs of decline, or if it declines and then rises again, the system is said to be unstable. However, in the

[4] For a discussion of equilibrium in this sense see Hayek (1937).

latter case we need not have cessation of all economic activity. The system may oscillate or change over time in a predictable fashion. The 'adjustment problem' involves the study of the properties of the *ex post* path of a system which is initially in disequilibrium.

The *ex post* path of a system will depend on two factors. First on individual plans, and second on the rules followed in determining actual behaviour when individual plans are incompatible. Economic theory provides a very satisfactory answer to the first question – the formation of individual plans given expectations – but no satisfactory answer to the second. In fact, it is in answer to the second question that economists were forced to introduce the *ad hoc* assumptions which escape the unifying maximization principle, and which are usually grouped under 'adjustment problems'.

When individual plans are incompatible we have to deal with the twin problems of (1) determining the relationship between desired and actual behaviour for each individual at each point of time, and (2) determining the effects of the divergence between desired and actual behaviour at some point of time t on desired behaviour at point $t + 1$. No assumptions which conform to the general principles of economic behaviour have yet been found to deal with these two problems, so such *ad hoc* assumptions have been devised as (1) quick revision of plans when individual plans are not consistent, without taking any action until such circumstances are created which make all desired actions realizable, or (2) some exchange may be allowed during the revision of plans, but that exchange is assumed to have no influence on the final state of equilibrium. In the particular case of price information the first alternative is associated with the names of Walras and Edgeworth, and the second with the names of Marshall and Hicks. In order to ensure that a process of plan revision does not extend over 'many' periods, Walras introduced a fictitious auctioneer who supplied all correct information efficiently, while Edgeworth avoided the problem of having to deal with 'mistakes' in trading by allowing 'recontracting'. Then individuals could revise contracts until everybody's desired action was realized.

Marshall dispensed with the fiction and allowed trading to take place at all prices, but only at the cost of the assumption that the typical market was 'a corn market in a country town'. If individuals spend only a small proportion of their incomes in a given market, then obviously mistakes in that market are not going to have a noticeable effect on the behaviour of that or other markets. Hicks (1946, pp.

127–9) paid more attention to the effects of trading at disequilibrium prices than the others, but his aim was to find a rationale for Marshall's neglect of the effects of mistakes rather than provide a systematic analysis of the adjustment problem when trading is allowed at all prices. Nevertheless, he noted that what he called 'false trading' produced additional wealth effects, by redistributing income through the exchange of commodities which would not have taken place at equilibrium, but he concluded, somewhat unconvincingly, that if 'enough intelligence is shown in price-fixing' the indeterminacy from the extra wealth effects may be ignored. However, he warned the reader that 'the situation appears to elude the ordinary apparatus of demand-and-supply analysis'.

Let us now consider more explicitly the adjustment of a system consisting of n commodities, traded in an equal number of atomistic markets. Suppose that each individual chooses a vector of demands and supplies, given his initial endowment, for each possible price vector that may prevail. If a price vector can be found such that all desired demands and supplies can be realized, then that price vector is said to be the equilibrium vector, and the system is in (Walrasian, demand-and-supply) equilibrium. The adjustment problem involves the dynamic analysis of the system given an arbitrary initial price vector, $\mathbf{p}_0$. In particular we would like to know whether optimal individual behaviour implies that $\mathbf{p}_0$ will move over time towards the equilibrium vector $\mathbf{p}^*$. The question usually asked in the literature is: what restrictions on individual behaviour and trading arrangements are required to ensure that $\mathbf{p}_0$ moves towards $\mathbf{p}^*$? The former question is obviously more relevant for the analysis of adjustment based on individual behaviour than the latter.

Let $\bar{\mathbf{x}}_{it}$ be the initial holdings of some individual i at period t, and $\mathbf{x}^*_{it}(\bar{\mathbf{x}}_{it}, \mathbf{p}_t)$ his desired holdings given his resources and market prices. Equilibrium prices are defined by the equality of demands and supplies for all goods, i.e. they are the solution to the equation

$$\sum_i \mathbf{x}^*_{it}(\bar{\mathbf{x}}_{it}, \mathbf{p}_t) = \sum_i \bar{\mathbf{x}}_{it}. \qquad (1)$$

Suppose a unique solution $\mathbf{p}^*_t$ exists. If the actual prices $\mathbf{p}_t$, at which trading takes place at t, happen to be equal to equilibrium prices $\mathbf{p}^*_t$, then the *composition* of the endowment vector $\bar{\mathbf{x}}_{it}$ is irrelevant for trading – what matters is solely its total value $\mathbf{p}^{*\prime}_t\bar{\mathbf{x}}_{it}$, which determines the 'income' of the individual. Thus in a market which is in Walrasian equilibrium the quantity of each good possessed does not enter the determination of excess demand functions, since equilibrium prices determine both the relative attractiveness of each good and the income of the individual.

Let now the actual price vector $\mathbf{p}_t$ be different from $\mathbf{p}_t^*$. Then, by definition equation (1) does not hold, so actual demands and supplies, $\mathbf{x}_{it}$, will be different from desired, $\mathbf{x}_{it}^*$, for some individuals i. The relationship between the actual and desired vector for every individual i will then be given by a *trading arrangement*, which may or may not be related to optimal behaviour. One would like to relate trading arrangements to individual behaviour, but as a first step a simple trading arrangement may be assumed which need not bear any relationship to optimization. The Walrasian equilibrium model ignores trading altogether, so the derivation of optimal individual behaviour *given* a trading arrangement is in itself a substantial step forward.[5]

Suppose we have a trading arrangement which yields a vector $\mathbf{x}_{it}$ for each individual i. If $\mathbf{x}_{it}$ is different from $\mathbf{x}_{it}^*$ for some i, these individuals will revise their plans and try to trade again. Thus the analysis of adjustment will have to consider a dynamic trading sequence, or alternatively a dynamic sequence of disequilibrium markets. Now clearly, given the trading arrangement, the composition of the actual vector $\mathbf{x}_{it}$ will depend on both desired demands and supplies $\mathbf{x}_{it}^*$, and on the composition of initial holdings $\bar{\mathbf{x}}_{it}$. For instance, if the trading arrangement postulates that the short side of the market dominates in exchange,[6] then the composition of an individual's initial endowment and its relationship to the aggregate will determine whether some of the demands of the individual will go unsatisfied or not. Under this arrangement an individual who has an excess demand for those goods which are in excess supply in aggregate (and conversely) will be able to attain his desired point; not one who does not 'go against the market'. Thus the composition of initial endowments

[5] The starting point of the literature which deals with the problems of this and the last paragraph was provided by Clower (1965). A growing literature was stimulated which attempts to introduce money in such trading sequences, and show that money has an explicit role to play as a medium of exchange, thus avoiding the embarrassment of having to deal with money in the Walras–Hicks–Patinkin fashion. See Hahn (1965), Clower (1967), Ostroy (1973) and references therein.

[6] That is, if x_{tj}^* is the total demand for commodity j, and $\bar{x}_{tj}$ the total supply of that commodity, $x_{tj} = \min(x_{tj}^*, \bar{x}_{tj})$.

at each period t will enter the determination of actual quantities ruling at the end of t, and through the influence of actual quantities on desired demands for $t + 1$, it will also enter the determination of future desired demands. History matters in this model.

The effect of the divergency between actual and desired quantities for some good j for an individual i on future behaviour may be broken up into what may be called *distribution* effects and *spillover* effects. Distribution effects arise out of the reallocation of wealth which takes place because of the 'false trading'. They may arise in both single and multiple markets – the only difference between these effects and the wealth effects of equilibrium economics is their cause of origin. Just as wealth effects introduce an indeterminancy into the equilibrium analysis of markets, distribution effects introduce an additional indeterminancy into the analysis of markets out of equilibrium and so make one more suspicious of a theory of markets which ignores wealth effects.[7]

The spillover effect goes deeper into the interaction of markets in disequilibrium. In choosing his demands and supplies the individual trader normally considers all markets in which he trades simultaneously. The planned demands and supplies he finally arrives at are those which achieve the optimal allocation of his resources in all markets, given prices. If now the realized transaction in one market does not coincide with the planned transaction, the equilibrium of the trader in all other markets is disturbed, so he will reconsider his planned action in all other markets. In the terminology of Patinkin (1965, p. 235) the divergence between the actual and the desired transaction in one market 'spills over' into other markets.

Normally the spillover effect takes the form of either (1) additional demand in some markets when some purchasing power goes unsatisfied in the markets where it was originally allocated (actual demand in the latter markets falls below desired), or (2) reduction in the planned expenditure in some markets when some of the planned sales in other markets are not realized (actual supply falls below desired). There is no reason, however, why complementarity and substitutability effects should not be present – for instance, if the demand for a product cannot be realized, the demand for its complements may fall, despite the additional purchasing power that is released in all other markets.

[7] Thus Hicks (1946, pp. 127–9) considered only the distribution effects of 'false trading' and neglected spillover effects.

Given the trading arrangement, the study of individual behaviour during adjustment involves the study of responses to the divergency between the actual and desired transaction in one or more markets. If a given divergency produces responses which lead to even greater divergencies then the system is inherently unstable, but if the divergency produces a self-correcting response the system is stable. Thus the problem of adjustment involves finding satisfactory trading arrangements and considering individual responses to disequilibrium quantities under these arrangements.[8]

Preview of the model

In the model of the following chapters we consider the adjustment of a static economy, where the total amount of resources available for production, the technology, and the preferences of individual agents are all fixed. In order to isolate the effects of disequilibrium in one market on the functioning of others we shall assume that only the labour market is out of Walrasian equilibrium, in that there is no central market organization which can set unique wage rates for labour of similar skill, and which can ensure that all desired supply and demand for labour can be realized at the ruling wage. Thus there will be a distribution of wage rates in the market for all skills, and no worker can be assured that he will be able to sell as much labour as he desires at an observed wage rate. Similarly, no firm can be assured that it will get as much labour as it desires at an offered wage, which may, nevertheless, attract some workers.

Trading in the labour market is decentralized, and the trading arrangement assumed is a variant of the sequential model of job search.[9] Thus firms offer jobs by choosing a wage rate and recruiting

[8] The literature on adjustment, as defined here, is growing so rapidly as to make a complete bibliography impossible. The most influential work in the area has been that of Clower (1965, 1967), Patinkin (1965, esp. ch. 13), Leijonhufvud (1968, esp. ch. 2), Stigler (1961, 1962) and Phelps *et al.* (1970). Related work of interest may be found in Negishi (1965) and other contributions in Hahn and Brechling (1965), Radner (1970), Arrow and Hahn (1971, chs. 11–14) Diamond (1971), Winter (1971), Barro and Grossman (1971), Fisher (1972, 1973), Ostroy (1973), Howitt (1974), and the survey by Rothschild (1973).

[9] Although non-sequential, Stigler's (1962) model provided the starting point of the literature on job search. Hutt (1939, chs. 3–4) preceded him by 23 years but his work is little known. See Alchian (1970) for a general discussion of the issues, and Reder (1969), Holt (1970), Phelps (1970), McCall (1970), Mortensen (1970*a*,*b*), Gronau (1971), Salop (1973*a*) and Whipple (1973) for analysis of the sequential model. Two partial surveys are available, Phelps (1969) and Rothschild (1973), and some discussion of the models as theories of the functioning of labour markets is included in Corina (1972, ch. 5).

workers. Workers are responsible for searching firms to find out about the wage rate they offer, and whether there are any vacancies for which they qualify. Therefore, under this arrangement prices are set by the buyers. Normally, we shall assume that the quantity traded is either that offered for sale at the observed wage, or zero, i.e. a firm is willing to let a man work as many hours as he wishes at the offered wage, provided the workman qualifies for the offered job. Put differently, the demand for hours from some worker will be either zero when the worker does not qualify for the job, or 'infinite' when he does qualify ('infinite' in quotation marks because by that we simply mean greater than whatever the workman is willing to supply). In some cases the quantity traded may, of course, be determined by other arrangements. For instance, a firm may wish to run a plant for ten hours a day in one shift. It will then be willing to buy exactly ten hours a day from each employee, no more no less. The actual quantity exchanged, then, will be either ten units or zero. The model is robust to such variations in arrangements about the quantity transacted.

The crucial restriction on the trading arrangement is that trading takes place bilaterally between offering firm and searching worker. Since there is no central organization to convey information about job offers and potential searchers, both employers and workers will be imperfectly informed about available market opportunities. Thus the trading arrangement gives rise to imperfect information and forces the individual to engage in sequential decision-making under uncertainty. Moreover, the information that each firm and each worker possess is influenced, to a large extent, by their own experience in the market.

It is shown that optimal individual behaviour under the postulated trading arrangement implies that a distribution of wage offers will be interacting over time with a distribution of job-acceptance levels. There will not necessarily be a tendency to any particular (non-stochastic) equilibrium in the short run. Thus there will be a sequence of labour markets which will not be in equilibrium in the aggregate, but whose participants will always be acting on the basis of an optimally chosen plan, given the information they have about the market.

Alongside this sequence of labour markets we shall assume the existence of a sequence of commodity markets which will be in momentary supply-and-demand equilibrium at all points of time. This sequence will be interacting with the labour market, so there will be distribution and spillover effects from the labour to the commodity markets. However, since the commodity markets are in supply-and-demand equilibrium whatever the situation in the labour market, there will be no disequilibrium effects acting the other way round. Thus the labour market will be of central importance in our model, and it will attract most of the attention of both the household and firm analyses.

There are at least three reasons for assuming that only the labour market is out of equilibrium. First, it is well known that scientific progress takes place in stages of increasing generality, and the analysis of the interaction of one disequilibrium market with a multiplicity of equilibrium markets should naturally precede the analysis of the interaction of a multiplicity of disequilibrium markets. Hicks's *Value and Capital* would have been less easily understood had economists not struggled for decades with partial analysis. Moreover, the main effects of disequilibrium, namely the transaction rules imposed on participants, the individual decision-making with respect to both prices and quantities, the distribution effects, and the spill-overs between markets, can be captured in a model of multiple markets where only a single market is out of equilibrium.

Second, labour is the single most important commodity traded in imperfect markets, so an analysis of job search and the offer of jobs, and their effects on consumption, wages and employment, is likely to have more than just academic interest. Thus the labour market model of the book, taken in isolation, may be regarded as a contribution to the more empirically oriented theory of the labour market, and the theory of frictional and involuntary unemployment in particular. There is ample evidence that the trading sequence we postulate is not an inaccurate description of actual arrangements in labour markets in a modern industrialized society.[10] Third, the labour market has traditionally attracted more attention from economists than any other market, and its slow adjustment to equilibrium has been emphasized

[10] This claim is so obvious that it does not need any justification. Nevertheless, there is ample evidence readily available: individual skill markets are more or less independent with only minor movement of adults between skills; labour markets are heavily localized with most exchange of jobs taking place directly between offering firm and searching worker; jobs are usually offered and accepted on a permanent basis. The relative success of vocational guidance agencies and the unpopularity of employment exchanges are further evidence for this. These features of modern labour markets were noted some time ago by Marshall (1920, pp. 474–7). See Phelps-Brown (1962, pp. 93–107) for more detailed description.

by both neoclassical and Keynesian economists. This is due, to a large extent, to the second factor, but the fact that economic literature has devoted so much attention and space to controversy about the functioning of labour markets makes it relevant on its own account. Although the main objective of the book will not be to clear controversy, a systematic analysis of controversial issues cannot but clear some of the controversy.

The framework we develop is also suitable for the analysis of exchange when there is a sole medium of exchange,[11] but in order to bring out more clearly the essentials of the interaction of markets in disequilibrium we shall abstract from the complexities of monetary exchange. We shall also abstract from the analysis of speculative exchanges, and the analysis of the functioning of stock markets, although, as Keynes emphasized some time ago, these institutions may gain central importance in the functioning of an economy such as the one we postulate.

[11] See the references in footnote 5 above.

PART I

Producers

2

The Supply of Labour to the Firm

When in an atomistic labour market exchange is conducted by a central market organization, which sets wages and ensures that all desired quantities can be exchanged at the ruling wage rates, the supply of labour to the firm at the ruling wage is infinitely elastic. If a firm does not obey the central organization's rules, and offers a higher wage rate than the one chosen centrally, it will be flooded with workers, so it will pay it to reduce wages; if it offers a lower wage than the one chosen centrally, it will be unable to obtain any labour at all, so it will be forced to increase wages if it wants to produce. The most important effect of the decentralization of exchange is that this 'perfectly competitive' result does not hold. In particular, the firm is now able to change the flow of workers to itself by varying its wage rate *vis-à-vis* the wage rates of other firms. During adjustment the firm is an 'imperfect' competitor, even if the market is atomistic, and so has some monopsony power.

This is a property of adjustment that Kenneth Arrow noted as long ago as 1959. By postulating a trading arrangement we expect to be able to go deeper into the nature of this monopsony power, its implications for the behaviour of wages and unemployment, and its properties over time.[1] The model of job search gives a very satisfactory answer to the first two queries, and a fairly satisfactory answer to the third, provided we consider the time path of the monopsony power of an individual firm.[2]

By 'monopsony power' we mean that the firm can control the supply of labour to itself by varying its wage rate. But other firms are also monopsonists in this environment, so the supply of labour to a particular firm also depends on the wage rates of all other firms. We shall consider each dependence in turn.

[1] As Rothschild (1973) has pointed out, if an adjustment model claims to be stable we should be told how this monopsony power is eroded over time, and what factors induce firms to move towards equilibrium and forego this power.

[2] See below, chapters 4 and 14.

The dependence on the firm's wage rate

Let w be the firm's per-hour wage rate, and denote the hours of work by y and the individual's initial (non-human) wealth by m'. We shall take the length of the period to be equal to unity, so y is the proportion of the period spent at work, and $1-y$ the proportion spent in leisure activities. The individual has a utility function defined over hours of work and total wealth, given by $u(m' + wy, y)$. Utility is monotonically increasing in total wealth and decreasing in hours of work in the interval $0 \leq y < 1$. We assume that as y tends to unity from below, utility tends to minus infinity, i.e. some leisure is absolutely essential for survival. The utility index is assumed cardinal in the von Neumann–Morgenstern sense.

Take first the simple case where a firm which offers a job fixes the wage rate w and lets the worker choose the number of hours he wishes to work at the offered wage. If the chosen number of hours, y^*, is zero, then the offer is rejected. Suppose the wage rate offered is determined by a central market organization and is the same for all firms. Then if y^* is zero the individual does not enter the labour market at all, but if y^* is positive he enters the market to find a firm with a vacancy. Since wage rates are equal across firms, the searcher will accept the first vacancy which he observes, so in this environment no firm offering jobs will find that searchers are refusing to accept their offer. A searcher's cut-off wage rate is by necessity below the market wage, because if it were not he would not have entered the market in the first place.

Now suppose each firm chooses its own wage rate and firms' wages differ. Let $f(w)$ denote the frequency distribution over wages, and suppose a worker is allowed to take only one drawing from $f(w)$, i.e. he can search only once. The expected utility from search, then, is given by $\sum_w f(w)\, u(m' + wy^*, y^*)$, where y^* is the chosen number of hours of work given a wage offer w. Denote this by V. If the individual decides to drop out of the labour force without searching, his utility will be equal to $u(m', 0)$, since in this case $y^* = 0$. So search will take place if $V > u(m', 0)$. The result that a firm can influence the supply of labour to itself by varying its wage rate follows immediately if we can demonstrate that a worker who chooses to enter the labour market and search for a job may find it optimal to reject an observed wage rate. If he does, then firms offering low wages will find that some searchers turn away, and that they can increase the supply of labour to themselves simply by raising their wage rates.

Consider any wage rate w. Maximizing $u(m' + wy, y)$ with respect to y subject to $0 \leq y < 1$, we obtain

$$\begin{aligned} y^* &= y(m', w) \quad && \text{if } u(m' + wy^*, y^*) \geq u(m', 0), \\ y^* &= 0 && \text{otherwise.} \end{aligned}$$

In the case where y^* is positive we may write the utility function in indirect form as $u^*(m', w)$. Then y^* is positive whenever

$$u^*(m', w) \geq u(m', 0), \tag{1}$$

i.e. whenever accepting the offer yields at least as much utility as rejecting it. The wage rate which satisfies (1) with equality is the individual's cut-off wage, or what we shall be calling his 'reservation' wage. Denote it by ω.

With knowledge of ω we are able to give a more explicit definition of the expected returns from search, V. Thus, since the indirect utility function is monotonically increasing in the wage rate, it follows that $y^* = 0$ when $w < \omega$, and $y^* > 0$ when $w \geq \omega$. So we may break up the summation giving V into two parts,

$$V = \sum_{w < \omega} f(w)u(m', 0) + \sum_{w \geq \omega} f(w)u^*(m', w). \tag{2'}$$

Let $w_{\min}$ denote the minimum wage offer in the market. Then the question of whether some searchers may find it optimal to reject some job offers reduces to the question whether it is possible that $w_{\min}$ falls below ω, given that $u(m', 0)$ is smaller than V.

This question can be put in a more convenient form. First rewrite (2′) as follows. Let a denote the probability of acceptance of the offer observed, i.e. $a = \sum_{w \geq \omega} f(w)$. Clearly, $0 \leq a \leq 1$. Moreover, let W denote the expected utility from *successful* search, i.e. the expected utility of the worker if he is told beforehand that he will definitely observe a w such that $w \geq \omega$. i.e.

$$W = E[u^*(m', w) \mid w \geq \omega] = \frac{1}{a} \sum_{w \geq \omega} f(w)u^*(m', w). \tag{3}$$

Writing also u_0 for $u(m', 0)$ we may rewrite (2′) as

$$V = aW + (1 - a)u_0, \tag{2}$$

i.e. the expected utility from search is equal to the expected utility from successful search, weighted by the probability of success, plus the utility from unsuccessful search, weighted by the probability of failure.

Now if there are offers which the individual decides to reject, a will be less than unity. On the other hand, search will take place if there is at least one offer which is acceptable, since if there is not, $a = 0$ and $V = u_0$ from (2), hence the condition $V > u_0$ is violated. Hence the searcher will never find it optimal to reject some offers if $V > u_0$ implies $a = 1$.

It is almost trivial to observe that $V > u_0$ does not necessarily imply $a = 1$. Using (2) $V > u_0$ implies

$$aW + (1 - a)u_0 > u_0.$$

Since $a > 0$, this becomes

$$W - u_0 > 0.$$

But given $a > 0$, W will exceed u_0 always, by the definition of the reservation wage in (1) and of W in (3). Hence some offers may be rejected. (In fact it is possible to obtain a stronger result by the converse argument. Thus, if $a > 0$, i.e. if there is at least one offer which is acceptable, we know that $W - u_0 > 0$. Multiplying by a, adding u_0 on both sides, and using (2) we obtain $V > u_0$. That is, if there is at least one job offer which is acceptable, search will definitely take place. This result, however, does not carry over to the general case because of costly search, whereas the converse does carry over.)

Thus we see that even within the simple framework of this model, workers will find it optimal to reject some offers, although they enter the market to search for a job. However, if all workers had the same reservation wage, firms would still have no monopsony power, since the supply of labour to themselves at all wages below the common reservation wage would be zero, and above that would be infinitely elastic. Hence firms will find that they can reduce their wage rates down to the reservation level and still obtain as much labour as they wish, so wage dispersion will disappear altogether. Dispersion of reservation wages is a necessary condition if firms are to have monopsony power and wage dispersion is to persist in the market.

Even in the single-period model we can find factors which will give rise to variations in reservation wages. Since the reservation wage ω is given by the solution to

$$u^*(m', \omega) = u(m', 0),$$

variations in tastes and initial wealth will give rise to variations in reservation wages. The most important factors that give rise to variations in reservation wages, however, are related to the nature of the trading arrangement itself (the decentralization of exchange) and the imperfect information that this implies. The way exchange between offering firm and searching worker acts to give rise to reservation-wage dispersion comes out more clearly in the more general model of job search which allows sequential exchange, so discussion will be postponed until chapter 13. At this stage we take it as given that the decentralization of exchange produces variations in reservation wages among individuals. Let $h(\omega)$ denote the frequency distribution over reservation wages.

Suppose a firm offers a wage rate w. The probability that a random searcher will accept its offer is equal to the cumulative sum $\sum_{\omega \leq w} h(\omega)$. Call this cumulative $r(w)$. If the number of searchers is 'large', approximately a ratio r of those searching the firm will be willing to accept its offer, whereas the remaining ratio of men, $1 - r$, will be unwilling to accept its offer. The *effective* supply of labour to the firm offering a wage rate w is equal to the total number of hours of work that those willing to accept the firm's offer supply. The hours supplied by those unwilling to accept the firm's offer are 'ineffective' from the point of view of the firm. It is the ratio of effective to ineffective supply that the individual firm can influence by varying its wage rate – the atomistic firm can do little to influence the total supply of labour (effective plus ineffective) in the short run. In neoclassical equilibrium, where no worker will ever find it optimal to reject an observed offer, the ineffective supply of labour is zero, and this is how the firm loses its power to control the effective supply of labour to itself. If individual wage rates differ, some labour supply will be ineffective, so the firm, by increasing its wage rate, can increase the effective supply and reduce the ineffective, whereas by reducing its wage rate it can reduce the effective and increase the ineffective supply. Although the hours supplied by each worker also depend on the firm's wage rate, it is mainly through the influence of the wage rate on the number of men willing to accept the offer that the firm is able to influence the short-run supply of labour to itself. Thus during adjustment the distinction between hours of work supplied and the number of men supplying them becomes very important. In contrast, in the full-equilibrium analysis of labour markets, where there is a unique wage rate, there is no meaningful distinction between the number of men and hours of work, since the theory is in terms of 'units' of labour, with no further restrictions on the nature of these units.[3]

In future we shall be talking of the 'supply of labour to the firm' meaning the effective supply. The ineffective supply will be ignored in this chapter, but it will be brought into the argument again in the next chapter, where it is demonstrated that it has a very important role to play in the adjustment process.

Now in order to demonstrate the dependence of the effective supply on the firm's wage rate, let $\bar{y}(w)$ be the average number of hours supplied by those willing to accept a wage rate w, and suppose the firm is searched by s men during the time interval that we are measuring supply. Then, to a first approximation, the total supply of man-hours to the firm within this time interval is

$$y^s(w) = s\bar{y}(w)r(w).$$

Differentiating with respect to w we obtain

$$(y^s)'(w) = s\bar{y}'(w)r(w) + s\bar{y}(w)r'(w),$$

where primes denote differentiation. The change in $\bar{y}$ may be decomposed into the standard income and substitution terms, where the former is negative if leisure is not an inferior good and the latter positive. Which one dominates on average is still a matter of controversy. In either case, the net effect on hours is not likely to be strong.[4,5]

It is mainly through its control over the number of men willing to work for it that the firm is able to control the supply of labour to itself. Thus the ratio of searchers willing to accept the firm's

[3] This inability of neoclassical theory to distinguish between men and hours may be one of the reasons for the poor performance of the neoclassical model of labour demand-and-supply in empirical studies. Feldstein (1967) and Craine (1973), and more implicitly Brechling (1965), suggested using men and hours as two separate factors in the production function. Although their empirical findings are better than those which do not distinguish between men and hours, their hypothesis is based on a very *ad hoc* argument.

[4] The issue is, of course, empirical. There has been a lot of work on this problem in the United States, but very little in Britain. The literature on labour force participation found that the substitution effect dominated in most cases, e.g. Bowen and Finegan (1969, p. 483), but recently Barzel and McDonald (1973) argued that an increase in wages has a negative effect on offered hours.

[5] Note that when we are talking of a change in $\bar{y}$ here, we mean a change in hours supplied by a firm's own employees. This is not the same as the change in the aggregate supply of labour analysed by the standard theory, e.g. in the references of the last footnote, because the latter, in as much as they discuss the issue at all, discuss the change in total man-hours (change in the number of men and the hours worked by each man) supplied to all firms simultaneously.

offer, $r(w)$, is an increasing function of w, and even if $\bar{y}(w)$ is a decreasing function of w, the positive effect of a wage increase on r is likely to outweigh the negative effect on $\bar{y}$. In our notation, the derivative $r'(w)$ is equal to the value $h(w)$ that the distribution over reservation wages takes at a reservation wage equal to w, provided the standard continuity requirements on $r(w)$ hold.

It should be clear now why the determination of hours of work – the quantity exchanged when a trade is agreed – assumes a peripheral interest in the theory of labour market adjustment. The same theory holds whether the number of hours of work is determined by the worker, the firm, or through bargaining, since the burden of adjustment falls on the number of men seeking work. Since Hicks's *Value and Capital* it has become customary to assume that the hours of work are determined by worker choice, but before that it was normally assumed that the number of hours of work was chosen by the firm.[6] Suppose the firm fixes the number of hours of work at $\bar{y}$. Then the utility of a job offer is given by the 'direct' function $u(m' + w\bar{y}, \bar{y})$, and not the indirect $u^*(m', w)$. There is no difficulty in dealing with the former instead of the latter, but there may be differences in behaviour. If w is the same in both cases, the indirect function cannot fall below the direct, and in general it will be above it, because by definition

$$u^*(m', w) = \operatorname*{Max}_{y} (m' + wy, y),$$

whereas $\bar{y}$ may not maximize utility. Thus a worker might be willing to accept a job if he were free to choose the number of working hours, but not if the firm fixes them at a level very different from that he desires.

The dependence on other firms' wages

In order to obtain the dependence of the supply of labour to some firm k on the wage rates paid by all other firms except k, we must abandon the single-period framework and look more explicitly into the possibility of searching more than one firm before accepting a job. However, the essentials of the dependence may again be brought out within a simple abstract model.

[6] For instance, Hicks in the *Theory of Wages* follows Chapman (1909) in assuming that the proportion of the day spent at work is chosen by the firm such that the firm obtains maximum per unit output from its workmen. See Hicks (1932, pp. 103–5). Robbins (1930) considered the choice of hours by workers before Hicks (1946).

Let $u(m' + wy, y)$ be a utility function defined over a job paying a wage rate w, and suppose the individual can search twice before accepting a job. The possibility of dropping out may be ignored at this stage, i.e. we assume that the individual can take two drawings from the pool of jobs, but he must take them sequentially: he must take the first, decide whether to accept it or not, and if he does not accept it he must put it back and take the second, which he will have to keep. The problem is to find the dependence of the reservation wage on the wage rates paid by those jobs which were not drawn out the first time.

Let $f(w)$ be the frequency distribution over wages for both draws. If the individual draws w_k the first time and accepts it he foregoes the chance of taking a second draw. Since he will have to accept the second draw if he rejects w_k and tries again, his expected utility from the second draw is given by

$$V = \sum_{w} f(w)\, u^*(m', w),$$

where $u^*(m', w)$ is, as before, the indirect utility obtained from a wage rate w. Thus the individual will accept w_k if and only if

$$u^*(m', w_k) \geq V = \sum_{w} f(w) u^*(m', w).$$

The reservation wage rate ω is therefore given by the solution to

$$u^*(m', \omega) = V. \tag{4}$$

Within this framework, we are able to identify two more factors that may lead to differences in the reservation wages of searchers. First, since $f(w)$ will in general be a subjective distribution over the wages that the individual expects to receive if he searches for a second time, it will be different for different individuals, so the Vs of different individuals will be different. Thus reservation wages will differ because information differs. Second, given $f(w)$, the higher the degree of risk aversion the lower V.[7] So differences in risk attitudes will give rise to differences in reservation wages: more risk-averse individuals will have lower reservation wages.

Now the reservation wage ω depends on V, so it also depends on the distribution over wages, $f(w)$. Let $\mathbf{w}$ denote the vector of all wage rates in the market. Clearly, for any w_i, $\partial V / \partial w_i > 0$. Differentiating (4) implicitly with respect to some w_i we obtain

[7] See Rothschild and Stiglitz (1970).

$$\frac{\partial\omega}{\partial w_i} = \frac{\partial V/\partial w_i}{\partial u^*/\partial\omega} > 0.$$

So an increase in the wage rate of some firm i increases the reservation wage ω, although if the number of firms is large the effect of a change in a single w_i on ω will be small. Thus we may write the reservation wage as a function of the wages paid by all firms in the market, i.e. $\omega(\mathbf{w})$ with $\omega' > 0$.

The influence of the wage rate of some firm i on the supply of labour to some other firm k may be obtained through the dependence of ω on $\mathbf{w}$. Thus let $h(\omega(\mathbf{w}))$ be the frequency distribution over reservation wages, and let $r(w_k, \mathbf{w})$ be the cumulative $\sum_{\omega \leq w_k} h(\omega)$. Clearly, if firm k is searched by s men during a given interval of time the supply of hours to itself during this interval is given by

$$y^s(w_k, \mathbf{w}) = s\,\bar{y}(w_k)\,r(w_k, \mathbf{w}),$$

where $\bar{y}(w_k)$ is the average number of hours supplied by those willing to accept the wage rate w_k, and hence depends only on w_k. (If searching takes place without replacement, as will usually be the case in a labour market if it does not take too long to search a firm, the vector $\mathbf{w}$ should not include the wage rate w_k, paid by the firm already searched, because $\mathbf{w}$ is the vector of wages expected after the second searching attempt. We shall make this assumption presently.) Differentiating now $y^s(w_k, \mathbf{w})$ with respect to w_i, $i \neq k$, we obtain

$$y_i^s(w_k, \mathbf{w}) = s\bar{y}(w_k)\,r_i(w_k, \mathbf{w})$$

where subscript i denotes differentiation with respect to w_i. The derivative $r_i(w_k, \mathbf{w})$ is negative, because an increase in w_i increases the reservation wage ω and so reduces r. Thus the supply of labour to some firm k is a decreasing function of the wage rate of all other firms $i \neq k$.

Now from equation (4) we immediately obtain that if the individual is indifferent to risk (i.e. if his utility function is a linear function of income) an increase in all wage offers other than w_k by the same absolute amount leads to an increase in the reservation wage by the same amount.[8] Thus the distribution over the reservation wages of those searching firm k shifts uniformly to the right by the same

[8] In the two-period model of this chapter the argument also holds for equi-proportional changes in wages. However, in a multi-period model the equi-proportional change has an additional effect on the reservation wage because of the resulting change in the shape of the distribution of offers (see below, ch. 10), so the result does not hold.

amount. If now firm k increases its offer by an equal amount, the ratio $r(w_k, \mathbf{w})$ of those willing to accept its offer will remain unaffected by the increase in the reservation wages. In other words a horizontal shift in the distribution of offers leaves the supply of labour to the firm unaffected, or more precisely the function $y^s(w_k, \mathbf{w})$ depends on the position of w_k in the scale of wage offers, apart from the dependence of the hours of work $\bar{y}$ on w_k. Thus it is not the absolute wage rate paid by each firm that is the main influence on the supply of labour to individual firms, but the differential between the firm's wage rate and those of other firms in the market.[9]

If individuals are not indifferent to risk the same result holds, but with an additional qualification. In this case equation (4) may be solved for the reservation wage ω under general conditions to give

$$\omega = \bar{w} - \rho,$$

where $\bar{w}$ is the mean wage offer and ρ is a risk premium.[10] The risk premium depends on the individual's attitude towards risk and on the shape of the distribution of offers, and it is positive for a risk averter, negative for a risk lover, and zero for an individual indifferent to risk. If now the distribution of wage offers shifts uniformly to the right, $\bar{w}$ will also increase by the same amount, but the effect on ρ will depend on the effect of the shift on the individual's attitude towards risk. If the individual is risk averse and satisfies the Arrow–Pratt criterion of reasonable risk-averse behaviour[11] then the rightward shift in the distribution of offers will lead to a fall in the risk premium. So in this case the reservation wage will increase by a greater amount than the increase in wage offers. But if the risk premium is independent of the absolute level of wage offers the reservation wage will change by the same amount as the mean wage offer, so the supply of labour to the firm will still be independent of the absolute level of wages.

[9] The usual assumption in the literature is that the supply of labour to the firm depends on the firm's *relative* wage, e.g. Mortensen (1970*a*, p. 183). This requires that $r(w_k, \mathbf{w})$ be homogeneous of degree zero in its arguments, which is not strictly correct given the argument of the last footnote.

[10] See Pratt (1964) and Pissarides (1974).

[11] See, in addition to Pratt (1964), Arrow (1965).

3

Production and the Demand for Labour

In the last chapter we identified the most important effect of the decentralization of exchange from the point of view of the firm – the dependence of the supply of labour to itself on its own and other firms' wages. We now come to a detailed examination of the behaviour of the firm during adjustment, where we shall pay attention in particular to the firm as a producer, and to the policy followed during the recruitment of labour, given a distribution of reservation wages and a distribution of wage offers by other firms. Both these last two assumptions, the existence of a distribution of reservation wages on the one hand, and of wage offers on the other, will be examined in some detail in subsequent chapters.

Profit maximization and marginal productivity theory

The firm produces with the aid of capital which it buys in a perfect capital market, and labour which it obtains by offering jobs to a decentralized labour market. It then sells the final output in a perfect commodity market at a known price.

Traditionally the decision of the firm with respect to the level of output and the optimal capital–labour mix is analysed by assuming that the firm produces to maximize profits. The demand for labour and other factors of production can then be shown to satisfy the marginal productivity conditions, which state, in general, the simple truth that the firm will be willing to employ additional units of a factor of production up to the point where the addition to revenue arising from the employment of the last unit is equal to the addition to cost due to the same unit.[1]

Stated in this general way marginal productivity theory would prob-

[1] The practice of analysing the demand for factors of production along these lines is very old, and reached a high point of sophistication as long ago as Marshall's *Principles*. For a comprehensive statement of the theory and its applications see Ferguson (1969).

ably command the approval of economists and non-economists alike, if only because of the apparent emptiness of the condition. But when the condition takes a more explicit form, depending on what additional restrictions one places on the objectives and the technology of the firm, and the market structure within which it operates, it invariably meets with criticism. Since the demand for labour will play a central role in the workings of our model we shall look here a little closer at the marginal productivity condition as applied to labour.

Most of the controversy surrounding marginal productivity theory appears to have been founded on the fact that early neoclassical economists used marginal productivity as the condition determining the level of *employment*, i.e. as the condition of *equilibrium* in the labour market. However, it was not realized until much later, and after a lot of wasteful discussion, that, as a condition of equilibrium, marginal productivity followed logically from a set of more primitive assumptions, so the theory stood and fell with these assumptions. Criticism therefore would have been better directed if it went straight to these assumptions.

From our point of view these assumptions may be separated into two classes. *As a condition of equilibrium*, marginal productivity theory requires (1) profit maximization by firms, and (2) the full list of the Walrasian assumptions of perfectly competitive product and factor markets. But *as a theory of the demand for labour*, marginal productivity does not need full Walrasian equilibrium in all markets. Marginal productivity may be used to give the restrictions on the demand for labour implicit in firm policy when (1) firms maximize profits, (2) the production frontier is continuous, so labour and capital may be employed in any proportion that the firm may please, and (3) firms are price-takers in labour markets.

It is important to be clear on these assumptions. When the latter group of assumptions is satisfied, the marginal productivity condition gives the demand for labour, i.e. the firm wishes to employ labour up to the point where the value of the product of the last man employed equals 'the' wage rate. (Note that since the firm is a price-taker in the labour market the wage rate is given.) If in addition the other assumptions required to achieve full Walrasian equilibrium in all markets are satisfied, then the same condition also describes the equilibrium relationship between employment and wage rates. But if there is no full Walrasian equilibrium in all markets, the marginal productivity relations may not hold, although they may still describe the demand for labour. Today, marginal productivity is not usually employed to give the conditions for equilibrium in the labour market, but to give the properties of the demand for labour when firms are profit maximizers. In most cases the particular features of the market necessitate modifications of the pure condition.[2]

Criticisms of marginal productivity theory as a theory of the demand for labour have concentrated on each one of the three assumptions required to achieve it, and we shall consider them briefly. The assumptions – profit maximization, substitutability between capital and labour, and price-taking in the labour market – are, as we shall see, in increasing order of vulnerability when exchange is decentralized. The last two in particular will be found to be too restrictive to enable unambiguous use of the theory in obtaining the demand for labour in a decentralized labour market.

Profit maximization has been criticized on two main grounds. First, there is a group of economists who criticize the assumption that profit is the only concern of the firm, arguing that each firm is a complex organization with many goals besides profit. Second, there is a group (not necessarily distinct from the first) who are willing to keep profit as the sole or main objective of the firm but reject the maximization assumption as such, proposing satisficing and similar rules as better alternatives.[3]

However, it appears that the first type of criticism has had little impact on the economic theory of the functioning of markets, either in or out of equilibrium. On the other hand the second criticism is beginning to have an impact, mainly because its proponents are able to develop some important market implications of their analysis, but also because satisficing and similar rules are particularly well suited where profit maximization is weakest, namely in the description of the firm's decision *process* under imperfect information.

Here we shall preserve profit as the sole short-run objective of the firm, and we shall assume profit maximization, but as we shall demonstrate below and in the next chapter the optimal sequential decision-making that takes place in the short run contains many features in it which have traditionally been associated with satisficing. In the long run the firm may have other objectives besides profit, but where we

[2] See Corina (1972, ch. 4) for a survey of marginal productivity theory as a theory of the demand for labour.

[3] See Papandreou (1952) and Williamson (1967) on the first criticism, and Cyert and March (1963) and Winter (1971) on the second.

shall touch on long-run decisions we shall assume expected-profit maximization as the sole objective.[4]

The other criticisms of marginal productivity theory are more damaging if the theory is to be used to give the short-run demand for labour in a decentralized labour market. First, the relevance of the theory in the short run may be questioned.[5] The method of production and the quality and quantity of capital may not be freely variable in the short run, so the firm may not be capable of changing the labour–capital mix every time their relative price changes. Marginal productivity theory requires that every time the wage rate is changed the demand for labour must be changed until the value of the marginal product of labour becomes equal to the new wage rate. If labour and capital cannot be employed in variable proportions in the short run this requirement will not in general be satisfied.

Second, the existence of imperfect information about workers' reservation wages, and in some cases about their efficiency, and the acquisition of labour through an offer–acceptance policy, imply that firms are not price-takers in labour markets, and is inconsistent with the assumption of realization of all plans. Although marginal productivity theory may be extended to deal with search and waiting costs,[6] giving a labour–demand function which satisfies the same broad properties as the static marginal productivity condition, it has yet to be shown whether this extension is relevant in a market where firms are *uncertain* about the efficiency and reservation wages of prospective employees. Since Mortensen's extension requires a unique relationship between the rate of change of the firm's labour force, and the relative attractiveness of its wage offer, it does not appear to be capable of handling a random flow supply of labour to the firm, where future firm policy is influenced to a large extent by its current experience in the market.

Thus, although in the long run we may view the firm as planning to employ labour up to the point where the addition of one more man adds as much to revenue as it adds to costs, in the short run the marginal productivity condition appears to be irrelevant as a theory

[4] A strong case for profit maximization in the long run may be made on evolutionary grounds, i.e. if there is free entry and exit and the firm does not maximize profits its long-run survival will be in doubt. See Alchian (1950).

[5] See Hicks (1932, pp. 19–21), Reynolds (1948), Salter (1960), Corina (1972, ch. 4, esp. p. 26), and Johansen (1972).

[6] See Mortensen (1970*a*, pp. 182–91).

of the realized demand for labour. So, to formulate the problem faced by the firm and its decision process over time given that labour searches the firm randomly, we must draw a sharp distinction between the short run and the long run. The sole objective of the firm in both runs is to maximize expected profits.

It is convenient to think of the firm as consisting of two departments, one responsible for short-run decisions and the other for long-run planning. The long-run planning department is primarily responsible for choice of technique, optimal allocation of funds to capital and labour, and choice of some long-term features of job offers. When considering the technique to adopt, the firm takes into account the availability of labour and capital, expected future conditions in factor markets, and its own position in factor and commodity markets. Once the technique is chosen it purchases and installs capital, and hands over the job of recruiting labour and producing and selling to the department responsible for short-run decisions. Capital is assumed to be fixed in the short run, so the short run may be defined to be the length of time between two capital-planning dates.

When capital is installed the department responsible for short-run policy is given the task of recruiting labour and producing and selling. We assume that in the short run there is no substitution between labour and other factors, so the coefficient of each worker in production is fixed. Moreover, there is a fixed upper bound on the amount of labour a firm can employ, imposed by its capital capacity. Since the frequency of capital replacement, the technique, and the nature and quantity of capital employed are all matters of firm policy, the coefficient of each worker in production is different for different firms. Also, workers of the same occupational group may be more or less efficient, so production coefficients vary between workers as well.

The firm's decision to offer a job involves the balancing of two opposing influences on its short-run profit. In the first place, the firm would like to obtain maximum labour from a given wage bill, so it would be better off if it offered a low wage and waited for the searchers with the lowest reservation wages to call. In the second place, a firm offering a low wage is likely to have to wait for a long time before finding somebody willing to accept its offer, at the cost of foregone production and idle capital. So in general a firm will be willing to offer a higher wage than the absolute minimum required to attract some labour, and recoup the additional wage costs by quicker production and sales. Thus when wages are flexible the problem facing the firm in the short run involves the choice of a wage offer to maximize its profit, given the two opposing influences of variations in wages on its profits.

If wages are rigid the problem is different, but the optimal decision again involves the balancing of two opposing influences on profits. Thus, when wages are rigid, the firm will have more profits from a given vacancy if the worker recruited to that vacancy is more efficient. But if the firm rejects all applicants except some very efficient ones, the higher profits from the recruitment of very efficient workers are likely to be counterbalanced by a longer waiting period before recruitment. The firm's problem when wages are rigid involves the choice of a 'recruitment standard', given that the higher the recruitment standard the longer the expected waiting period before recruitment, but also the higher the expected profit from the production of those actually recruited.[7]

The short-run decision process

The firm wishes to enter into a transaction with workers when it has at least one vacancy. Thus during sequential exchange it is natural to assume that not more than one worker per vacancy is offered a job by the firm at a point of time. To make this more formal we assume that the short run is divided into elementary periods, such that not more than one worker per vacancy is offered a job during the period. If the worker who is offered a job in period t is willing to accept it, he starts producing in period $t + 1$. If not, the firm makes a new job offer for the vacancy in period $t + 1$.

In the first elementary period the firm reorganizes its labour force on the basis of the changes in capital and (perhaps) technique that have just taken place, decides whether to renew the contract of existing employees, observes any quits because of the new conditions, and observes whether there are any vacancies after the reorganization.

[7] The possibility of recruiting workers on a temporary basis will not be taken into consideration although it may be used in some cases by firms taking on men temporarily to fill a vacancy until a more suitable worker is found. In practice such policies are rare because of the existence of administrative costs in recruiting and dismissing employees, and because workers are usually willing to accept an offer only if the firm offers some kind of guarantee about the job, e.g. in the form of a contract which stipulates a minimum length of employment. Casual labour offers an exception which need not concern us here.

If it has vacancies it makes a job offer to the labour market, one for each vacancy, producing at the same time with the labour force already employed.

Since the sole concern of the firm is to maximize profits, production coefficients are fixed, and product markets are competitive, the firm may consider its employment policy for each vacancy in isolation – the cost and contribution of each man under these conditions is independent of that of other employees. (However, the firm may have to offer broadly similar wages to employees of the same skill.) Jobs are offered sequentially either until all vacancies have been filled or until the end of the short run, which is assumed to consist of T elementary periods. In the long run new capital and job offers will be planned.

We shall assume as a first approximation that T is fixed, and that capital does not depreciate in the short run. This implies that capital lives for exactly T periods, and in each one of these periods it is as good as new, but dies suddenly in period $T + 1$, whether it was standing idle or used in production in the previous T periods. This assumption will be shown in the next chapter to have a rather important influence on the optimal policy. Although at first sight it may appear unreasonable, it is in fact not too restrictive. First, it should be emphasized that the assumption that capital does not depreciate but dies suddenly is not important, and is only made to simplify the exposition. Second, when the capital is employed, the assumption that T is fixed is not crucial and the model may be adapted easily to a world where the date of capital replacement is a matter of firm policy and is influenced by events in the short run up to period T. What is crucial in the assumption is that the capital lives the same number of periods whether it is being actively employed or standing idle. This may be justified by the fact that over time new technological improvements may render the firm's capital obsolete, so if the firm wishes to maintain its competitiveness it should replace its capital after a finite number of periods whether that capital has been employed at every period or whether it stood idle for some periods. Also, if capital is not perfectly divisible, a unit of capital may be capable of supporting a number of vacancies, so if some of these vacancies are standing idle the capital still depreciates because it produces with those already employed. Finally, the fact that capital has to be maintained and interest costs borne even when it is idle implies that the entrepreneur is not indifferent about the time he takes a worker on, even if he knew his capital would live exactly T periods from the time of the start of production. Although the latter is not precisely the same thing as a finite horizon, it can be shown to have the same effects on the optimal policy as the latter.

Thus the firm should choose its short-run recruitment policy knowing that after T periods it will have to replace its capital whatever the waiting period before an employee is being taken on. In this environment the firm may follow one of two extreme policies, or any combination of the two, in its short-run recruitment of labour. The first one may be referred to as *flexwage*, and the second as *fixwage*.

In flexwage the firm is willing to accept any worker applying for a vacancy, but adjusts its wage offer according to the worker's contribution in production. The trade-off in this case is between a higher wage which may be needed to attract labour quickly, and foregone production because of the unwillingness of workers to accept a low wage. In fixwage the firm keeps the wage rate offered fixed, and formulates recruitment sets for each period in the short run. If a worker who searches a vacancy in period t belongs to the recruitment set for the same period, and is willing to accept the firm's offer, he is taken on and the job offer withdrawn from the market. If not the firm chooses a new recruitment set for period $t + 1$ and makes the offer again. The trade-off in this case is between a lower contribution to production given that more efficient workers may be willing to accept the job offer, and foregone production when the firm refuses to recruit inefficient workers, hoping to find more efficient ones to take the job in the future.[8]

At period T no job offer will be made, since the job which was to be offered will cease to exist the following period, which was the period in which a successful applicant was to begin work. In period $T + 1$, of course, some new jobs will be created, so the firm may be able to find employment for any men recruited in period T, but it will be to its advantage to wait another elementary period (which will not in general be long) when it will know more definitely about long-term

[8] In general there are two dimensions along which the firm may vary wages. First, wages may be flexible or rigid over workers with different efficiencies; second, they may be flexible or rigid over time. Here we defined flexwage as complete flexibility along both dimensions and fixwage as rigidity along both dimensions. Other combinations may be analysed by using similar techniques, so the details of the analysis will be omitted. In chapter 14 we shall argue that rigidity across workers implies that firms will change their wages infrequently over time, so it is the rigidity across workers which is the crucial restriction in fixwage.

planning and the new production programme. It can then make a more definite job offer.

The production function in the short run exhibits fixed coefficients of labour, so the average and marginal products of labour are equal to some constant q. To isolate the effects of imperfect information which arise from the decentralized trading between offering firm and searching worker, we assume that at the time an individual searches a firm the firm can ascertain his production coefficient q from interviews, evidence of educational and other qualifications, screening devices, and others; and that a worker is equally productive in all elementary periods in the short run. However, the coefficient of different workers will in general be different, and also the coefficient of the same worker at different firms will be different.[9]

The profit obtained in period t from an employee with coefficient q, discounted to the present, is given by

$$z(t)y(t) \equiv [qp(t) - w(t)]y(t),$$

where $p(t)$ is discounted product price at t, $y(t)$ is hours worked, and $w(t)$ is the discounted per-hour wage rate. If the searcher calling at period t is accepted and his production coefficient is q, the total short-run profit to the firm from this man will be $\sum_{t'=t+1}^{T} z(t')y(t')$. At time $T + 1$ the firm will reorganize production, so production coefficients will vary in a way now unknown to the firm. Under conditions of imperfect information and search, labour input is not freely variable because the firm cannot lay off one employee and employ a more suitable one immediately, so having a ready labour force at the time of long-term planning cannot be less, and in general it will be more, advantageous to the firm than if it had to wait for a random search process for acquiring employees. Thus a man taken on at any period in the short run will have some expected long-run return to the firm, which will in general be positive and dependent on the man's efficiency in the short run. So the total profit from a man with production coefficient q, recruited in period t, is the sum of the short-run profit and the expected long-run returns from this man.

However, we shall obtain the short-run recruitment policy of the firm by assuming that the long-run return from a man is zero, partly

[9] Those familiar with Spence's (1973) work will recognize his model of imperfect information and 'job signalling' as the complement of the search model presented here. Thus the two models may be combined into a more general model of the functioning of decentralized labour markets under imperfect information.

to simplify the exposition, but also because a positive long-run return can be shown to be of no consequence in the determination of the optimal recruitment policy in the short run. Thus we shall write the total profit from a worker with coefficient q, taken on at t, as

$$Z_t(q) = \sum_{t'=t+1}^{T} z(t')y(t') \quad (t = 1, \ldots, T-1).$$

At period T, as we argued above, no job offer will be made, so no recruitment will take place.

In most cases we shall find it convenient to work with the assumption that prices are equal in all periods t, and that the hours of work offered by a worker are independent of the wage rate. The first assumption will be relaxed explicitly in chapter 5, where we shall consider the effects of changes in current and future prices, whereas the second, although obviously unrealistic, can be shown to have no effect on the properties of adjustment implicit in the optimal firm and worker policy.[10] If we let $\beta(t)$ denote the discounting factor at t,[11] then discounted price $p(t)$ is equal to $\beta(t)p$, where p is the common price. The hours worked in each period will be denoted by y.

Since a firm may consider its employment policy for each vacancy in isolation, and each vacancy can only be filled by one man, it may also consider the recruitment of each man independently of other recruits. We shall investigate the optimal job offer (recruitment) policy first in the flexwage, and second in the fixwage system, for a single such 'typical' vacancy.

Wage choice under flexwage

In flexwage the firm that has a vacancy makes a job offer to the market and waits for searchers to call. When it is searched by a man it observes his production coefficient and offers him an appropriately chosen wage rate for every hour's work supplied. Since when a worker searches a firm the firm can ascertain his production coefficient, and it also knows prices, the choice of a wage rate is equivalent to the choice of a profit level: for every hour's work supplied,

[10] This should be obvious from the discussion of chapter 2, esp. pp. 19–21. We shall not demonstrate how the results are altered when the dependence of hours on wage rates is made explicit, to avoid unnecessary repetition, although it should be obvious how this can be done in each case from the method used to derive each result.

[11] i.e. if there is a unique and constant rate of interest ρ then $\beta(t) = 1/(1 + \rho)^{t-1}$.

profits vary linearly and inversely with wage payments when the production coefficient and product prices are given. Thus, in order to obtain the optimal policy we may either consider the choice of a wage rate for every hour's work supplied, or the choice of a profit level for every hour's work.

The fact that a prospective employee may reject the firm's offer at the time of search, implies that the firm's realized profits will not in general be equal to chosen profits. Thus the wage offer should be chosen to maximize *expected* profits, given that the lower a wage offer the higher the probability that the offer will be rejected, and hence the higher the probability that realized profits will be equal to zero. During recruitment the firm is assumed to follow the dynamic 'principle of optimality', which states that whatever the initial state and initial decision are, the remaining decisions must constitute an optimal policy with regard to the state resulting from the initial decision.[12]

Since the short run consists of T elementary periods and the firm can make a job offer at every one of them except the last one, the firm has $T - 1$ opportunities to choose a wage and offer it to those searching it. Let V_t be the returns from an optimal wage policy in the future when t of these opportunities have already elapsed, and there are $T - t - 1$ opportunities remaining. Suppose the firm chooses to offer a wage rate w_t to the worker searching it at t, and w_t is such that the per-hour profit from this man in each future period $t + 1, \ldots, T$ is equal to z_t. Now if the firm offers w_t, the searcher at t will be willing to accept its offer with some probability $r(w_t) \leq 1$.[13] So if the wage offer at t is w_t, there will be a probability $r(w_t)$ that the firm will have a profit of Z_t (defined more fully below) from this vacancy, representing the returns from success of the policy at t, and a probability $1 - r(w_t)$ that the firm will have a profit V_t, giving the returns from failure of the policy at t and continuation of the optimal policy in the future. Hence the expected profits from this vacancy when the firm offers w_t in period t and follows an optimal policy thereafter are

$$r(w_t)Z_t + [1 - r(w_t)]V_t. \tag{1}$$

[12] See Bellman (1957, ch. 3).

[13] The dependence of $r(\cdot)$ on the wage offers of all other firms will not be made explicit in this chapter. See below, chapters 5 and 14 for a discussion of the implications of this dependence.

Since w_t is chosen such that the per-hour profit from this vacancy is always z_t in the future, Z_t in this case is equal to[14]

$$Z_t = \sum_{t'=t+1}^{T} \beta(t') z_t y \equiv B_t z_t y = B_t(pq - w_t)y, \qquad (2)$$

where B_t is equal to the sum $\sum_{t'=t+1}^{T} \beta(t')$.

The optimal wage offer at t is that w_t which maximizes (1). Therefore, the returns from an optimal policy in period t and thereafter, V_{t-1}, are given by

$$V_{t-1} = \underset{w_t}{\text{Max}} \{r(w_t)B_t(pq - w_t)y + [1 - r(w_t)]V_t\}$$
$$(t = 1, \ldots, T-1). \quad (3)$$

Equation (3) is a functional equation in the V_ts. With a terminal condition giving the returns from zero opportunities to offer the job, i.e. giving the value for V_{T-1}, this functional equation system gives unique solutions for the expected returns from an optimal offer policy in all periods in the short run. But at $T - 1$, when the entrepreneur has exhausted all his chances for recruiting a man, his returns from the vacancy will be zero. Thus,

$$V_{T-1} = 0,$$

which together with (3) completes the system.

With knowledge of the sequence of expected returns $V_1, \ldots, V_{T-1}$, the properties of the sequence of wage offers $w_1, \ldots, w_{T-1}$ may be obtained directly from the maximization condition satisfied by (3). Thus, setting the first derivative of the right-hand side of (3) equal to zero we obtain the first-order maximization condition

$$r'(w_t)B_t(pq - w_t)y - r(w_t)B_t y - r'(w_t)V_t = 0. \qquad (4)$$

Now $r(w_t)y$ is what we called in the last chapter the 'supply of labour to the firm', and $r'(w_t)y$ denotes the rate of change of that supply when the firm varies its wage offer (under the assumption $y'(w_t) = 0$). Letting r_t denote $r(w_t)$ and r'_t its derivative with respect to w_t, we may

[14] In this expression we ignore the probability that a worker will quit before the end of the short run if he is taken on at t. This is not very serious because our aim in this chapter is to find the optimal wage policy when the firm has some vacancies to fill, and not to obtain its optimal labour turnover in a dynamic environment. Workers who find an offer acceptable at t will quit after t only if some changes have taken place in the market as a whole. This has some important implications for the workings of the market over time and is raised again in Part III.

solve (4) to give the optimal wage offer at t as

$$w_t = pq - \frac{r_t}{r_t'} - \frac{1}{yB_t}V_t \quad (t = 1, \ldots, T-1). \tag{5}$$

The per-hour profit level implied by this wage offer, which may be referred to as the optimal or chosen profit level, is given by

$$z_t = pq - w_t = \frac{r_t}{r_t'} + \frac{1}{yB_t}V_t \quad (t = 1, \ldots, T-1).$$

Substituting w_t from (5) into (3) we obtain the more explicit functional equation form satisfied by the V_ts as

$$\left.\begin{aligned} V_{t-1} &= V_t + \frac{r_t^2}{r_t'}yB_t \quad (t = 1, \ldots, T-1), \\ V_{T-1} &= 0. \end{aligned}\right\} \tag{6}$$

Thus the optimal wage-offer policy when wages are as flexible as prices is described by equation (5) for every period $t = 1, \ldots, T-1$ in the firm's short run. The value of V_t which enters (5) is given by the solution to the functional equation system (6). This system forms the heart of the firm's policy during adjustment in flexwage, and it will be used in subsequent chapters to obtain the properties of that adjustment process.

Recruitment-standard choice under fixwage

If wages are not as flexible as prices the recruitment policy of firms will be different from that followed when wages are flexible, even if the other features of the economy – the behaviour of searchers in particular – and the firm's objectives are the same under both regimes. We turn now to the derivation of the equations which replace the basic flexwage equations (5) and (6) when wages are rigid.

If wages are completely fixed there is no way in which the firm can change the supply of labour to itself, but there is a way in which the firm can control the profit it receives. Since the efficiency of prospective employees, as measured by their production coefficient q, varies, the firm can make a higher profit by employing workers with high efficiency. Thus if a worker searching the firm at t has a low q, the firm may refuse to recruit him in the hope of finding a more efficient worker to take the job in the future. The problem facing the firm is that by refusing to take on a man with low q it produces nothing from now to the period a new recruit is taken on; but by taking him on it produces below the maximum it can produce with a man with a higher q, provided of course that there are more efficient men willing to accept the historically given wage rate. Thus the crucial factor in the supply of labour to the firm when wages are fixed is not the ratio of the searchers willing to work for the firm at the offered wage, as under flexwage, but the differences in the efficiency of those willing to accept the firm's offer.

Let the wage rate be fixed at w, and let the pair $[q_i, \omega_i(t)]$ denote, respectively, the production coefficient of individual i in the production line of the firm in question, and the reservation wage of the same individual in period t. The supply of labour to the firm in period t under fixwage may be described by the distribution over the production coefficients of those willing to accept the firm's offer in t, given by

$$g_t(q) = g(q_i | \omega_i(t) \leq w) = \frac{g_t(q, w)}{r_t(w)},$$

where $g_t(q, w)$ is the probability that a searcher with coefficient q will be willing to accept the wage offer w, and $r_t(w)$ is, as before, the ratio of those searchers willing to accept w.

Thus when wages are completely fixed the firm should choose that recruitment policy which maximizes expected profits given that the production coefficients of those willing to work for it are distributed according to $g_t(q)$ in each period $t = 1, \ldots, T - 1$. Now, if wages are not completely fixed but 'rigid', in that they may change from time to time but they do not change as frequently as prices, we may still use the same framework to analyse recruitment. If, for instance, w increases in some period t, the ratio of those willing to work for the firm, r_t, increases, whereas the probability that more efficient workers will be willing to accept the offer also increases, since more efficient workers will usually seek higher wages. Thus the distribution over the production coefficients of those willing to accept the firm's offer, $g_t(q)$, shifts to the right; if the wage offer falls it shifts to the left. So if we derive an optimal recruitment policy for any sequence of distributions $g_1, \ldots, g_{T-1}$, infrequent wage changes may be accommodated by considering the effects of variations in the sequence $g_1, \ldots, g_{T-1}$ on the optimal policy.[15]

[15] This topic will be considered in greater detail in chapter 5. In this chapter fixwage may be taken to mean completely fixed wages.

If the wage offer is fixed but the production coefficients of searchers variable, the firm is certain of the cost of a vacancy if filled, but it is uncertain of the returns from that position. Since workers search the firm sequentially, it may be optimal for the firm to refuse to take on a man whose contribution to production does not make the costs of the job worth while. If the firm was searched only once, the worker would be taken on if and only if his contribution to total revenue did not fall below the costs of the job. But with sequential search the firm will in general have more stringent recruitment standards.

In general the firm's recruitment policy in fixwage is described by recruitment sets $Q_1, \ldots, Q_{T-1}$, such that a searcher calling at the firm in period t and willing to accept its wage offer is recruited if and only if his coefficient q belongs to the recruitment set Q_t. Thus the problem facing the firm is to find the recruitment sets implied by an optimal policy. This problem can be solved by a method similar to the one which gave the optimal wage offer under flexwage.

Let V_t denote again the expected profit from a vacancy when there are $T - t - 1$ periods remaining in which the firm can take on a man, and when it follows an optimal recruitment policy in each one of these periods. Now if a man with coefficient q searches the firm in period t, and the firm offers him the job, the net returns from this man will be $Z_t(q)$, given by (2), if the man accepts the offer. (Since in the fixwage system w is not tied to pq, in that p or q may change and w remain fixed, Z_t will depend on q – unlike the flexwage system where the firm planned to make the same profit on each one of its employees taken on at t.) But if the firm refuses to recruit this worker, its expected net returns from the vacancy will be V_t, since now there are $T - t - 1$ periods left in which the firm can try again. Thus the man is recruited if and only if $Z_t(q) \geq V_t$, and so the recruitment set for period t is given by

$$Q_t = \{q | Z_t(q) \geq V_t\} \quad (t = 1, \ldots, T - 1). \tag{7}$$

Once q is known $Z_t(q)$ can immediately be obtained from (2), so the problem facing the firm which wishes to choose an optimal sequence of recruitment sets reduces to the choice of the profit-maximizing value of V_t for all periods $t = 1, \ldots, T - 1$. These values may be shown to satisfy a simple functional equation system similar to that satisfied by their counterpart values in flexwage. Thus, since the qs of those willing to accept the firm's offer at t are distributed according to $g_t(q)$, and since the returns from taking on a man with coefficient

q are given by $Z_t(q)$, whereas the returns from not taking him on are equal to V_t, the expected returns from an optimal policy in period t and thereafter, V_{t-1}, are given by

$$V_{t-1} = \sum_{Q_t} g_t(q)Z_t(q) + \left[1 - \sum_{Q_t} g_t(q)\right] V_t \qquad (t = 1, \ldots, T-1). \qquad (8)$$

With a terminal condition giving the value of V_{T-1}, this functional equation gives a unique solution for each V_t $(t = 1, \ldots, T-2)$.[16] But if the firm reaches period $T - 1$ and the vacancy is still unfilled, its returns from that vacancy will be zero, so $V_{T-1} = 0$. Given $V_{T-1} = 0$, the functional equation (8) gives the values of $V_1, \ldots, V_{T-2}$ which are used in (7) to give the recruitment sets implied by an optimal policy.

The functional equation relating successive V_ts may be put into a more convenient form with some rearranging of its terms and the introduction of some new notation. Thus, by rearranging the terms of (8) we obtain

$$V_{t-1} = V_t + \sum_{Q_t} g_t(q)\left[Z_t(q) - V_t\right] \quad (t = 1, \ldots, T-1).$$

Furthermore, let b_t denote the probability of recruiting the searcher at t, i.e.

$$b_t = \sum_{Q_t} g_t(q),$$

and Y_t the expected profit from those taken on at t, conditional on their recruitment, i.e.

$$Y_t = E\left[Z_t(q) \mid q \in Q_t\right] = \frac{1}{b_t} \sum_{Q_t} g_t(q)Z_t(q).$$

Using this notation in (8) the functional equation system under fix-wage becomes

$$\left.\begin{aligned} V_{t-1} &= b_t Y_t + (1 - b_t)V_t \quad (t = 1, \ldots, T-1), \\ V_{T-1} &= 0. \end{aligned}\right\} \qquad (9)$$

Since b_t is the probability of success at t, Y_t the expected profit from successful recruitment, and V_t the expected profit from unsuccessful recruitment, equation (9) expresses the expected returns from an optimal policy in period t and thereafter as the expected value of the

[16] See, in addition to Bellman (1957), Karlin (1962).

returns from successful and the returns from unsuccessful recruitment at t.

Now a searcher with coefficient q calling at period t will be taken on if $Z_t(q) \geq V_t$. The firm's 'recruitment standard' may be taken to be given by the minimum value of q that satisfies this condition, since this value of q sets the minimum standards of efficiency that potential employees must satisfy. Denote this minimum value of q by ξ_t. Using (2) we obtain

$$B_t(p\,\xi_t - w)y = V_t \quad (t = 1, \ldots, T - 1).$$

Solving this for ξ_t we obtain the firm's recruitment standard at t as

$$\xi_t = \frac{w}{p} + \frac{1}{pyB_t} V_t \quad (t = 1, \ldots, T - 1), \tag{10}$$

an expression which formally looks very similar to the equivalent expression for flexwage, (5).

It follows by the continuity of $Z_t(q)$ that the recruitment set for period t may be written as

$$Q_t = \{q \,|\, q \geq \xi_t\}, \tag{7'}$$

i.e. a worker is taken on if and only if his efficiency does not fall short of ξ_t. Equations (10) and (9) are therefore the fixwage counterparts of (5) and (6), and may be used to obtain the firm's policy during adjustment when wages are rigid. This system of equations will serve as the background to our discussion of the fixwage system in subsequent chapters, just as the latter system will provide the background for the flexwage system.

Summary and conclusion

In this chapter we derived the short-run recruitment policy of the firm when the production function exhibits fixed coefficients and the firm attempts to maximize profits. We considered two extreme cases of recruitment. In the first place, a firm may be willing to vary its wage offer as frequently as prices, and so use the wage rate to control the supply of labour to itself. The problem facing the firm in this system, which we called flexwage, is that by increasing its wage rate it incurs greater costs, but it also reduces the expected waiting period before a worker can be found to work for it. The optimal wage offer in each period t was shown to be given by a simple equation which contained a functional form as one of its arguments. The optimal value of this functional form was shown to satisfy a recursive relation, so the recursive relation system and the equation giving the optimal wage offer specify completely the optimal recruitment policy under flexwage (see equations (5) and (6)).

If the firm does not vary its wage offer it has no control over the supply of labour to itself. But it can control its profits by choosing to reject inefficient workers and recruit only the highly efficient ones. Thus in this system, which we called fixwage, the recruitment policy is described by 'recruitment sets', one for each period, such that a worker is taken on if and only if he belongs to the recruitment set of the period he searches the firm. The problem facing the firm in fixwage is that by choosing to recruit inefficient workers the firm reduces the waiting period before successful recruitment, but it also foregoes the chance of finding more efficient workers in the future. The optimal recruitment sets were shown to be completely specified by a 'recruitment standard' which gives the minimum efficiency that the firm is willing to tolerate from potential employees. The recruitment standard depends on a functional form which is similar to the one obtained in flexwage, and satisfies a similar recursive system. So formally the flexwage and fixwage recruitment policies are similar, although in interpretation and properties they may be different (see (7′), (10) and (9)).

It is to the interpretation and the analysis of the properties of these optimal policies to which we shall turn in the following chapters. Since the optimal policy is partly given by a recursive system, the exact solution to the critical values involved in each case is hard to obtain, and it is doubtful whether they can be obtained without imposing some strong restrictions on the functions involved, and without the use of numerical techniques. However, as economists we have learned to obtain our best results not by obtaining exact solutions to complicated functional systems, and then analysing these solutions, but by analysing the *structural* properties of our systems, and deducing strong restrictions on the optimal policy implicit in those systems, without ever knowing what that optimal policy is.[17] This is the method which we shall be utilizing here, so the analysis naturally falls into the domain of 'pure theory'. Econometric estimation will have to be another story.

[17] But we need to know that a solution exists. This, of course, is the method of 'theoretical' economics, not econometrics. Compare, for instance, the way the Slutsky restrictions on demand functions are obtained, and the additional restrictions needed for econometric estimation of demand functions. The former is logically prior to the latter.

4

Job Offers: Dynamic Properties

If a firm is forced to follow either a fixwage or a flexwage policy, it will do so to recruit labour and produce when expected profits do not fall below zero. But if it is free to follow any one of these extremes, or any combination of the two, and its objective is to maximize profits, it will normally choose that policy which gives higher profits, both in the short and the long run. If flexwage proves a more profitable alternative, then profit maximization in the postulated environment implies that money wages are as flexible as prices, whereas if fixwage is found to be more profitable money wages will be more rigid than prices. For this and other reasons the choice between flexwage and fixwage is of extreme importance, in particular with respect to the dynamic movement of the system as a whole.[1] But at the same time it is also a very difficult problem to deal with, and if anything at all can be said about it, it will have to await a more detailed investigation of the worker and firm decision problem than we have at this stage. So we shall postpone this issue until much later. In the meantime, we shall talk of flexwage and fixwage as two alternative systems, with some firms preferring one and some the other, and we shall analyse the properties of each one separately without saying what factors might induce a firm to choose one or the other.

The nature of the solution

The similarities and differences between a flexwage and a fixwage policy may be brought out most sharply if we consider the nature of the solution in each case. Before doing this, however, we should emphasize that both flexwage and fixwage are *recruitment* policies, i.e. they are policies which describe the behaviour of the firm when it has one or more vacancies, and when it is trying to increase its

[1] See below, chapter 14.

labour force. So they both describe the policy of the firm during adjustment, and they are not relevant to the production process itself. Production takes place with the aid of labour and capital already possessed by the firm, and it is independent of the way that labour and capital was obtained. The neoclassical theory of production, of course, does *not* have a theory of how the firm obtains its factors of production, i.e. it does not have a theory of the trading sequence in labour and capital markets. In this model we also do not have a theory of how capital is obtained, but we do have a theory of how labour is obtained. All the other features of our model are neoclassical, so the model may be regarded as an extension of the standard neoclassical model to a situation of decentralization and bilateral trading in the labour market. For this reason it is on the analysis of the trading sequence in the labour market that we shall concentrate, and in particular on the optimal policy of firms and households given the trading arrangement.

The nature of the trading sequence in the labour market, whereby the firm makes a job offer and waits for suitably qualified workers to search it, implies that the firm is uncertain of the type of labour it will be able to find, and also of the number of periods it will have to wait before finding it. By choice of an optimal policy we mean the choice of that wage offer or recruitment standard which will maximize its expected profit, given these uncertainties and the behaviour of labour under the postulated trading arrangement. Once a vacancy is filled, however, all uncertainty is resolved; the firm is certain of the efficiency of the worker once recruited, and it is certain of the price that the final product will fetch in the market. So uncertainty in this model is purely a feature of adjustment, and it disappears as soon as the firm adjusts its labour force fully to its capital. If the firm finds it optimal to change its capital at the end of the short run, a new process of adjustment will begin, that of adjusting the old labour force to the new conditions. So there will be new uncertainties, and a new recruitment policy will have to be formulated to ensure that expected profit is as high as possible under the new conditions.[2]

[2] The capital decision is analysed in chapter 13. The assumption that uncertainty is solely a feature of disequilibrium is a methodological device used extensively in the consumption–search model, so it is discussed again in some detail in chapters 6 and 7. The same principles, however, underlie the firm recruitment model during adjustment.

In flexwage the firm maximizes the expected profit from each one of its vacancies by choosing an appropriate wage rate. This choice problem is not different in principle from that involved when the firm has some monopsony power in the labour market. In general the firm has monopsony power when the supply curve of labour to itself is upward sloping, i.e. when it has to put up its wage rate to attract more labour. The same constraint holds here in the short run. The firm can only expect to attract additional labour within a specified period of time if it puts its wage offer up, since only then will the ratio of those searching the firm and willing to accept its offer go up. The difference between the general monopsony model and the present one lies in that now the *source* of the monopsony power is known, and further that the firm cannot be certain of the exact amount of labour that a given wage offer will attract. Thus, the source of the monopsony power lies in the nature of the trading arrangement itself, in particular in the search process which allocates labour to the various firms in the economy. This same process gives rise to the uncertainty about the exact outcome of a particular wage offer, but if the firm maximizes expected profits this uncertainty will have no effect on its optimal recruitment policy, because it will be indifferent to risk.

Thus the flexwage problem appears to be the natural extension of the standard neoclassical labour-demand problem to a decentralized labour market. However, the fixwage problem is only superficially different from the flexwage in this particular respect. Since both the flexwage and fixwage firms face the same labour-supply constraint, they are both monopsonists in their recruitment roles. And since they both attempt to maximize profits, they both try to exploit this monopsony power to their advantage. In fact, the relationship between the real wage rate and the marginal product of labour in the two systems is remarkably similar, and it is itself a special case of the general relationship holding in monopsonistic competition.

Thus, just as the monopsonistic firm will plan to make positive profits by paying a wage rate which is below the value of the marginal product of labour, the firm in the decentralized labour market will also plan to make a positive profit, by ensuring that none of its workers is getting paid as much as the value of his marginal product. The knowledge of the source of the monopsony power which we have in this model enables us to get a formal expression for this divergency between the real wage rate and the marginal product of labour, and also to obtain how this divergency moves over time.

Producers

Consider first flexwage. The optimal (money) wage offer under flexwage is given by

$$w_t = pq - z_t \quad (t = 1, \ldots, T - 1), \tag{1}$$

where p is the price of output, q is the production coefficient of the worker, and z_t is the per-hour profit level obtained from those recruited at t, given by

$$z_t = \frac{r_t}{r'_t} + \frac{1}{yB_t} V_t \quad (t = 1, \ldots, T - 1). \tag{2}$$

V_t is the expected profit from the vacancy when the firm is following an optimal recruitment policy after period t, and satisfies the functional equation system

$$\left.\begin{aligned} V_{t-1} &= V_t + \frac{r_t^2}{r'_t} yB_t \quad (t = 1, \ldots, T - 1), \\ V_{T-1} &= 0. \end{aligned}\right\} \tag{3}$$

B_t is equal to the sum of the discounting factors $\beta(t + 1), \ldots, \beta(T)$, y is the hours worked per period, assumed fixed, $r_t = r(w_t)$ is the proportion of those searchers calling at t who are willing to accept the firm's offer, and $r'_t = r'(w_t)$ is the derivative of that ratio with respect to w_t. The firm's monopsony power arises because when it puts its wage offer up, more workers are willing to accept its offer, i.e. the derivative r'_t is positive.

Clearly, when production coefficients are fixed, marginal product equals average product equals the production coefficient q. Thus the firm offers less than the worker's marginal product at t if planned profits z_t are positive. Now, from (3)

$$V_{t-1} - V_t = \frac{r_t^2}{r'_t} yB_t > 0 \quad (t = 1, \ldots, T - 1),$$

so the expected profits from an optimal policy fall over time. Since $V_{T-1} = 0$, expected profits are positive in all periods in the short run, except the last one when they fall to zero.[3] It follows directly from (2) that z_t, the per-hour profit level obtained from those ac-

[3] It is tempting to interpret this along Arrow (1959) lines. If the firm has T periods to adjust, it should have more monopsony power at first, than when some of these periods have elapsed. Just before T the monopsony power disappears altogether. So if the expected profit reflects monopsony power, it should be positive and falling over time, until it reaches zero just before T. This, in fact, is the behaviour of the V_ts implied by the optimal policy.

tually recruited at t, is positive in all periods in the short run. So the firm's real wage offer w_t/p, at t, falls short of the worker's marginal product by the real value of per-hour profits, z_t/p. The real wage rate is *always* less than the marginal product of labour, although as we shall show in the next section it is tending towards it over time.

In the standard theory of the firm in monopsonistic labour market conditions we learn that the firm can fix either the wage rate or the quantity of labour employed, but not both. If it fixes its wage rate the supply schedule of labour gives the quantity that will be employed; if it fixes the quantity the same gives the wage rate. This simple rule extends in the flexwage system in a straightforward manner, with the difference that now time plays a more explicit role. Thus, if the firm fixes its wage rate the supply schedule gives the *expected* quantity of labour that will be supplied *within a specified period of time*; if it chooses its expected quantity of employment and the time period within which it wants to have this employment, the supply schedule gives the wage rate.

The decentralization of exchange implies that the firm cannot adjust automatically from one position to another – given its wage offer and the expected quantity of employment, the time period required to adjust is given by the supply schedule. Thus, although the firm in the decentralized labour market has monopsony power, its problem is different from that of the monopsonistic firm in a centralized market, because of the sequential nature of the trading arrangement which gives rise to the monopsony power in the former. In the (timeless) centralized market model when the firm has monopsony power, there are one-to-one pairs of the form (w, y), giving the number of hours of work that will be supplied at the wage rate w. The firm can move automatically and costlessly to any feasible pair (w, y). In the decentralized labour market, however, the constraint is a triple of the form (w, y, t), giving the expected number of hours that will be supplied at a wage rate w as a function of the waiting period t. Thus if (w, y, t) is a feasible triple, the firm can expect to get y hours after t periods if it offers w. If it wants to reduce the expected waiting period it will have to put its wage rate up, i.e. if (w', y, t') is also feasible, w' must be greater than w if t' is less than t.

The same adjustment costs exist in the fixwage system, but the firm's problem is different, because the heterogeneous nature of the labour force and the constancy of the wage rate imply that the firm can make a different profit on different employees. This leads to the choice of a recruitment standard, i.e. a minimum acceptable efficiency level required of one's employees. Since wages and prices are known, the recruitment standard also sets a minimum acceptable profit level from each employee, so if a searcher is just capable of qualifying for the job the firm takes him on and receives the minimum acceptable profit from his production. But if another searcher is more efficient and so yields the firm a higher profit the firm also takes him on at the same rate, and has more profits from him. Thus, a man is taken on if and only if he is efficient enough to yield the firm above an optimally chosen profit level, which we denoted by V_t. If the man's contribution to the firm's profits does not fall below V_t at period t the firm is willing to keep him, but if at some other period t' his contribution falls below $V_{t'}$ it will dismiss him. Any profit above V_t that the workman is capable of yielding is 'economic rent', i.e. it is a bonus to the firm, and it does not affect its short-run policy when it rises or falls.

Thus the recruitment policy of the fixwage firm has some 'satisficing' features.[4] The minimum acceptable profit levels V_t $(t = 1, \ldots, T-1)$ may be referred to as *reservation profit levels*, since the firm will never let its actual profits from a man fall below V_t in any period t. So in this environment satisficing behaviour arises as an optimal decision rule during adjustment when the *a priori* intention is to *maximize* profits. This is in contrast to 'behaviourist' theory, which introduces satisficing theory *a priori* as a better description of the decision process than maximization when there is imperfect information. Maximization, it is argued, offers very limited scope for the analysis of a decision *process*.[5]

The derivation of a policy with satisficing features from more primitive assumptions about individual behaviour is obviously a strength of the model. It also makes the fixwage decision process a markedly different one from that involved in flexwage. Nevertheless, the remainder of this and the next chapter will argue that the two systems satisfy the same broad properties, in that the firm will be behaving similarly in both fixwage and flexwage, given that wages in the former are rigid. Thus fixwage is the 'dual' of flexwage – in the latter the firm manipulates wage rates (short-run production costs) to maximize profits, whereas in the former it manipulates recruitment

[4] See Simon (1959) for a survey of satisficing and maximizing theory.
[5] See for instance Winter (1971).

standards (short-run contribution to production) to achieve the same objective.

We first establish that the fixwage firm ensures that the marginal product of each one of its employees is greater than the real wage rate, just as the flexwage firm ensures that the offered wage rate falls below the value of its employees' marginal product. In the next section we consider the dynamic properties of each policy more explicitly.

The recruitment standard at time t is given by

$$\xi_t = \frac{w}{p} + \frac{1}{pyB_t} V_t \quad (t = 1, \ldots, T - 1), \tag{4}$$

where ξ_t is the minimum coefficient level (efficiency) that the firm is willing to accept from those recruited at t, and all the other variables are as before. V_t now satisfies the functional equation system

$$\left.\begin{aligned} V_{t-1} &= V_t + \sum_{Q_t} g_t(q)\left[Z_t(q) - V_t\right] \quad (t = 1, \ldots, T - 1), \\ V_{T-1} &= 0, \end{aligned}\right\} \tag{5}$$

where Q_t is the recruitment set at t, given by

$$Q_t = \{q \,|\, Z_t(q) \geq V_t\} = \{q \,|\, q \geq \xi_t\},$$

$g_t(q)$ is the distribution of coefficient levels of those willing to accept the firm's offer at t, and $Z_t(q)$ is the total profit derived from a man with coefficient q recruited at t, from $t + 1$ to the end of the horizon.

Now from (5) we have

$$V_{t-1} - V_t = \sum_{Q_t} g_t(q)\left[Z_t(q) - V_t\right] > 0 \quad (t = 1, \ldots, T - 1),$$

so, as with flexwage, the expected profits from a vacancy (which is the same as the reservation profit level in fixwage) are positive and declining over time until they reach zero at the end of the adjustment period.[6] It follows from (4) that the reservation coefficient level ξ_t is greater than the real wage rate w/p in all periods in the short run, except the last one when it is equal to it. Thus the firm is never willing to recruit anybody who will contribute to production less than the real wage rate, and, apart from the last period in the short run when it runs out of all opportunities to take on a man, it will demand a marginal product above the real wage rate even from the most inefficient

[6] Thus footnote 3 applies in fixwage as well.

of its employees. The similarity with the flexwage policy, and that of the firm under monopsonistic conditions in general, is obvious.

The dynamic path of wage offers and recruitment standards

During the adjustment period there is a positive probability that the firm will be searched by some individuals who, after observing its wage offer, will walk out without offering their labour services for sale at the observed wage. The question arises as to how the firm will respond to this if it occurs, i.e. how will the flexwage firm adjust its wage offer, and the fixwage firm its recruitment standard, if at all. This is the question that we shall investigate in this section. Everything else in the system will be assumed fixed, so we shall continue assuming that market conditions are stationary. That is, every period may be thought of as identical to the previous one, apart from the fact that the firm now knows that the worker who searched it last period walked out again without offering his labour services for sale.

Since we have assumed that there is only a finite number of periods T in the short run, and that the firm has only $T - 1$ opportunities in which it can take on a workman, when a searcher turns down an offer the firm knows that there is one period less in which it can take on a worker, and that one more period has elapsed without any production forthcoming from that position. This waiting cost turns out to be crucial in the determination of the optimal recruitment policy. In fact, it is the existence of this waiting cost that leads to the fall in the expected profits from a vacancy when the firm is unsuccessful in finding a suitable worker to take it. If the horizon were infinite and the firm was not impatient, every period would be identical to every other period, since the firm could always look ahead to an infinite number of opportunities to take on a man and produce with the capital available, so the expected profits from a vacancy would be the same at all periods.

Now consider more explicitly the dynamic path of wage offers in a flexwage system when the firm is unsuccessful in finding a man to take its offer. The path, of course, is implicit in equations (1) – (3) which describe the optimal policy. To derive it more explicitly we assume that $r'_t = r'(w_t)$, the slope of the supply function, is constant and independent of the wage rate. This, in fact, is a rather mild restriction, since it simply asserts that the supply curve of labour to the firm is a straight line, rising upwards from left to right.

From (1) and (2) we obtain, for any pair of consecutive wage offers

$$w_{t-1} = pq - \frac{r_{t-1}}{r'} - \frac{1}{yB_{t-1}} V_{t-1},$$

$$w_t = pq - \frac{r_t}{r'} - \frac{1}{yB_t} V_t,$$

where r' is the common slope of the supply function. Subtracting we obtain

$$w_{t-1} - w_t = \frac{r_t}{r'} + \frac{1}{yB_t} V_t - \frac{r_{t-1}}{r'} - \frac{1}{yB_{t-1}} V_{t-1}. \tag{6'}$$

Now if the wage rate at $t-1$ is higher than that at t, the ratio r_{t-1} of those willing to accept the firm's offer at $t-1$, will be higher than the ratio r_t of those willing to accept the offer at t. Similarly, if $w_{t-1} < w_t$ then $r_{t-1} < r_t$, and if $w_{t-1} = w_t$ then $r_{t-1} = r_t$. It follows that the difference $w_{t-1} - w_t$ always has the opposite sign of the difference $r_t - r_{t-1}$. Writing (6′) as

$$w_{t-1} - w_t = \frac{1}{r'}(r_t - r_{t-1}) + \frac{1}{y}\left(\frac{1}{B_t} V_t - \frac{1}{B_{t-1}} V_{t-1}\right) \tag{6}$$

we immediately obtain that $w_{t-1} - w_t$ must have the same sign as the difference

$$\frac{1}{B_t} V_t - \frac{1}{B_{t-1}} V_{t-1}, \tag{7}$$

for all $t = 2, \ldots, T-1$.

This difference will always be negative when the firm has only two opportunities in which it can take on a worker. Writing $t = T-1$, we know from the functional equation system (3) that $V_{T-1} = 0$, and $V_{T-2} = yB_{T-1}\, r^2_{T-1}/r' > 0$. So in a two-period model, or when the firm has exhausted all its opportunities for recruitment apart from the last two, the wage offer will certainly increase in the second period if recruitment in the first period is unsuccessful.

This intuitive result does not, unfortunately, extend to the multi-period horizon under all conceivable circumstances. However, it can be shown that the difference in (7) will be negative in all periods t for all 'reasonable' values that the parameters may take. To show this we write (7) as

$$\frac{1}{B_{t-1}}\left(\frac{B_{t-1}}{B_t}V_t - V_{t-1}\right) = \frac{1}{B_{t-1}}\left[\frac{\beta(t)}{B_t}V_t - (V_{t-1} - V_t)\right], \quad (7')$$

since $B_{t-1} = \beta(t) + B_t$. So (7) has the same sign as the difference in the square brackets on the right-hand side of (7′). From the functional equation system (3) we know that $V_{t-1} - V_t = yB_t r_t^2/r'$, whereas by substituting successively $V_{T-1}, V_{T-2}, \ldots, V_{t+1}$ from (3) into itself we obtain

$$V_t = \frac{y}{r'}(B_{t+1}\, r_{t+1}^2 + \ldots + B_{T-1}\, r_{T-1}^2).$$

Hence (7) has the sign of

$$\frac{\beta(t)}{B_t}(B_{t+1}\, r_{t+1}^2 + \ldots + B_{T-1}\, r_{T-1}^2) - B_t r_t^2. \quad (8)$$

Recalling that r_t represents the ratio of those willing to accept the firm's offer at t (or alternatively the probability that a random searcher would be willing to accept the firm's offer at t), we would not expect large variations between the values of r in consecutive periods, even if wage rates change frequently. But if r_t^2 is not 'much' smaller than its counterparts in future periods, the sign of (8) will be the same as the sign of the difference in the coefficients

$$\frac{\beta(t)}{B_t}(B_{t+1} + \ldots + B_{T-1}) - B_t, \quad (9)$$

which is certainly negative if $\beta(t) = 1/(1 + \rho)^{t-1}$ and $B_t = \sum_{t'=t+1}^{T} \beta(t')$, as it would be when there is a single discount rate ρ.

If r_t^2 is much smaller than its counterpart values in the future then (8) may, of course, become positive, in which case the wage rate will be reduced from period $t - 1$ to period t. However, considering the difference in the coefficients in (9) we can show that, on average, future wage offers must be such that about one-and-a-half times the number of the workers willing to accept the firm's offer in the current period should be willing to accept it in the future.[7] Only then will the wage rate be reduced from period $t - 1$ to period t; i.e. a firm will

[7] This may be shown by taking the ratio of the coefficients in (9) and summing the terms in the brackets. To avoid complicated manipulations, the same result may be obtained by considering reasonable values of the discount rate and length of horizon. For instance, for a discount rate of 3 per cent, and ten remaining periods in the horizon ($t = 2$, $T = 12$), (8) becomes positive when $\bar{r} \geq 1.56\, r_t$, where $\bar{r}$ is the average of $r_{t+1}, \ldots, r_{T-1}$.

consider not increasing its wage offer in the current period only if it plans to increase it rapidly in the future, such that many more workers will be willing to accept its offer in the future than now. The shorter the future that the firm looks ahead the more likely it is to increase its wage offer. If it looks ahead to only one more period it will definitely increase its offer.

Thus the mathematical restrictions implied by the optimal policy when wages are flexible say that a firm may not consider increasing its wage offer when a man searches it but walks out again without taking the job, if and only if it expects a lot more men to search it, and if it plans to increase its offer very rapidly if the same happens in future. They also say that if 60 per cent or more of all searchers are willing to accept the firm's offer, the offer will definitely be raised over time when it is turned down by a searcher. But if, say, only 40 per cent of searchers are willing to accept the offer, the firm may actually lower its offer now, planning to raise it in future such that on average over 60 per cent of searchers would be willing to accept it. This has the rather paradoxical implication that it is the low-wage firm that may consider not raising its wage offer at all periods, the high-wage one being certain to raise it. However, it is not *any* low-wage firm that may lower its offer, but only those that look ahead to a long future, and plan to raise their wage offers again in future, well above the level prevailing in the current period. Thus over long periods of time those firms which are unsuccessful in recruiting labour will certainly raise their offers, although there may be temporary reductions in some offers.

We may infer from this that the typical firm will raise its wage offer by a little when it is searched by someone who is not willing to accept its offer. Thus when a firm opens up new vacancies it may offer a wage rate which is well below the worker's marginal product. If it finds a worker quickly to take this low offer then it will have very high profits from this man's production. But if the workers who search the firm at first are unwilling to accept its offer, it will gradually raise it towards the value of the marginal product of potential employees, but, as we have seen, it will never quite raise it up to that level.

This result has the important implication that if a firm is lucky enough to find a workman to take the job quickly, it will be paying less wages than one which had to wait longer before finding an employee. Each firm's experience in the market will therefore influence the wage rate that it offers. Since searchers call, to a large extent, at random, the experiences of firms are likely to diverge. So optimal firm behaviour under the offer–acceptance arrangement implies that firms' wage rates will diverge – even if firms are identical in all other respects – because their market experience will diverge.[8]

If the firm is operating in a fixwage system it will respond to the fact that expected profits fall over time if it is unsuccessful in its recruitment policy by changing its recruitment standard. The recruitment standard, as we have seen, gives the minimum efficiency that the firm will tolerate from its employees, and it is given by equation (4). The formal similarity between equation (4) and equation (2), giving the optimal profit level under flexwage, implies that the dynamic properties satisfied by the flexwage profit level and the fixwage recruitment standard should be broadly similar. Since the profit level is linearly and inversely related to the wage offer, the dynamic properties of the recruitment standard are similar to those of the wage offer but opposite in direction.

Thus, along the lines of the result obtained in the flexwage system, it can be shown that the recruitment standard will very likely be falling during unsuccessful recruitment, i.e. the firm will lower its recruitment standards if the worker applying for the job at period t is not good enough to qualify. Subtracting ξ_t from ξ_{t-1}, as they are given in (4), we obtain

$$\xi_{t-1} - \xi_t = \frac{1}{py}\left(\frac{1}{B_{t-1}} V_{t-1} - \frac{1}{B_t} V_t\right), \qquad (10)$$

so the difference $\xi_{t-1} - \xi_t$ has the same sign as the difference in the brackets. This result is the fixwage counterpart of the result in (6) and (7), so using the functional equation system (5), just as we used (3) in flexwage, we can obtain the properties of the path of the recruitment standard over time.

Thus in a two-period model (or when there are only two opportunities remaining in which the firm can take on a man) the recruitment standard will certainly fall. Putting $t = T - 1$, and $V_{T-1} = 0$, $V_{T-2} > 0$, in (10) we immediately get $\xi_{T-2} > \xi_{T-1}$. The change in the recruitment standard in any other period t may be obtained from (10) and the functional equation system (5) along the lines of the discussion of the change in wage rates in the flexwage system so we shall not repeat

[8] This meets one of the most damaging criticisms made to the traditional flexwage model of Phelps (1970) and Mortensen (1970*a*), in particular by Rothschild (1973). See also below, chapter 13.

the same argument here. However, it can also be obtained more directly as follows. Solve equation (4) for V_t, and write also the corresponding expression for V_{t-1}. Subtracting V_t from V_{t-1} we may write the difference as

$$V_{t-1} - V_t = B_t py(\xi_{t-1} - \xi_t) + \beta(t)y(p\xi_{t-1} - w).$$

But from the functional equation (5) this difference is equal to

$$\sum_{Q_t} g_t(q)\,[Z_t(q) - V_t] = B_t py \sum_{Q_t} g_t(q)(q - \xi_t).$$

Equating these we obtain that ξ_t exceeds ξ_{t-1} (i.e. the recruitment standard rises from $t-1$ to t) if the discounted per-hour reservation *profit* $\beta(t)(p\xi_{t-1} - w)$, in period $t-1$, exceeds the expected discounted accumulated *gross revenue* made per hour's work supplied in all periods in the horizon after t, over and above the reservation level, $B_t p \sum_{Q_t} g_t(q)(q - \xi_t)$. Clearly, this is unlikely to occur in practice, and the more heterogeneous the labour force, the more likely it is to be violated.[9] If it is violated, the firm will lower its recruitment standard if the searchers calling at $t-1$ are not recruited.

Thus, just as wage offers in the flexwage system will vary according to each firm's experience in the market, recruitment standards in the fixwage system will also vary according to each firm's experience in the market. A firm which has just opened up some new vacancies is likely to have higher recruitment standards than one whose vacancies have been standing idle for some time, even if their wage offers are identical. So if a worker finds that a firm paying a wage rate w is unwilling to recruit him, although it has some vacancies, he need not take that as implying that he should search for a lower wage: another firm paying w, or even above it, may be willing to take him on.

Summary and conclusion

In this chapter we touched on some of the most important features of the workings of the firm during adjustment. We first showed that the two extreme systems of recruitment which we described in the last chapter, flexwage and fixwage, satisfy the same broad properties and differ only in points of detail – in the first one firms respond to changes in their environment by changing their wage rate, whereas

9 See below, pp. 64–5.

in the second by changing their recruitment standard. The objective when changing them is the same in both systems: to maximize the expected profits from an optimal recruitment policy in the future.

The firm in the decentralized labour market exploits its power to influence the supply of labour to itself and acts as a monopsonist. Thus the wage rate is always less than the value of the marginal product of labour, so the firm plans to make a positive profit on each one of its employees. By using the recursive nature of the recruitment policy we were able to introduce time explicitly into the process of wage formation, something which has eluded the more traditional analysis of labour markets. First, we showed that time, and the firm's experience over it, is one of the factors that influence the firm's recruitment policy, whether it be choice of a wage rate or choice of a recruitment standard. Since there is a probability between zero and one that a random searcher would be willing to accept the firm's offer (and, in fixwage, that the firm would be willing to take him on) firms' experiences are likely to diverge right from the first period of search. Thus wage rates and recruitment standards will differ across firms, even if firms are identical in all other respects.

Second, wage offers and recruitment standards will not vary at random over time, but they are likely to follow a well-defined dynamic path. When the firm opens up one or more vacancies it will normally offer a low wage, or fix a high recruitment standard, at first, but it will raise its wage rate and lower its recruitment standard when the workers who search the firm walk out again without taking the job. Thus, the discrepancy between the value of the marginal product of labour and the wage rate will fall over time if the firm is not successful in finding enough workers to take its vacancies quickly. However, this discrepancy will never decline to zero in the short run – even the firm which manages to find a worker only after a long waiting period is unwilling to offer as high a wage as the value of his marginal product.

The result on the dynamic path of wage rates is clearly related to the more traditional stability problem, analysed in the literature without exploring its foundations in optimizing individual behaviour. In this book we have chosen to shift the balance and concentrate on the underlying individual behaviour, so we shall not attempt a full coverage of the stability properties of the model. However, we shall return to it again in the last two chapters, where we shall set the stage for the analysis of the market implications of the model.

5

Changes in the Supply of Labour and Prices

In the last two chapters we obtained the profit-maximizing behaviour of firms when exchange in the labour market is decentralized and takes place according to an offer–acceptance arrangement. If the firm offers a wage rate w_t and has a recruitment standard ξ_t, the probability of finding a worker to take the vacancy at t is $b_t = \sum_{q \geq \xi_t} g(q, w_t)$, and if $\xi_t = 0$ this becomes equal to $r(w_t)$. Thus there is a probability between zero and one, equal to $(1 - b_1) \ldots (1 - b_{t-1})b_t$, that the vacancy will be standing idle for t periods exactly.

In a neoclassical world, where all markets are centralized and trading does not take time, it does not take the firm any time to find the workers it needs to fill all its vacancies. Thus in a sequential environment the waiting period between the time of the opening up of vacancies and the time of recruiting labour to them is always equal to unity if the world is neoclassical, but it may be greater than unity in our model. The *expected* waiting period in our model is equal to

$$\sum_{t=1}^{T-1} (1 - b_1) \ldots (1 - b_{t-1})b_t t,$$

which is greater than one if $b_t < 1$ for all t. We may call the waiting period between the opening up of new vacancies and the recruitment of labour to them as the period of adjustment, since it is the period during which the firm is trying to adjust its labour force from the current level to the desired level given its capital.[1]

In this chapter we shall investigate the response of the firm during its adjustment period to changes in its environment. When the adjustment period is of non-trivial length the environment within

[1] The period of adjustment is more interesting in the model of job search, because it may be related to temporary unemployment. Since the formal structure of the job-searching and recruitment models is the same, the discussion of the properties of the length of adjustment is postponed until chapter 11, where it is related more explicitly to unemployment.

which the firm operates may change. We should then expect the firm's policy during adjustment to respond to this change, such that expected profits are maximized both before and after the change.

We shall consider the effects of two general types of changes, changes in current and expected prices, and changes in the supply of labour to the firm. These, in turn, may be the result of several types of changes which fall into two main classes, exogenous changes in the environment and changes due to the actions of other firms and individuals. The inter-relationships between firm actions during adjustment is of considerable interest, and it will be investigated in some detail.

The effects of changes in prices and the supply of labour are, of course, two of the central questions occupying traditional theory, and two questions for which traditional theory provides a clear-cut answer. Thus, in a neoclassical world where the demand for labour is determined by the marginal productivity conditions, an increase in the price of output increases the demand for labour and raises the money wage rate, whereas a decrease in the supply of labour (increase in the supply price of labour) reduces the quantity demanded and raises the wage rate. As it will be shown below, the response of the firm during adjustment is remarkably consistent with the response of the firm in neoclassical equilibrium, whatever the system within which the firm is adjusting. We shall first investigate the effects of changes in the supply of labour and then derive the effects of changes in prices.

Changes in the supply of labour

By supply of labour we mean two things. First, the distribution of the production coefficients of those searching the firm, and second the distribution of the reservation wages of searchers. The first factor determines the productivity of potential labour input, whereas the second determines the willingness of labour to accept the firm's offer, and hence the expected waiting period before recruitment and production.

Flexwage. The policy of the firm during adjustment in flexwage is described by the following set of equations.

$$w_t = qp - z_t \qquad (t = 1, \ldots, T - 1), \tag{1}$$

$$z_t = \frac{r(w_t)}{r'(w_t)} + \frac{1}{yB_t} V_t \quad (t = 1, \ldots, T - 1), \tag{2}$$

$$\left.\begin{aligned} V_{t-1} &= V_t + \frac{r^2(w_t)}{r'(w_t)} yB_t \quad (t = 1, \ldots, T - 1), \\ V_{T-1} &= 0. \end{aligned}\right\} \tag{3}$$

In this system the firm is indifferent between the efficiencies of its potential employees, and it plans to make the same profit on all men, whatever their efficiency. Therefore a change in the supply of labour under flexwage has a non-trivial effect on policy only if it is manifested through a change in labour's reservation wage. We shall consider the case of a fall in the supply of labour, or equivalently, a rise in reservation wages. The firm is affected by this change to the extent that a lower proportion of searchers will be willing to accept a given job offer.

Thus, suppose the ratio r, of those willing to accept the firm's offer, falls in some period t. From the functional equation (3), V_t and all other values of V after t are unaffected, whereas from (2) z_t, the optimal profit level chosen at t, falls. Hence the wage rate offered at t rises. This will compensate, to some extent, the decline in the ratio of those willing to accept the firm's offer, since the increase in the wage rate has made the firm's job offer more attractive, but not to the full extent. Hence V_{t-1} will also decline, and from the functional equation (3) all other Vs prior to $t - 1$ will also go down. Since the Vs decrease, optimal profits at all periods prior to t also decrease, and so the wage offer is increased in all periods prior to t.

To obtain the effect more formally suppose the ratio in period t depends on a parameter θ which changes, and, as before, treat the derivative $r_t' = r'(w_t)$ as a constant. Furthermore, write $\partial r/\partial\theta = 1$ for period t, and zero for all other periods. Differentiating (1) with respect to θ we obtain the effect on period t's wage offer, w_t, as

$$\frac{\partial w_t}{\partial\theta} = -\frac{\partial z_t}{\partial\theta}.$$

Differentiating now (2) with respect to θ we obtain

$$\frac{\partial z_t}{\partial\theta} = \frac{1}{r'}\left(r'\frac{\partial w_t}{\partial\theta} + 1\right),$$

so we may solve for the effect of the wage offer at t to obtain

$$\frac{\partial w_t}{\partial \theta} = -\frac{1}{2r'}. \tag{4}$$

Since r' is positive, a fall in θ leads to an increase in the wage offer at the rate $1/2r'$. To obtain the effect on wage offers before t we differentiate (2) with respect to θ for $t' = 1, \ldots, t-1$ and use (1) to obtain

$$\frac{\partial w_{t'}}{\partial \theta} = -\frac{1}{2yB_{t'}}\frac{\partial V_{t'}}{\partial \theta} \quad (t' = 1, \ldots, t-1). \tag{5}$$

Differentiating also the functional equations (3) and using (4) and (5) we obtain

$$\frac{\partial V_{t'}}{\partial \theta} = 0 \quad (t' = t, \ldots T-1),$$

$$\frac{\partial V_{t-1}}{\partial \theta} = \frac{2r_t}{r'} yB_t \left(r' \frac{\partial w_t}{\partial \theta} + 1\right) = \frac{r_t}{r'} yB_t,$$

$$\frac{\partial V_{t'-1}}{\partial \theta} = 2yr_{t'}B_{t'}\frac{\partial w_{t'}}{\partial \theta} + \frac{\partial V_{t'}}{\partial \theta} = (1 - r_{t'})\frac{\partial V_{t'}}{\partial \theta}$$
$$(t' = 1, \ldots, t-1).$$

Thus a change in θ causes a change in the expected returns from recruitment in all periods before t in the same direction. Since $r_{t'}$ is positive and less than one for all t', the change in some period t' is greater the closer period t' is to t. Using equation (5) and noting that $B_{t'}$ increases as t' falls towards unity we obtain that when θ falls in some period t all wage offers prior to t increase, and the increase is greater as we approach t. The wage increase in period t is the greatest of all.

Thus the effects of changes in the supply of labour on wages conform to the effects obtained by standard theory under conditions of wage flexibility: a fall in the supply of labour leads to an increase in the optimal wage offer. The reasons for the particular dynamic effect obtained here, where the increase becomes greater as we move towards period t, emerge immediately if we consider the problem within the framework of our model. A fall in the supply of labour in some period t is taken by the firm as a worsening of conditions in the labour market in that particular period. If the firm manages to find a worker for each one of its vacancies before t it will not suffer from that worsening of conditions, but if it still has vacancies on offer at t it will suffer. By offering higher wages before t the firm reduces the probability that it will reach period t with vacant positions, whereas at the same time it is incurring some additional wage costs. As the chances of finding a worker before t decline (i.e. as we move towards t) the probability that there will be vacancies at t increases, so the wage offer is put up further to compensate for this increase in the probability. Thus the flexwage firm spreads the costs of the tightening of the labour market at t in all periods in its horizon in the form of higher wage offers before t, and hence higher wage payments after t as well if a worker is recruited before t.

Fixwage. Consider now the effects of a change in the supply of labour in a fixwage world. In a flexwage world we could push the differences in the efficiency of workers to the background by assuming that the firm plans to make the same profit on all the recruits of each period, whatever their efficiency. Since the firm first learns of the worker's efficiency and then offers him a suitably chosen wage rate this assumption is consistent with the spirit of the model, and it should be taken as part of the features of a flexwage world – i.e. the firm in a flexwage world will very rarely be able to make a higher profit on more efficient workers, because these workers will normally have higher reservation wages.

In the fixwage system, however, the differences in the production coefficients of searchers cannot be pushed to the background. First, since wages are fixed the firm will make a higher profit on more efficient workers and less on less efficient ones. Second, and largely *because* of this, the firm is only willing to take on employees who are able to contribute to production above a critical reservation value. So a fall in the supply of labour in a fixwage world may be either taken to mean a fall in the production coefficients of searchers *or* an increase in the reservation wages of searchers, i.e. a fall in the ratio of those willing to accept the firm's offer.

Both of these changes, however, will have the same effect on the supply of labour to the firm, so they will also have the same effect on the firm's policy. In chapter 3 we defined the supply of labour to the fixwage firm in some period t as the distribution of production coefficients of those willing to accept the firm's offer. So if production coefficients fall with reservation wages fixed, or if reservation wages rise with production coefficients fixed, the distribution of production coefficients of those willing to accept the firm's offer, $g_t(q)$, will shift to the left. So the effect of a fall in the supply of labour in a fixwage world may be obtained by considering the effects of leftward shifts in the distributions $g_t(q)$ used in the derivation of the optimal policy.

Before obtaining these effects, we may consider an additional influence on g_t which is likely to be of some importance. We defined a fixwage world as one where wages are more rigid than prices, i.e. wage rates are changed infrequently and only under continuous pressure. Wage rates do not have to be fixed at the same level at all times, and in fact they will never be. Now suppose the supply of labour is unchanged, and a fixwage firm lowers its wage offer. Then there will be fewer workers than before willing to accept the firm's offer, and if more efficient searchers also have higher reservation wages, the efficiency of those willing to accept the firm's offer also goes down. So if a firm keeps its wage rate fixed in all periods up to t, but lowers it at t, the distribution of production coefficients of those willing to accept its offer shifts to the left at t, and if it keeps the lower wage rate for a few more periods into the future, as it will do if it is operating in a fixwage world, the distributions beyond t also shift to the left. Thus the effects of (infrequent) changes in wage offers under fixwage may also be obtained via the effects of shifts in the distributions $g_t(q)$. An increase in the wage offer at t onwards shifts g_t and all other distributions beyond t to the right, whereas a fall shifts them to the left.

The optimal recruitment policy in a fixwage system, for a given sequence of distributions $g_1, \ldots, g_{T-1}$, is given by the following set of equations:

$$Q_t = \{q \mid Z_t(q) \geq V_t\} \quad (t = 1, \ldots, T-1), \tag{6}$$

$$Z_t(q) = B_t(qp - w)y \quad (t = 1, \ldots, T-1), \tag{7}$$

$$\left.\begin{aligned} V_{t-1} &= V_t + \sum_{Q_t} g_t(q)\left[Z_t(q) - V_t\right] \quad (t = 1, \ldots, T-1), \\ V_{T-1} &= 0 \end{aligned}\right\} \tag{8}$$

where Q_t is the recruitment set and w is the historically given wage rate. The recruitment policy, however, can be expressed more conveniently in terms of the recruitment standard ξ_t, defined as the minimum efficiency level that the firm is willing to tolerate from potential employees. From (6) and (7) the recruitment standard is given by

$$\xi_t = \frac{w}{p} + \frac{1}{pyB_t} V_t \quad (t = 1, \ldots, T-1). \tag{9}$$

Let θ be an additive shift parameter in the distribution $g_t(q)$, such that $dq/d\theta = 1$. A fall in θ shows a uniform decline in the efficiency of those willing to accept the firm's offer at t (so θ may stand for the wage rate). Differentiating the functional equation (8), with respect to θ we obtain

$$\frac{\partial V_{t'}}{\partial \theta} = 0 \quad (t' = t, \ldots, T-1),$$

$$\frac{\partial V_{t-1}}{\partial \theta} = \sum_{Q_t} g_t(q) \frac{\partial Z_t(q)}{\partial q} \frac{dq}{d\theta} = b_t py B_t, \tag{10}$$

$$\frac{\partial V_{t'-1}}{\partial \theta} = (1 - b_{t'}) \frac{\partial V_{t'}}{\partial \theta} \quad (t' = 1, \ldots, t-1),$$

where $b_t = \sum_{Q_t} g_t(q)$. Thus, as with flexwage, a shift in the distribution at period t has a positive effect on the reservation profits in all periods prior to t, and the effect is stronger the closer the period is to t.

In a fixwage world the firm will react to these changes by adjusting its reservation coefficient level in all periods prior to t. From the definition of the reservation coefficient level, (9), we obtain

$$\frac{\partial \xi_{t'}}{\partial \theta} = \frac{1}{pyB_{t'}} \frac{\partial V_{t'}}{\partial \theta} \quad (t' = 1, \ldots, t-1), \tag{11}$$

so the reservation coefficient level changes in the same direction as the reservation profit level. Substituting for the effect on $V_{t'}$ from (10) this may be written as

$$\frac{\partial \xi_{t'}}{\partial \theta} = \frac{B_t}{B_{t'}}(1 - b_{t'+1}) \ldots (1 - b_{t-1}) b_t \quad (t' = 1, \ldots, t-1).$$

Thus if the entrepreneur expects the labour market to tighten in some future period t, in the sense that fewer workers are willing to accept his offer, or that the efficiency of those willing to accept his offer declines, he will lower his recruitment standards in all periods before t. In view of the lower efficiency of potential searchers at t, it is optimal to do so because it will increase the chances of finding an employee before t, and so not having to bear the full costs at t. By doing so the firm allocates the costs of the tightening of the market in t in all periods in its horizon, since if it recruits an inefficient worker before t it will normally keep him after t as well (since the recruitment standard will be falling over time for all sequences $g_1, \ldots, g_{T-1}$ if no exogenous influence induces the firm to raise it again later).

Now if the shift in g_t was caused by a fall in the wage offer at t, the firm will reduce its recruitment standard before t, as we have just seen. But it will also reduce it in t and in all periods following t if the wage rate is not put up again, both because the distributions, $g_{t+1}, \ldots, g_{T-1}$ will also shift to the left, and because when wage costs at t are reduced, the firm can afford to recruit low-efficiency workers and still make the same profit. Thus, just as the flexwage firm offers more or less depending on the efficiency of the worker, the fixwage firm fixes a higher or lower recruitment standard depending on its real wage rate. The dependence is linear in both systems, although there will normally be repercussion effects from changes in expected and reservation profits.

Finally, we may consider briefly the effects of changes in the heterogeneity of the labour force. Since the differences in the efficiency of workers are important in the operation of a fixwage system, changes in these differences are also of some importance.

An increase in the heterogeneity of the labour force may be represented by an outward multiplicative shift in the distribution g_t.[2] Let θ now denote a multiplicative shift parameter in the distribution at time t, i.e. we may write each q as

$$q(\theta) = q + \theta(q - \bar{q}_t),$$

where q is the original coefficient evaluated at $\theta = 0$, $\bar{q}_t$ is the expected value of coefficients at t, and $q(\theta)$ is the coefficient which is observed with the same probability as q was before the change in θ.[3] Differentiating with respect to θ we get $\mathrm{d}q(\theta)/\mathrm{d}\theta = q - \bar{q}_t$, so the effect of a multiplicative shift in $g_t(q)$ may be obtained by substituting this value in (10) instead of $\mathrm{d}q/\mathrm{d}\theta = 1$. Substituting we obtain, for the effect on V_{t-1},

$$\frac{\partial V_{t-1}}{\partial \theta} = B_t p y \sum_{Q_t} g_t(q)(q - \bar{q}_t). \tag{12}$$

Now Q_t includes all values of q *above* the critical value ξ_t. Had it included all values of q, i.e. had we put $\xi_t = 0$ in (12), $\partial V_{t-1}/\partial\theta$ would

[2] Changes in the shape of the distributions, of course, may also be caused by changes in the information possessed by households and firms. If workers become more informed of firms' policies, or if firms learn more of each other's policy, the distributions are likely to shift inwards. The effects of these shifts may be obtained along the lines of the argument that follows. Shifts in the shape of a distribution are considered again in some detail in the search model, chapter 10.

[3] This method of analysing the effects of shifts in probability distributions was first used by Kenneth Arrow (1965).

have been equal to zero, since by definition $\bar{q}_t = \sum_{\text{all } q} g_t(q)q$. But if $\xi_t > 0$, very small values of q are excluded from the summation, so the positive terms of the difference $q - \bar{q}_t$ will now dominate the negative ones. Hence the net effect of an outward shift in the distribution g_t on V_{t-1} will be positive. By (10) and (11) the reservation coefficient level will rise in all periods prior to t.

The reason the firm responds by raising its recruitment standard when the heterogeneity of the labour force increases is that now it learns that the efficient workers become more efficient, whereas the inefficient ones become more inefficient. Since it was planning to reject very inefficient workers the firm is not affected by the further deterioration in their efficiency, whereas it knows that it will be better off if it can find a worker whose efficiency has increased. By raising its recruitment standard the firm ensures that it does not 'waste' a vacancy on a relatively inefficient worker, and the longer waiting period before recruitment that this entails is counteracted by the prospect of finding a very efficient worker in the future. Thus an increase in the heterogeneity of the labour force makes life for the average employee more difficult – recruitment standards will tend to move against him.

Changes in prices

We shall analyse the effect of a change in the price of output in a single period t, since the effects of simultaneous changes in more than one period's price may be obtained by adding up the individual effects. We shall concentrate on changes in the price of output of a single firm, all other prices remaining fixed, which is the standard problem investigated in the microeconomic literature. The effects of simultaneous changes in all prices may be obtained by combining the results of this section and the last, since the effects may be decomposed into the effects of changes in the price of output and the effects of the change in the supply of labour, provided labour is free of money illusion and interested in its real wage rate.

Flexwage. In chapter 3 we obtained the policy of the firm during adjustment in the flexwage system by assuming that the price of output was expected to remain constant over time. This enabled us to simplify the exposition enormously, since we could talk about 'the' price of output and 'the' wage offer without ambiguity. When prices are expected to change, however, this is not possible. Suppose the firm expects the sequence of output prices to be $p(1), \ldots, p(T)$. On the basis of this it will offer a wage sequence $w_1(2), \ldots, w_1(T)$ to those calling in period one, a sequence $w_2(3), \ldots, w_2(T)$ to those calling in period two, and so forth.[4] Let $\langle w_t \rangle$ be the sequence offered to those calling in period t. Then the probability that a caller will be willing to accept the firm's offer is a function of the whole sequence $\langle w_t \rangle$, whereas the profit obtained from a man recruited in period t is now equal to

$$Z_t = \sum_{t'=t+1}^{T} \beta(t')[qp(t') - w_t(t')]y \quad (t = 1, \ldots, T-1). \quad (13)$$

The problem facing the firm now is to choose the sequence $\langle w_t \rangle$ to maximize expected profits.

We shall simplify the exposition and at the same time make it more intuitive by assuming that despite the variation in prices the firm plans to pay the same wage rate in all periods to those calling in period t. That is, for each wage sequence $\langle w_t \rangle$ the firm offers a flat rate, so $w_t(t') \equiv w_t$ for all $t' = t+1, \ldots, T$. This assumption simplifies the exposition because we can talk again about 'the' wage offer at t, and removes the ambiguity about the optimal sequence that arises when searchers are indifferent about the timing of their receipts. When there is a perfect capital market searchers will, in general, be interested only in the present discounted value of the wage stream that is being offered. So the firm can influence the supply of labour to itself by changing the present discounted value of the stream, and not by offering compensated variations in the terms of the stream. Since the firm is also indifferent about the timing of wage payments, given their total discounted value, the exact relationship between the individual wage rates in a wage sequence cannot be determined uniquely. Our assumption that all terms in the sequence are equal simplifies the exposition by removing this ambiguity.

Given this assumption we can write (13) as

$$Z_t = qy \sum_{t'=t+1}^{T} \beta(t') p(t') - yB_t w_t. \quad (13')$$

[4] For instance, the firm may offer a 'basic' wage, on the basis of this period's price level, and an automatic adjustment for changes in the price level, e.g. a 1 per cent change in the basic wage for every 1 per cent change in the price level. This system is what is referred to as a system of wage indexation, and is related to the 'threshold' agreements introduced in Britain in 1974.

This generalization does not change the structure of the problem, since the term that is generalized consists wholly of exogenous variables. Hence we can immediately write down the equation which gives the optimal wage offer and which replaces equations (1) and (2):

$$w_t = \frac{q}{B_t} \sum_{t'=t+1}^{T} \beta(t')\, p(t') - \frac{r(w_t)}{r'(w_t)} - \frac{1}{yB_t} V_t \quad (t = 1, \ldots, T-1). \tag{14}$$

The functional equation (3) remains the same as before since prices do not appear directly in the equation.

When the price of a single firm changes in some period t the supply of labour to this and other firms is not directly affected by this change, since the firm is small in relation to the size of the market. Concentrating on this type of change we obtain immediately from the functional equation (3) and the condition for the optimality of the wage offer (14) that the optimal policy in period t and thereafter is not affected by the price change at t. Thus $V_t, \ldots, V_{T-1}$ remain constant when $p(t)$ changes. To obtain the effect on the policy before t we differentiate (14) with respect to $p(t)$ for all $t' = 1, \ldots, t-1$ to obtain

$$\frac{\partial w_{t'}}{\partial p(t)} = \frac{\beta(t)}{2B_{t'}} q - \frac{1}{2yB_{t'}} \frac{\partial V_{t'}}{\partial p(t)} \quad (t' = 1, \ldots, t-1). \tag{15}$$

Thus a change in some price $p(t)$ influences the wage offer before t in two ways. First, the profit expected from the production and sales of period t changes in the same direction as price. This results in a change in the wage offer before t also in the same direction. Second, the price change causes a change in the expected returns from recruitment in the future. The change is in the same direction as the price change, but when the expected returns from the policy change, the wage offer changes in the opposite direction. For instance, if the expected returns from a future policy increase, the firm can afford to reduce its current wage offer because the resulting fall in the probability of finding a worker to take the offer is compensated by the increased returns from the future policy. The net effect on the wage offer is the outcome of these two opposing influences.

Differentiating now the functional equation (3) for period $t - 1$ we obtain

$$\frac{\partial V_{t-1}}{\partial p(t)} = 2yB_t \frac{\partial w_t}{\partial p(t)} = 0. \tag{16}$$

So the effect of the price change on w_{t-1} is

$$\frac{\partial w_{t-1}}{\partial p(t)} = \frac{\beta(t)}{2B_{t-1}} q,$$

i.e. the wage offer at $t - 1$ changes in the same direction as the price change. The effect on the wage offer in other periods may be obtained by differentiating (3) and using this result:

$$\frac{\partial V_{t-2}}{\partial p(t)} = 2yB_{t-1} r_{t-1} \frac{\partial w_{t-1}}{\partial p(t)} = \beta(t) yqr_{t-1} \tag{17}$$

$$\frac{\partial V_{t'-1}}{\partial p(t)} = \frac{\partial V_{t'}}{\partial p(t)} + 2yB_{t'} r_{t'} \frac{\partial w_{t'}}{\partial p(t)}$$

$$= \beta(t) yqr_{t'} + (1 - r_{t'}) \frac{\partial V_{t'}}{\partial p(t)} \quad (t' = 1, \ldots, t - 1). \tag{18}$$

Thus the expected returns from recruitment in all periods prior to t also change in the same direction as the price change. Substituting $\partial V_{t'}/\partial p(t)$ from (18) into (15) and doing some rearranging we obtain

$$\frac{\partial w_{t'-1}}{\partial p(t)} = \frac{1 - r_{t'}}{2yB_{t'-1}} \left[\beta(t) yq - \frac{\partial V_{t'}}{\partial p(t)}\right].$$

Thus the wage offer at $t' - 1$ moves in the same direction as price if

$$\frac{\partial V_{t'}}{\partial p(t)} < \beta(t) yq.$$

Now it follows immediately from (16) and (17) that this inequality is satisfied for periods $t - 1$ and $t - 2$, so the wage offer at $t - 2$ and $t - 3$ changes in the same direction as the price at t. Substituting from (17) into (18) for period $t - 3$ we obtain

$$\frac{\partial V_{t-3}}{\partial p(t)} = \beta(t) yqr_{t-2} + (1 - r_{t-2})\, \beta(t) yqr_{t-1}$$

$$= \beta(t) yq \left[r_{t-2} + (1 - r_{t-2})\, r_{t-1}\right],$$

which is certainly less than $\beta(t)yq$ because the expression in the square brackets is less than one. Hence the wage offer at $t - 4$ also changes in the same direction. Doing the same substitution recursively for periods $t - 4, \ldots, 2$ we obtain that the wage offer changes in the same direction in all periods prior to t.

This result is analogous to the result obtained in traditional theory when the price of output changes. There is a good intuitive explanation within the framework of our model for this kind of behaviour. Thus, if a price increase is expected in a single period, the entrepreneur expects to gain from the sales of that period, and the gain will be in proportion to the total production of the period; but if a vacancy is unfilled at the time of the price increase the gain will be zero, because production and sales from that position will be zero. Thus if the firm has any idle vacancies when expected prices rise, it raises its wage offer to increase the probability of finding a man before the price increase, so production and sales from the vacancy are non-zero and some gain is enjoyed. The additional gain should be just enough to compensate for the loss from the additional wage costs. Wage offers in the flexwage system should therefore increase during booms and decrease during depressions.

Fixwage. In the fixwage system changes in prices cannot affect the wage rate, by definition, but they do affect the firm's recruitment standard. To obtain formally the effects of a change in price $p(t)$ in fixwage we must also abandon the assumption that prices are identical in all periods, and generalize the optimality conditions (6)–(9), as we did with flexwage. The generalization is again straightforward. Equations (6) and (8) remain the same as before, whereas equation (7) generalizes to

$$Z_t(q) = qy \sum_{t'=t+1}^{T} \beta(t')\, p(t') - ywB_t. \tag{7'}$$

Equation (9) generalizes to

$$\xi_t \sum_{t'=t+1}^{T} \beta(t')\, p(t')y = ywB_t + V_t. \tag{9'}$$

To obtain the effect of a change in $p(t)$ on the recruitment standard in all periods before t we differentiate (9′) with respect to $p(t)$ to give

$$\frac{\partial \xi_{t'}}{\partial p(t)} \sum_{\tau=t'+1}^{T} \beta(\tau)\, p(\tau) y = \frac{\partial V_{t'}}{\partial p(t)} - \beta(t) y\, \xi_{t'} \quad (t' = 1, \ldots, t-1). \tag{19}$$

(The effect on the policy at t and thereafter is equal to zero.) Equation (19) is the fixwage counterpart of equation (15), which gives the effect of the price change in a flexwage world. The effect on the recruitment standard is again decomposed into two terms, so to obtain the net effect we have to evaluate the effect of the change on the reservation profit levels V. Differentiating the functional equation (8) for period $t - 1$ we obtain,

$$\frac{\partial V_{t-1}}{\partial p(t)} = \sum_{Q_t} g_t(q) \frac{\partial Z_t}{\partial p(t)} = 0, \tag{20}$$

and substituting this in (19) we immediately obtain that the recruitment standard in period $t - 1$ changes in the opposite direction of the price change. Differentiating now for $t - 2$ and using (20) and (7′) we obtain

$$\frac{\partial V_{t-2}}{\partial p(t)} = \sum_{Q_{t-1}} g_{t-1}(q) \frac{\partial Z_{t-1}}{\partial p(t)} = \beta(t)y \sum_{Q_{t-1}} g_{t-1}(q)q.$$

The recruitment standard at $t - 2$ will therefore change in the opposite direction of the price change if

$$\xi_{t-2} > \sum_{Q_{t-1}} g_{t-1}(q)q. \tag{21}$$

The right-hand side of (21) is a weighted sum of all q which are greater than ξ_{t-1}. Thus if ξ_{t-1} increases, the sum in (21) declines, whereas we know that ξ_{t-2} will in general be above ξ_{t-1}. It follows that if we can prove that (21) is true for the lowest possible recruitment standard it is also true for all other recruitment standards. But the lowest recruitment standard is the one that is chosen in period $T - 1$, which is the last period during which the firm can offer the vacancy. Substituting (7′) and (9′) into the functional equation for period $T - 1$ we immediately obtain that (21) will always be true if the recruitment standard for $T - 2$ is not 'very' different from that for period $T - 1$. It is not possible to establish *a priori* whether there are any cases which violate (21), but it is also not possible to exclude the possibility. Thus, although we would expect in most cases the recruitment standard to move against the change in price, we cannot prove that perverse behaviour will never be observed.

Thus, if the price at period t increases, we can show that the recruitment standard will definitely fall in period $t - 1$, but it may not fall in other periods. (The effect in periods other than $t - 2$ may be obtained by differentiating recursively the functional equation, as we did with the flexwage system, so the argument will not be repeated.) Given that we may observe some perverse behaviour, is it possible to establish the conditions under which we may observe it? In the last paragraph we argued that if recruitment standards do not decline very rapidly no perverse behaviour will be observed. But even if they do decline rapidly behaviour will only be perverse in exceptional cases. The conditions under which it may arise may be established by considering the inequality in (21). The right-hand side of this inequality is always below the mean efficiency of those searching the firm, since the weighted sum of the qs is equal to the mean efficiency only if taken over all possible values of q. But the recruitment standard cannot fall below the real wage rate, so the sum in (21) is taken, at most, over those qs which exceed the real wage rate. Since the left-hand side of (21) must also exceed the real wage rate, if the real wage rate is not much below the mean efficiency level (21) is certainly satisfied. In practice we would expect the real wage rate to be in the neighbourhood of the mean efficiency level, although in monopolistic situations firms may be able to sustain a real wage rate below the mean efficiency level.

Thus a necessary condition for the existence of perverse behaviour is that the real wage rate be a good deal below the mean efficiency level of labour, a situation which is unlikely to arise when the wage rate is not subject to violent short-run fluctuations but remains fixed over considerable periods of time. However, even if the real wage rate is very low, (21) will be violated only if the recruitment standard is also very low. Thus perverse behaviour requires the additional condition that the labour market be very tight, i.e. the opportunities of finding good workmen must be so low as to force the firm to reduce its recruitment standard to the minimum level which is needed to ensure survival. The latter situation is the nearest we can get to full employment in a fixwage world, so the existence of this situation undermines the earlier assumption that the real wage rate be very much below the mean efficiency level. As we argued in chapter 3, and we shall argue again in chapter 14, wages in the fixwage system do change under continuous pressure, so in conditions of full employment the wage rate is unlikely to be very much below the mean efficiency level.

Thus we have shown that if the recruitment standard is not very low, i.e. if there is no full employment, an increase in any price $p(t)$ leads to a lowering of recruitment standards in all periods before t. If there is full employment there *may* be some perverse behaviour when the real wage rate is very much below the mean efficiency level of labour. Since under conditions of full employment wages are not likely to remain fixed at very low levels for long, perverse behaviour is not likely to arise in practice, even if it were possible to construct counter-examples within the individual recruitment model.

If the price change is expected in more than one, or even in all periods, the effects may be obtained by adding up the individual effects. Thus, if a boom is thought to be imminent, or has just set in, current recruitment standards will fall rapidly, and if a depression is expected recruitment standards will rise. Workers will therefore find it easier to find employment during booms, and more difficult during depressions. Also, during a depression some of the firm's own employees may be dismissed, because although they were efficient enough to qualify for the job when the recruitment standard was low, they may not be capable of qualifying now that standards have become more stringent. These effects of booms and depressions are normally observed in industrialized labour markets, where wages tend to be more rigid than prices. They are, respectively, the fixwage counterparts of an increase and a fall in wages, i.e. manifestations of an increase or a fall in the demand for labour with supply remaining fixed.

Summary and conclusion: preliminary analysis of the workings of the market

In the last chapter we found that the flexwage firm will offer at first a relatively low wage rate and revise it upwards every time it is searched by potential employees who find the offer too low and turn it down. The fixwage firm will similarly fix a high recruitment standard at first, and lower it until it finds an employee who is good enough to qualify for the job. Thus both systems carry similar implications – in a sense the one is the dual of the other.

The same duality also arises in the analysis of the effects of changes in prices and the supply of labour. An increase in prices induces the flexwage firm to increase its wage offer and the fixwage firm to reduce its recruitment standard, whereas a fall in the supply of labour leads, similarly, to an increase in the wage offer and a fall in the recruitment standard. Thus the price increase leads to an increase in the demand for labour, and the fall in supply (increase in the supply price of labour) to an improvement in conditions from the point of view of labour – although each effect is manifested differently in each system according to the decision variable of each.

These effects are also those obtained by standard theory under similar conditions, but only when the production function exhibits variable coefficients. In particular, there are no comparable results to the ones found here for the changes in the supply of labour in the neoclassical theory of labour-demand *when production coefficients are fixed.* A change in the efficiency of labour has no effect in the short run on the demand for labour, although in the long run an increase in the supply price of labour may induce substitution of capital for labour and so reduction in the quantity of labour demanded.[5] On the other hand if production coefficients are not fixed, a fall in the supply of labour always reduces the quantity demanded, or alternatively it increases the wage rate employers have to pay. In the sequential model of recruitment entrepreneurs are also willing to offer higher wages for men with the same productivity, but in a fixwage environment the usual short-run response will be to lower the recruitment standard. With fixed prices and wages the latter measure produces results which are similar to an increase in the wage offer, namely a reduction in expected output and profits.

We considered two factors as causes of the fall in the supply of labour to the firm, a fall in the efficiency of searchers and an increase in reservation wages. However, the nature of the supply of labour to the firm, as we obtained it in chapter 2, also implies two other causes of changes in the supply of labour to the firm. One of these has played a crucial role in the literature on the microeconomic foundations of the Phillips curve,[6] whereas the other is intimately related with the inter-dependencies of different firms' wage offers, a topic which has largely been neglected by the adjustment literature but which will occupy us again later on.[7] Without anticipating too much the analysis of chapter 14, we may conclude this chapter by introducing these two causes.

We defined the supply of labour to the firm as the ratio of those searchers willing to accept the firm's offer. Now, that same ratio is also the probability that a random searcher would be willing to accept the firm's offer, and also the probability that the firm will find an employee in some period t, given its wage offer. The latter prob-

[5] See Reynolds (1948, pp. 295–301) for the differences in short-run and long-run behaviour.

[6] See in particular Phelps *et al.* (1970).

[7] However, it has played a central role in the theory of monopolistic competition since Cournot. Since the atomistic firm during adjustment is like a monopsonist, we would expect those results to carry over, *mutatis mutandis.* See also chapter 14.

ability, however, varies directly with the number of searchers in relation to the number of vacancies in the market, so the more searchers in the market in relation to total vacancies the more likely is a firm to find an employee within a given period of time. Thus, a fall in the number of searchers leads to a fall in the supply of labour to the firm as we defined it here, and an increase in the number of searchers leads to an increase in supply. It follows that the flexwage firm raises its wage offer when the total number of searchers falls and reduces it when it rises. A relation like the Phillips curve may be shown to arise from such a mechanism, with firms responding to changes in the stock of searchers via the effects on the supply of labour to themselves, and searchers responding, in their turn, to the change in firms' recruitment policy.[8]

The second cause of changes in the supply of labour to itself, which provides a link between different firms' wages, follows directly from the analysis of chapter 2. In that chapter we argued that the searcher is faced with a distribution of wage rates, which may be written as a vector of wage rates ruling in the market, and that the probability that he will accept a given wage rate w_i depends mainly on the relative attractiveness of w_i, i.e. the position of w_i on the scale of all wage rates; i.e. if we write $\mathbf{w}(i)$ for the vector of all wage rates except that of firm i, and w_i for that of firm i, the supply of labour to firm i is written in general as $r[w_i, \mathbf{w}(i)]$ and satisfies the restrictions $\partial r/\partial w_i > 0$ and $\partial r/\partial \mathbf{w}(i) < 0$: an increase in the firm's wage rate raises the supply of labour to itself whereas an increase in any other wage rate reduces it.[9] Thus other firms' wage rates play the role of shift parameters in the supply of labour to a particular firm.

This provides a link between the wage rates of different firms. Even if firms are completely unaware of the wage rates of other firms, a change in other firms' wages will lead to a change in the supply of labour to the firm, and via this to a change in this firm's wage rate. Thus, a rise in the wage rate of some firm j leads to a fall in the supply of labour to all other firms, and so leads to a rise in all other wage rates. It follows that wage rates move always in the same direction, even if firms are completely unaware of each other's wages. This interdependency between wage rates is a crucial element in the workings of a decentralized labour market, because it may contradict

[8] See chapter 14 for the details of the analysis.
[9] See above, chapter 2.

the crucial requirement that there is a distribution of wage rates, i.e. that wage rates vary sufficiently across firms to induce some workers to turn down an observed wage rate and search for another. Fortunately, it is possible to find reasonable conditions which support sufficient wage variability, so we shall continue making this assumption until we come to chapter 13, where we shall examine the interdependency between firms' wages in greater detail.

PART II

Workers and Consumers

6
Job Search

The trading arrangement in our labour market requires firms to fix the wage rate for every unit of labour services supplied, and labour to contact firms individually and arrange a bilateral exchange. Thus the function of labour in this system is one of job searching. In the second part of the book we shall analyse this problem.

As we have already seen, the crucial factor in our model is whether the two parties agree to an exchange, given the offered wage and the efficiency of labour on the one hand, and their expectations for future opportunities on the other. The actual quantity exchanged (the number of hours of work) is of no special interest, and the same conclusions about adjustment hold whether hours are exogenously fixed, or whether they are fixed by the firm or by labour, *mutatis mutandis*. Thus we shall have much more to say about whether a searcher will agree to an exchange or not, than about the properties of the optimal number of hours he wishes to work at the offered wage.

Like the firm, the wage-earner is capable of influencing, to some extent, the wage he receives in a market where there is no central organization to establish Walrasian equilibrium. Thus when firms' wages differ, the individual can choose to reject an offered wage and try to obtain a higher one somewhere else – in contrast to the Walrasian market where he will have to accept the centrally chosen wage. By turning down a wage offer to look for a higher one, the individual increases his chances of actually receiving a higher wage, but he also increases the waiting period before he starts earning a wage. The waiting period is costly in terms of foregone earnings, so when offered a job, the individual can either accept it and earn the offered wage without any waiting, or reject it and bear the cost of waiting for a little longer, hoping to find another job paying a higher wage. Thus the formal structure of the problem is similar to that facing the firm, and with some differences in detail the same techniques may be used to analyse it.

The decision process

Consider an unemployed individual who is faced with the option of either not entering the labour market and remaining unemployed, or entering the labour market to look for a job. The individual will take his decision on the basis of his preferences for income and leisure, and his chances of finding work, as evaluated by him. If he chooses to enter the labour market to look for a job he is said to be willing to *participate* in the labour market, although before he starts work and during search he will have to remain unemployed. But if after a few periods' search the worker is still unemployed, he may find it optimal to terminate the search and drop out of the labour market. We may then say that the worker is *discouraged* by his experience in search, and he chooses to terminate his participation in the labour market.

There is a number of questions that may be asked in relation to the participation and search decision. First, whether a worker who chooses to participate will ever be discouraged before the end of his working life, and if so what factors will induce his discouragement. Second, whether a discouraged worker will decide to participate again. Third, what policy should he follow during search, and how does his policy affect his participation decision and his chances of becoming employed quickly. We shall tackle these questions by starting from the last one – the determination of his optimal acceptance policy. This is the most important question, since the answer to all the other questions depends on the policy followed during search.

Our trading sequence requires that search take place sequentially, a restriction which has recently attracted a lot of attention with favourable results.[1] We shall assume that the individual is searching for a permanent job, i.e. a worker will accept a job only if he plans to stay in it until the end of his working life. The worker may, of course, discover after acceptance that he over-estimated the merits of the job, or with the passage of time labour market conditions may change such that searching for a new job becomes a more viable proposition than staying in the same one. He will then try to find another one, either by quitting his current job to search whilst unemployed, or by searching on-the-job. However, when searching the worker is assumed to be looking for a permanent job, so he will never accept a

[1] See footnote 9 of chapter 1, p. 9.

job which he does not want to keep permanently and continue searching on-the-job.[2] It is obvious from this that the worker may be either employed or unemployed during search. Although the empirical interpretation of the analysis may be different when the searcher is employed than when he is unemployed, the formal structure of the search model is precisely the same in both cases. So, to avoid the cumbersome 'either or' during the development of the formal problem, we shall talk of the searcher as an unemployed person, until we come to the empirical interpretation of the analysis (chapter 11), where we shall consider the implications of unemployed search and on-the-job searching separately.

Given the assumptions of sequential search and permanent job-acceptance the typical individual's problem during search is to compare the utility which he may derive from an observed offer with that expected from additional search. If the former exceeds the latter he accepts the offer and terminates the search. But if the expected utility from search exceeds the utility from the job offer, he rejects the offer and continues the search. The formal structure of the problem is similar to that of recruitment in fixwage.

Thus, time is divided into elementary periods such that not more than one offer is observed per period. The individual's working life is assumed to consist of T^* elementary periods, whereas the maximum amount of search planned before discouragement will be taken to be equal to T periods. T^* will be referred to as the *work horizon* and T as the *search horizon*. Clearly, if the worker is currently unemployed he will participate in the labour market if the optimal search horizon is greater than zero, whereas discouragement will take place if the search horizon is smaller than the work horizon, and search is unsuccessful in all periods in the search horizon. Thus the answers to the questions on participation and discouragement depend on the chosen search horizon. We approach the problem of simultaneous choice of search horizon and acceptance policy by obtaining first the optimal acceptance policy for any arbitrary search horizon $T \leq T^*$ (chapters 6–11) and then showing how the optimal search horizon is chosen (chapter 12).

Let $\mathbf{J}_t$ be the individual's *lifetime* job if he accepts the offer observed at period t (defined more fully below). If the firm searched at t makes no job offer to the individual we say that the offer observed at t is null,

[2] But see chapter 11, where the question of temporary employment and on-the-job search is raised again.

and denote it by $\mathbf{J}_{ot}$. We assume that the individual cannot be certain that the firm searched at some period t will make him a job offer, or alternatively he does not know which firms have the vacancies for which he qualifies. A worker can only hold one job at a time, and if a job is offered and accepted in period t, work begins in period $t + 1$.

The individual's search policy for a fixed horizon (number of search opportunities) T is described as follows. At the beginning of each period t the individual chooses an acceptance set S_t for the period. He then searches one firm and observes $\mathbf{J}_t$ (say). If $\mathbf{J}_t \in S_t$ he accepts the offer and stops the search; if $\mathbf{J}_t \notin S_t$ a new acceptance set S_{t+1} is chosen and the process is repeated, *unless* the state of unemployment belongs to S_t; if $\mathbf{J}_{ot} \in S_t$ the worker terminates the search and drops out of the labour force. However, if the search horizon is chosen optimally, it is possible to show that $\mathbf{J}_{ot} \notin S_t$ for all $t = 1, \ldots, T - 1$, whereas $\mathbf{J}_{oT} \in S_T$ (see chapter 12). So if no offer was accepted in periods $1, \ldots, T$ the worker is discouraged at T. For this reason we shall obtain the optimal acceptance policy ignoring the possibility $\mathbf{J}_{ot} \in S_t$ for $t = 1, \ldots, T - 1$.

Thus the problem with T fixed is to find the acceptance sets S_1, $\ldots$, S_T implied by the optimal policy. Before we do this a few more concepts must be defined.

The individual's lifetime job and the utility function

The individual derives utility from the amount of income and leisure he consumes in all periods in his lifetime. By a 'job' in some period t we mean a two-dimensional vector (m, y), giving respectively the total amount of money received by the individual in the period and the number of hours he has worked.[3] If the individual is unemployed during a period we may then write $m = m_o \geq 0$, where m_o is unemployment insurance and $y = 0$; if he is searching we write $m = m_o - c$, where c is the monetary cost of search in a period, such as the cost of transport, and $1 > y = y_s > 0$, where y_s is the time spent searching during the period, and the length of the period

[3] In general, of course, the attractiveness of a job depends, as Adam Smith (1776, p. 112) noted, on 'the ease of hardship, the cleanliness or dirtiness, the honourableness or dishonourableness of the employment', and a large number of other such 'non-pecuniary' features of the job. Since the theory of job search which we shall develop is independent of the dimension of the vector of 'job characteristics', any number of job characteristics may be taken into account by considering an n-dimensional instead of a two-dimensional vector.

is equal to unity; and if the individual is employed and receives a wage rate w for every hour he works we have $m = wy > 0$ and $1 > y > 0$. Non-wage earnings and the possibility of transferring wealth from one period to others through saving and dissaving will be ignored in this chapter but analysed in the next chapter.

By a *lifetime* job we mean the labour market condition of the individual in all periods in his lifetime. For instance, if the individual's lifetime consists of three periods only, and if in the first period he is unemployed and searching, in the second he is working y hours and earning w per hour, whereas in the third he is unemployed and retired, his lifetime job situation is given by the vector

$$\mathbf{J} = [(m_o - c, y_s), (wy, y), (m_o, 0)].$$

Our assumptions of sequential search and acceptance of jobs on a permanent basis imply that we can narrow down to manageable proportions the types of lifetime jobs relevant to the analysis.[4] Thus, an individual who is seeking work should expect to spend a few periods searching, and after finding a job he should expect to stay in it until the end of his lifetime (assumed equal to his working life). Then, in general, a lifetime job may be partitioned into two components, the first one describing the state of the individual during search and the second describing his state in the job accepted in the last period of search. Suppose the individual has searched in periods $1, \ldots, t-1$ unsuccessfully, accepted the offer observed at t, and spent the rest of his work horizon in the new job. We denote the lifetime job under these conditions by $\mathbf{J}_t$. The first component of $\mathbf{J}_t$ is a t-dimensional vector whose typical element is the pair $(m_o - c, y_s)$ giving the state of the individual during search, whereas its second component is a $(T^* - t)$-dimensional vector whose typical element is the pair (wy, y), giving the state of the individual in the new job. Denote these components, respectively, by $\mathbf{J}_t^1$ and $\mathbf{J}_t^2$, hence

$$\mathbf{J}_t = (\mathbf{J}_t^1, \mathbf{J}_t^2).$$

Suppose the individual is discouraged by his experience in search, i.e. after searching for t periods unsuccessfully he drops out of the labour market and remains unemployed until the end of his lifetime. Clearly, the first component of the lifetime job when there is dis-

[4] If it was impossible to restrict the types of lifetime jobs that the individual could have, the definition of a lifetime job would be so general as to make it a useless tool of analysis. This is one of the greatest advantages of the sequential assumption.

couragement at t is the same as that for $\mathbf{J}_t$, $\mathbf{J}_t^1$, with typical element $(m_o - c, y_s)$; whereas the second component will be different, because the worker will now be unemployed. The typical element of the second component will now be $(m_o, 0)$, since the individual will now be receiving unemployment benefit for zero hours of work. The $(T^* - t)$-dimensional vector with typical element $(m_o, 0)$ is denoted by $\mathbf{J}_{ot}^2$, and the lifetime job when there is discouragement at t by $\mathbf{J}_{ot}$, where

$$\mathbf{J}_{ot} = (\mathbf{J}_t^1, \mathbf{J}_{ot}^2).$$

Thus by a lifetime job $\mathbf{J}_t$ we mean the state of the individual when he is unemployed and bears the cost of search in the first t periods in his work horizon, terminates the search at t, and spends the remaining T^*-t periods in the job observed at t. Subscript zero to a lifetime job means that the individual was discouraged at t, i.e. he was either not offered a job at t, but still terminated the search, or if he was offered one he rejected it and remained unemployed for the rest of his working life. This is the only type of 'lifetime job' that need concern us in the analysis of sequential search, and when temporary jobs are not normally accepted. Thus the utility function may be taken to be defined over the set of such feasible lifetime jobs, and since in general there is uncertainty about the outcome of search, utility may be assumed to be cardinal in the von Neumann–Morgenstern sense. Utility must be increasing in all desirable characteristics of jobs (wages), and decreasing in all undesirable characteristics (hours of work), but it need not be continuous or concave. A lifetime job $\mathbf{J}$ is at least as preferred as another job $\mathbf{J}'$ if and only if

$$U(\mathbf{J}) \geq U(\mathbf{J}').$$

Performing search is assumed to be always costly, i.e.

$$U(\mathbf{J}_{ot}) > U(\mathbf{J}_{ot+1}) \quad (t = 1, \ldots, T^* - 1),$$

where $\mathbf{J}_{ot}$ denotes search in t periods and $\mathbf{J}_{ot+1}$ search in $t + 1$ periods, with all their other characteristics equal.

Clearly, unsuccessful search in all periods in the work horizon imposes a lower bound on the utility from the lifetime job. Thus we may fix the origin of the utility scale by the utility obtained from unsuccessful search in all periods in the work horizon. The unit of measurement of the scale may be fixed by the utility of some job $\mathbf{J}^*$, which is the best possible job that the individual could be offered.

The unit of measurement is finite because jobs are offered by profit-maximizing firms, so the utility index is well defined.

In order to isolate the effects of decentralized trading and searching on behaviour, we shall assume that the only type of uncertainty existing in the system is uncertainty about job *offers*. That is, once a job offer is observed there is complete certainty about the characteristics of the offered job in all current and future periods.[5] Thus the uncertainty about the lifetime job is confined to (1) not knowing the period t in which an acceptable job will be found, and (2) not knowing the exact nature of the job that will be found, i.e. not knowing the wage rate it pays. Thus the individual does not know the lifetime job $\mathbf{J}_t$ that will result from acceptance at t, even if he knows that search will terminate at t. Since the optimal search policy imposes some restrictions on the possible outcomes of the search process, it also imposes some restrictions on the nature of the uncertainty existing in the system. Given these restrictions, and the distribution of job offers prevailing in the market, the worker is able to derive a probability distribution over the possible lifetime jobs that will result from search. The power of the model in yielding such a distribution is one of its strongest features, because once we are able to derive a distribution over the possible outcomes of search, given an optimal policy, the problem becomes similar to the standard economic problem under uncertainty, with the difference that now the distribution over outcomes is not taken as given, but it is derived from more primitive concepts and it depends on individual action.

Before obtaining the optimal search policy, and hence the probability distribution over outcomes, we show how the distribution of job offers relevant for household decisions during search can be obtained from the model of firm behaviour of chapters 3–5.

Let $\varphi(w_t)$ denote the distribution of wage offers in period t. Since when a worker accepts a job in period t he starts getting paid in period $t+1$, when the distribution $\varphi(w_t)$ is translated to the terminology of this section it should be taken to be defined over the second component

[5] This is a methodological device which simplifies the model enormously, preserving at the same time its new features without restricting their generality. The assumption may be relaxed along Arrow (1953) and Debreu (1959, ch. 7) lines, but little will be gained at the cost of increased complexity and even more prohibitive notation. In Arrow–Debreu language here we are analysing behaviour when the true event is known, but there is a distribution of wages associated with each event and not a unique wage. See also pp. 98–9, and p. 44 for the corresponding assumption on firms.

of the lifetime job, because it is this component that denotes the job offer observed in period t. But since when $\mathbf{J}_t^2$ is known, the first component of the lifetime job, $\mathbf{J}_t^1$, is also known by the assumption that there is complete certainty about everything except job offers, if the individual expects to be offered a job $\mathbf{J}_t^2$ with probability $\varphi(\mathbf{J}_t^2)$, he should also expect to be 'offered' a lifetime job $\mathbf{J}_t$ with the same probability. Thus the distribution φ may be taken to be defined over the lifetime job $\mathbf{J}_t$.

If all firms follow a flexwage policy the worker is recruited to any job that he wishes to accept, since the firm will adjust its wage offer according to the worker's efficiency such that the recruitment of the worker is profitable. So in a flexwage world, the distribution of job offers relevant for decisions during search is the same as the distribution over wage offers which results from firms' actions.[6] But if one or more firms follow a fixwage policy, the worker may be willing to accept a job offered to people of his broad occupational class, and yet the firm may refuse to take him on, because his efficiency is below the firm's recruitment standard. The searcher should take this possibility into account when deriving the distribution over the lifetime job which he uses to obtain his optimal policy.

Suppose firms' recruitment standards are distributed according to $\psi(\xi_t)$ where ξ_t is the reservation coefficient level of the fixwage firm. In general ξ_t will be an increasing function of the wage offer, i.e. the higher the wage offer the more stringent the recruitment standard. Now if the coefficient level of some individual is q, he should expect to be recruited to some job paying w_t with probability $\sum_{\xi_t \leq q} \psi(\xi_t(w_t)) \leq 1$, denoted by the cumulative $\Psi(q, w_t)$, and expect to be turned down with probability $1 - \Psi(q, w_t)$. The distribution over job offers which the searcher uses in arriving at his optimal policy should therefore be the distribution arrived at after taking

[6] In general, of course, the individual will not be able to estimate the distribution of wage offers precisely, so he will search on the basis of a subjective estimate of the distribution and revise his beliefs according to the information which he receives during search. So search performs the subsidiary role of an information-gathering activity for those who have incomplete information about the distribution of job offers. Here we shall concentrate on the primary role of search as a job-finding activity and as the process which allocates labour to firms in a decentralized market. Recently some authors have studied the information-gathering role of search, e.g. Rothschild (1974*b*) and Kohn and Shavell (1974), and concluded that although it may imply additional restrictions on the optimal policy when taken into account, ignoring it does not undermine any of the results related to its job-allocation function.

into account the job offer of each firm, $\varphi(w_t)$, discounted by the probability of being turned down by the offering firm, $1 - \Psi(q, w_t)$; i.e. the probability that the individual with efficiency q will be offered a job paying a wage rate w_t is given by

$$f(w_t) = \varphi(w_t)\,\Psi(q, w_t),$$

whereas the probability that he will be offered no job is given by

$$f(0) = 1 - \sum_{w_t} \varphi(w_t)\,\Psi(q, w_t).$$

Clearly the distribution of job offers f depends on the worker's efficiency. By changing his efficiency, through education or more practical training, the individual may change the distribution of offers in his favour, since in general an improvement in q will shift $f(w_t)$ to the right. We shall not make this dependence explicit, and we shall not consider the choice of q by individual workers, since this is, strictly speaking, a long-run decision. Once the worker enters the labour market to search for a job there is little he can do to change his efficiency, and since our main interest will be in the search process we may simplify the analysis by assuming that q is fixed for each individual.[7] However, later on we shall consider the effects of shifts in the distribution of job offers, and changes in q may be one cause of such shifts. Other causes are changes in wages, changes in the recruitment standard, and changes in information flows.[8]

Now, just as φ could be taken to be defined over the lifetime job, the distribution f may also be taken to be defined over the lifetime job $\mathbf{J}_t$. The first component of $\mathbf{J}_t$, then, becomes a shift parameter in f, but since $\mathbf{J}_t^1$ is known with certainty when t is known, f has the same shape whether it is defined over w_t or $\mathbf{J}_t$; and since the utility function is defined over $\mathbf{J}_t$ it is more convenient to assume that f is defined over $\mathbf{J}_t$. To make clearer the dependence of f on a number of shift parameters which depend on t, including q and $\mathbf{J}_t^1$, we shall write the distribution of job offers at t as $f_t(\mathbf{J})$, and talk of a job offer $\mathbf{J}$ meaning that given the time it is observed, and the wage rate it offers, the lifetime job from acceptance will be $\mathbf{J}$. Similarly, we shall talk of $f_t(\mathbf{J})$

[7] But see chapter 13. This area is clearly of high potential interest, because it may provide a link between the literature on human capital and the literature on job search. See Whipple (1973) for analysis of changes in efficiency within a sequential-search framework, and Spence (1973) for a more radical treatment.

[8] See chapter 10.

as the distribution of job offers at t, without making explicit whether the system is flexwage, in which case f_t will coincide with $\varphi(w_t)$, or whether it is fixwage, in which case it will depend on $\Psi(q, w_t)$.

The optimal acceptance policy

The optimal acceptance policy is derived using the same extension of the dynamic programming model as we used for the firm in fixwage. Thus, for any initial state and decision, the searcher is assumed to follow an optimal policy in the future with respect to the state resulting from the initial decision. Let V_t be the expected returns from search when an optimal policy is followed in all periods after t, and there are $T - t$ opportunities to search remaining. Suppose the individual searched in period t and observed $\mathbf{J}_t$. If he accepts this his utility will be $U(\mathbf{J}_t)$, whereas if he rejects it and continues the search his maximum returns will be V_t, since he now has $T - t$ opportunities to search remaining. Thus $\mathbf{J}_t$ is accepted if and only if $U(\mathbf{J}_t) \geq V_t$, giving an acceptance set for period t equal to[9]

$$S_t = \{\mathbf{J} \,|\, U(\mathbf{J}) \geq V_t\} \quad (t = 1, \ldots, T).$$

Thus the acceptance policy in each period t depends on the expected returns from subsequent search V_t, and so the properties of the optimal policy may be obtained from the properties of the optimal sequence $V_0, V_1, \ldots, V_T$.

As with recruitment, the V_ts may be shown to satisfy a simple recursive relation which yields a unique solution for each V_t, $(t = 1, \ldots, T)$, and also for the expected returns from search in all T periods, V_0. Thus, since the job offers observed in period t are distributed according to f_t, the expected returns from a maximum of $T - t - 1$ opportunities when an optimal policy is followed in period t and thereafter are,

$$V_{t-1} = \sum_{S_t} f_t(\mathbf{J})\, U(\mathbf{J}) + \Big[1 - \sum_{S_t} f_t(\mathbf{J})\Big] V_t \quad (t = 1, \ldots, T), \tag{1'}$$

where the first term of the right-hand side denotes the expected utility from acceptance of the offer at t and the second that from rejection.

[9] If the utility function is additive over time, the state of the searcher in all periods prior to t is irrelevant for search in period t, because it is the same for both the utility function U and the critical values V_t. However, if utility is not additive there may be complementarity effects which influence the utility of jobs in the future, not always in the same direction.

Rearranging and omitting the arguments of the functions for notational convenience we obtain the discrete-time functional equation form

$$V_{t-1} = V_t + \sum_{S_t} f_t(U - V_t) \quad (t = 1, \ldots, T). \qquad (1)$$

Equation (1), with a terminal condition giving the value of V_T, may be solved recursively to give the unique solutions for $V_0, V_1, \ldots, V_T$. But if T is known, the terminal condition giving V_T may be derived immediately, since if the individual has exhausted all his search opportunities without success, he will be 'discouraged' at T. That is, he will drop out of the labour market and remain unemployed until the end of his working life, enjoying a lifetime job given by $\mathbf{J}_{oT}$.[10] Thus we have

$$V_T = U(\mathbf{J}_{oT}),$$

which together with (1) completes the system.

The formal similarity between the acceptance policy of the searching worker and the recruitment policy of the fixwage firm imply that the two policies satisfy the same broad properties. In particular, the acceptance policy contains satisficing features, and the V_ts play the role of *reservation utility levels*. Despite this formal similarity, however, the interpretation of many of the features of the model, and their empirical relevance, is very different, and each case warrants consideration on its own merits.[11] For this reason we shall obtain the properties of searching behaviour in much the same way as we obtained the properties of recruitment behaviour, but to avoid repetition we shall emphasize the interpretation of the properties more than their formal derivation. In the case of the individual, however, there is an additional feature not relevant in the case of the firm. The individual offers to forego some leisure because with the proceeds from his work he can purchase consumption commodities. By saving or dissaving he can allocate his income over time so as to maximize

[10] See above, p. 83–4.

[11] A parallel may be drawn between the similarity of the acceptance and recruitment models during adjustment, and the equally striking formal similarity between the consumer and producer models in neoclassical economics. As Samuelson (1947) noted, the formal structure of the latter models is similar and it is based on the constrained maximization of an objective function, whereas the economic content of each model is different. It is such formal similarities that make economics one unified science.

the utility from his lifetime job situation. Thus we must also show how the consumption-saving decision is related to the searching process, and how it interacts with it. This is done in the next two chapters. By way of summary of the formal structure of the acceptance policy we conclude this chapter with some new notation and rewriting of the recursive system. This corresponds largely to the notation employed in the fixwage recruitment model.

Let a_t be the probability that the offer observed at period t is acceptable to the searcher when he follows an optimal policy, i.e.

$$a_t = \sum_{S_t} f_t(\mathbf{J}). \tag{2}$$

Now suppose the individual has searched unsuccessfully in periods $1, \ldots, t-1$, but has accepted the offer observed at t and terminated the search. The sequence of observed job offers $\mathbf{J}_1, \ldots, \mathbf{J}_t$ satisfies

$$\begin{aligned} &\mathbf{J}_{t'} \notin S_{t'} \quad (t' = 1, \ldots, t-1), \\ &\mathbf{J}_t \in S_t. \end{aligned} \tag{3}$$

Hence the probability of observing a sequence of job offers which satisfies condition (3) is, using (2),

$$P(t) = (1 - a_1) \ldots (1 - a_{t-1}) a_t. \tag{4}$$

Now, $P(t)$ is the probability of terminating the search at period t when an optimal policy is followed throughout. Let W_t denote the expected utility from acceptance of the offer observed at t, conditional on acceptance, i.e.

$$W_t = E[U(\mathbf{J}_t) | \mathbf{J}_t \in S_t] = \frac{1}{a_t} \sum_{S_t} f_t(\mathbf{J})\, U(\mathbf{J}).$$

Substituting W_t and a_t in (1′) we obtain

$$V_{t-1} = a_t W_t + (1 - a_t) V_t \quad (t = 1, \ldots, T), \tag{5}$$

so V_{t-1} is the sum of the expected utility W_t, from successful search at t, weighted by the probability of success, a_t, plus the expected utility from failure and continuation of search, V_t, weighted by the probability of failure, $1 - a_t$. Substituting successively $V_1, V_2, \ldots, V_T$ from (5) into itself, and using (4), we obtain the total returns from search with horizon T as

$$V_0 = \sum_{t=1}^{T} P(t) W_t + \left[1 - \sum_{t=1}^{T} P(t)\right] U(\mathbf{J}_{0T}). \tag{6}$$

Thus V_0 is the sum of W_t for all $t = 1, \ldots, T$, denoting successful termination of search in some period t, plus $U(\mathbf{J}_{oT})$ denoting failure in all T searches, each weighted by its respective probability of occurrence. The dependence of $P(t)$ and W_t on the optimal acceptance policy implies that the value of V_0 given by (6) is the maximum of all V_0s obtained by considering alternative policies. Thus, the optimal acceptance policy could also be interpreted as the choice of that configuration of the probabilities of success and failure that maximizes (6). Derivation of the optimal policy in the latter manner, however, involves the manipulation of technically messy formulae which is avoided by the dynamic programming technique.

7

Consumption and Savings

The main reason for spending money and effort in the search for a good job is the need for consumption and the income necessary to fulfil that need. Thus a worker, by improving his job, is also improving his consumption possibilities, so the utility derived from a job is largely indirect. In general, however, the worker derives both direct and indirect utility from his job – he spends a large proportion of his time at his place of work, so the location and general conditions of life at work also influence his utility. Thus a job will in general influence consumption from two directions. First, the non-pecuniary features of the job may enter the utility function directly and influence the pattern of tastes over commodities, e.g. a movie star will have different tastes from a top civil servant, even if they earn precisely the same income. Second, given the individual's initial wealth, the budget and physical (time) constraints are completely specified by the job situation. Thus the job situation influences demand both directly via the utility function and indirectly via the budget and time constraints. The direct influence acts mainly on the *direction* of expenditure, whereas the indirect affects their *volume*, so the former is of more interest to a micro-oriented analysis and the latter to a macro-oriented one.

The novelty of our approach, of course, lies in our assumption that the labour market is ridden with imperfect information and the exchange of labour services takes place sequentially between searching worker and offering firm. Thus the most important elements in the model are those which describe the interaction of consumption decisions and decisions with respect to choice of job *during job search*. Now, if the search in a period is successful, the individual will receive a certain wage from the offered job, so he will be able to choose his demand functions for commodities in all periods in his work horizon along the familiar Hicksian lines. But if the search is unsuccessful the individual will receive no income now, and he will be uncertain of the income he is likely to receive in the future, because it will depend on the outcome of a random search process. So in the current period consumption will be constrained by the individual's past savings, and by his income prospects.

There are two implications of this. First, the effects of search on consumption are felt mainly through the budget constraint, and second, the existence of search implies that future income is uncertain, so the individual should choose his consumption and savings in the current period by taking into account the uncertainty accompanying search. Thus the essential features of the interaction between searching and consumption-and-saving decisions may be brought out by a simplified model where the dependence of the direction of expenditure on the particular job accepted is ignored. The relative prices of goods may therefore be assumed constant and commodities may be grouped into a single Hicksian aggregate, whereas we may continue assuming that no non-pecuniary job characteristics enter the utility function other than hours of work.

The timing of consumption decisions and the resolution of uncertainties

In the model of the last chapter we implicitly assumed that the individual spends all his income on consumption at the time it is received, i.e. the timing of consumption expenditure coincides with the timing of income receipts. Thus savings in the model are identically equal to zero at every period in the individual's work horizon. This assumption is obviously unrealistic and should be relaxed. First, when jobs are accepted via a process of search the income stream of the individual is likely to show strong irregularities, because income receipts will be very low during search and high when a job is accepted. Also, if a job change takes place with some intervening unemployment, the income stream of the individual is likely to drop to very low levels during the intervening periods, although the new job may be better than the old one. If there are such irregularities in the income stream, savings are likely to play the role of a buffer stock, falling when search is unsuccessful and increasing when the individual is gainfully employed. Thus the consumption stream is likely to show less ups and downs than the income stream.[1] Second, since search gives rise to income un-

[1] See Modigliani and Brumberg (1954) and Friedman (1957).

certainty, the individual will choose between consuming and saving his income subject to that uncertainty. Income uncertainty usually influences the saving decision – the 'precautionary' demand for savings is one of Keynes's original motives, and it is usually taken to be positive. More recently, a number of authors showed that the relationship between savings and income uncertainty is not as clear-cut, but in any case the 'reasonable' risk-averse individual probably saves more when there is income uncertainty than when there is not.[2] One thing that no author doubted, however, is that uncertainty does influence savings, so ignoring the role of savings during search is clearly restrictive.

In order to isolate the effects of decentralized trading and searching on behaviour in the multi-market model we assume that commodity markets are frictionless and are always in supply-and-demand equilibrium. It is then a matter of convenience whether we use continuous or period analysis to analyse the properties of these markets over time, provided the period in the period analysis is not too long. If we also assume that there is no uncertainty about market-clearing prices, the period of the sequence of commodity markets may be made equal to the period of the labour market sequence, and so the two sequences may be analysed simultaneously. Thus, suppose that alongside the labour-market sequence there is a sequence of commodity markets, and that exchange in the latter takes place once per period at market-clearing prices. Let $\mathbf{x}(t)$ denote a vector of commodities in period t and $\mathbf{p}(t)$ denote the vector of market-clearing prices in the same period, discounted to the present. The vector $\mathbf{x}(t)$ may contain bonds and money but, following Patinkin (1965), we treat monetary goods like any other commodity. It may be more accurate to think of $\mathbf{x}(t)$ as a vector of real goods and services and a single bond whose price is used for discounting the prices of commodities to the present. In this way we abstract, at this stage of development, from the complexities of monetary exchange and asset-portfolio choice. We shall also assume that the relative prices of goods are constant so all commodities in a period t may be aggregated into a single Hicksian aggregate, denoted by $x(t)$, with price index $p(t)$. Prices may then be normalized by assuming that the price index in the current period, $p(1)$, is identically equal to unity. No loss of generality is suffered by these simplifications, so we shall adopt them in what follows.

[2] See Leland (1968) and Sandmo (1970).

We continue assuming that once a job offer is accepted, the individual knows precisely his job situation throughout his lifetime.[3] Thus uncertainty about the future arises only when the individual decides to search, and is resolved as soon as he accepts a job offer. Suppose the individual is currently unemployed, so his condition is described by the pair $(m_o, 0)$, denoting, respectively, non-wage income in the form of unemployment benefit and zero working hours. (If the individual is currently employed and considering whether to search for a new job his condition will be described by a pair $(w_o y, y)$ where w_o is the per-hour wage he is currently receiving, and y the hours of work. The analysis that follows holds in both cases, provided we employ the appropriate pair in each case.) If the expected utility from an optimal search policy does not exceed the utility from remaining unemployed the individual does not search and drops out of the labour market, so his condition in all periods in his work horizon is described by the pair $(m_o, 0)$. Let the T^*-dimensional vector of such pairs be denoted by $\mathbf{J}_o$ (the null job). This job situation involves no uncertainty, so the individual is able to choose his optimal consumption sequence $x(1), \ldots, x(T^*)$ under complete certainty about his constraints.

Now suppose he decides to search either until he finds an acceptable job offer or until he has completed T searches. If he observes a job offer which promises to pay a per-hour wage rate w_1 for ever, the individual's condition under acceptance of this offer will be described by the pair $(w_1 y, y)$. So his lifetime job will consist of a pair $(m_o - c, y_s)$ describing his condition in the first period, during which he was unemployed and searching, and a $(T^* - 1)$-dimensional vector with typical element $(w_1 y, y)$ describing his condition in the new job. This is the vector which we denoted by $\mathbf{J}_1$ in the last chapter. However, it will be more convenient to distinguish explicitly between the different wage offers available in each period, since there is more than one wage offer which the searcher may find acceptable, and his income will depend on the magnitude of the wage offer accepted, and not just on whether the offer was acceptable. Thus let w_{kt} be the typical wage offer available in period t, and denote by $\mathbf{J}_{kt}$ the lifetime job which results from acceptance of w_{kt}.

Suppose again that the individual has searched in period one and observed w_{k1}. If he accepts this his lifetime job will be $\mathbf{J}_{k1}$, so the

[3] See above, p. 85.

uncertainty about the lifetime job is resolved in the first period. The individual knows that his state throughout his work horizon will be described by the pair $(m_o - c, y_s)$ in the first period, and by (yw_{k1}, y) in all other periods. But if he decides to reject the offer observed in period one, the uncertainty about the lifetime job will persist for at least another period, because although he will know that his condition in the first two periods will be described by $(m_o - c, y_s)$ he will be uncertain about the wage offer that will be observed in the second period of search. In particular, the individual will be uncertain about whether he will be offered a wage rate at all, and whether that wage rate will be acceptable, and also about the exact magnitude of that wage rate if it is acceptable.

Consumption decisions have to be taken sequentially, i.e. the decision to consume $x(1)$ has to be taken before the outcome of the search in period two is known, but may be taken at any time before that. Clearly, it is to the individual's advantage to wait until the outcome of the search in period one is known and then choose $x(1)$. Thus there is a chance a_1, equal to the chance of observing an acceptable offer in period one, $\sum_{S_1} f_t(\mathbf{J})$, that the uncertainty will be resolved in period one and the individual will be able to choose his consumption sequence under complete certainty. If the observed offer is w_{k1} we denote this consumption sequence by

$$\mathbf{x}_{k1} = [x_{k1}(1), \ldots, x_{k1}(T^*)],$$

so subscript $k1$ to a consumption sequence means 'accept offer w_k in period one'. The probability of this event obtaining is

$$\Pr(i_{k1}) = f_1(\mathbf{J}_{k1}) \quad \text{for all } \mathbf{J}_{k1} \in S_1.$$

If the individual rejects the offer observed in period one and continues the search, the uncertainty about the lifetime job will persist at least until the offer of period two becomes known. Consumption in period one will therefore have to be chosen under *imperfect* information about the lifetime job – the only thing that the individual knows for certain is that search (and the uncertainty about the lifetime job) must continue for at least another period. This information may be referred to as the 'information signal' received during search in period one.[4] It provides some information about the

[4] See Marschak and Radner (1972, chs. 1–3) for a concise analysis of the theory of information and information-gathering.

outcome of search, but not complete information. Denote the event 'reject the offer observed in period one and continue searching' by $I(1)$. The probability of $I(1)$ obtaining is $1-a_1$.

Under $I(1)$ search goes into period two, during which the individual observes some other job offer, denoted by w_{k2}. If he accepts w_{k2} the uncertainty will again be resolved and his lifetime job situation will be described by the pair $(m_o - c, y_s)$ in the first two periods of search, and by the pair (yw_{k2}, y) in all other periods. Denote this lifetime job by $\mathbf{J}_{k2}$ and the event of that obtaining, i.e. 'accept offer w_k observed in period two', by i_{k2}. The consumption sequence from period two onwards under i_{k2} will be chosen under complete certainty, but the consumption chosen in period one will be that chosen when event $I(1)$ was observed, i.e. before i_{k2} became known. So we may denote the consumption sequence when $\mathbf{J}_{k2}$ is the true job situation (and hence i_{k2} the true event) by

$$\mathbf{x}_{k2} = [x_I(1), x_{k2}(2), \ldots, x_{k2}(T^*)].$$

The probability of i_{k2} obtaining is, clearly,

$$\Pr(i_{k2}) = (1 - a_1) f_2(\mathbf{J}_{k2}) \quad \text{for all } \mathbf{J}_{k2} \in S_2.$$

If the offer observed in the second period is rejected as well, the uncertainty will go into period three. Like the first period's consumption when the offer observed in period one was rejected, the consumption in period two will have to be chosen under imperfect information about the lifetime job. The information signal received during search is that period two's offer as well is unacceptable, so the individual has more information now than he had when he chose $x_I(1)$, but still less than perfect information. Let the event 'reject the offer observed in period two' be denoted by $I(2)$, and the consumption chosen for period two by $x_I(2)$. The probability of $I(2)$ obtaining is $(1 - a_1)(1 - a_2)$.

The uncertainty about an individual's job is certainly resolved at the end of period T (the last period of search). Denote the event 'accept offer w_k observed in period T' by i_{kT}, and the event 'reject offer and remain unemployed' by i_{oT}. The probability of i_{kT} obtaining is

$$\Pr(i_{kT}) = (1 - a_1) \ldots (1 - a_{T-1}) f_T(\mathbf{J}_{kT}) \quad \text{for all } \mathbf{J}_{kT} \in S_T,$$

and that of i_{oT} obtaining is

$$\Pr(i_{oT}) = (1 - a_1) \ldots (1 - a_T).$$

Thus information is becoming known to the individual sequentially during search and he is able to influence this information flow through his choice of search policy. The sequential development of information may be illustrated in a tree diagram (Fig. 7.1).

This tree may be contrasted with the one drawn by Debreu (1959, pp. 98–9) for the Arrow–Debreu economy. Whereas the Arrow–Debreu sequence of events is exogenously given by acts of nature and is the same for all agents,[5] in the present model the sequence of events depends partly on the random workings of the system and partly on the actions of the individual. Indeed, the individual may choose to forego all uncertainties by deciding not to search, or accept the first offer observed. In perfect competitive equilibrium it will be optimal to do so, since all offers are identical from the point of view of the individual for people of his skill, so no uncertainty arises. Thus un-

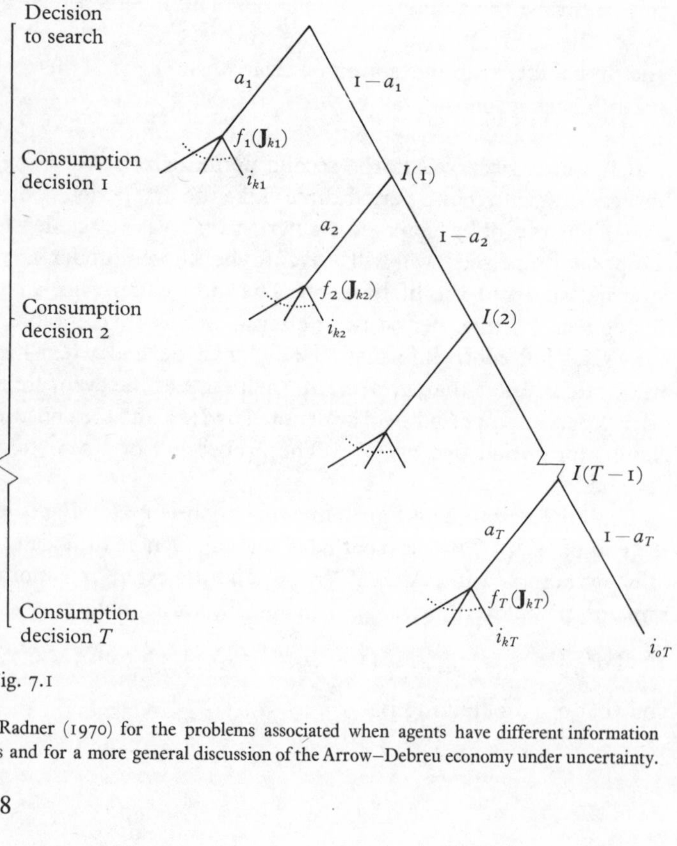

Fig. 7.1

[5] See Radner (1970) for the problems associated when agents have different information structures and for a more general discussion of the Arrow–Debreu economy under uncertainty.

certainty in this model is a purely disequilibrium phenomenon which arises because of the absence of a central market organization which can transmit perfect information to agents about the location and nature of job offers and enable quick adjustment in labour markets. Once adjustment stops for the individual all uncertainty is resolved.

But although the flow of information, and so the probability distribution over future income, depends on individual actions, if we assume that the individual always follows an optimal policy in search, whatever his consumption sequence, we can obtain a probability distribution over the present value of his income stream, comparable to that found in equilibrium economics. Thus, it is evident from the discussion of this section that once the individual knows the true event i_{kt}, associated with a lifetime job situation $\mathbf{J}_{kt}$, he also knows his lifetime income stream. For instance, if i_{kt} is the true event, the individual will be receiving m_o in the first t periods in his work horizon, and yw_k in the remaining $T^* - t$ periods. This income stream and his initial asset position enable him to estimate with certainty the total wealth which he can make available for consumption. Thus the probability distribution over all events i_{kt} (for all $\mathbf{J}_{kt}$ and $t = 1, \ldots, T$) is also a probability distribution over total wealth. Since the optimal search policy enables one to estimate the probability of i_{kt} as

$$\Pr(i_{kt}) = (1 - a_1) \ldots (1 - a_{t-1}) f_t(\mathbf{J}_{kt}) \quad (t = 1, \ldots, T, \\ \mathbf{J}_{kt} \in S_t \text{ and } \mathbf{J}_{kt'} \notin S_{t'} \text{ for } t' < t),$$

and

$$\Pr(i_{oT}) = (1 - a_1) \ldots (1 - a_T) \quad (t = 1, \ldots, T, \mathbf{J}_{kt} \notin S_t)$$

one is also able to take the distribution $\Pr(i_{kt})$ as being defined over total wealth.

The utility function and the constraints on consumption

The utility function utilized in the derivation of the optimal job search strategy was totally unrestricted, in that any function defined over a vector of job characteristics which is increasing in the desirable characteristics and decreasing in the undesirable ones could serve. Thus the utility of a job may be direct (derived from liking or disliking of some of the features of the job), indirect (derived from the consumption possibilities that the job opens up), or a combination of both. In general, of course, the utility of a job will be a combination of both, but as we argued in the introduction to this chapter the novel features of the model may be captured by a utility function which is largely indirect. Thus in the analysis of consumption and saving decisions we shall use the dynamic analogue of the consumption–leisure function, i.e.

$$U = U[x(1), \ldots, x(T^*), y(1), \ldots, y(T^*)],$$

where as usual $x(t)$ is consumption in period t and $y(t)$ hours of work in the same period. Some further restrictions are placed on U which are needed to ensure that there is a unique local and global maximum with respect to consumption choice. Thus U is increasing in consumption and decreasing in hours of work, tending towards minus infinity as hours of work tend towards the maximum length of the period from below, and as consumption tends towards zero from above. Moreover, it is real-valued, concave, continuous and twice differentiable in all its arguments. Concavity implies that the individual is risk-averse in his saving decision and his acceptance policy during search.

The constraints on consumption are fully specified by the individual's job situation throughout his lifetime and by his initial wealth. The constraints fall into three main classes – informational, physical and monetary constraints. We shall consider each in turn.

The *informational constraints* are related to the information that the individual has at the time of consumption choice, and they have already been alluded to in this chapter. They only arise during search and they constrain the individual to choosing the consumption for period t without knowing the job offers that will be observed after t.

Suppose that during search the individual satisfies the von Neumann–Morgenstern consistency axioms, so he chooses that consumption sequence which maximizes the expected value of his utility function. Let again $x_{kt}(1), \ldots, x_{kt}(T^*)$ denote the consumption sequence when i_{kt} is the true event, and let $y_{kt}(1), \ldots, y_{kt}(T^*)$ denote the sequence of working hours in the same event. (Note that we are assuming that the firm offers a per-hour wage rate and the worker supplies the desired number of hours – see also below pp. 103–5.) Then since the probability of event i_{kt} obtaining is known, the problem at the beginning of the first period and before any job offers are observed is to choose a consumption and working-hours sequence to maximize the function

$$\sum_{k} \sum_{t=1}^{T} \Pr(i_{kt})\, U[x_{kt}(1), \ldots, x_{kt}(T^*), y_{kt}(1), \ldots, y_{kt}(T^*)], \qquad (1)$$

with the summation over job offers taken only over those offers which are acceptable given the period they are observed, and if $t = T$, k takes the value o if the observed offer at T is not acceptable. The informational constraint then, states that if t, the period in which the uncertainty is resolved under event i_{kt}, lies after some other period t', then the consumption at t' must be the same whatever the true event that will become known in the future. Moreover, the 'hours of work' at t' must be equal to y_s, the time needed to search a firm.[6] More formally, the informational constraint states

$$\text{if } t > t' \text{ then } x_{kt}(t') = x_I(t')$$
$$\text{and} \quad y_{kt}(t') = y_{kt}(t) = y_s \quad \text{for all } i_{kt}. \tag{2}$$

The *physical constraints* include such factors as time constraints and effort requirements. Since our main interest will be in other aspects of the consumption–search sequence we shall make strong and simple assumptions on these which will simplify the main part of our analysis.[7] Thus we assume that every lifetime job situation $\mathbf{J}_{kt}$ has a consumption possibility set X_{kt} associated with it, which gives the physical constraints imposed by job $\mathbf{J}_{kt}$ on consumption. A consumption vector $\mathbf{x}_{kt}$ may be chosen if and only if $\mathbf{x}_{kt} \in X_{kt}$, so by our assumption of concave utility, if X_{kt} is convex for all $\mathbf{J}_{kt}$ then there exists a unique global and local utility-maximizing consumption sequence. Now, we have taken the length of the period to be equal to unity, and we have also assumed that as y tends towards unity, utility tends towards minus infinity. So the chosen y must be less than unity, i.e. it is always optimal to choose some leisure time, $1 - y$, in all periods. In what follows, we shall assume that the individual's wealth always constrains him before the physical constraints become binding, i.e. wage rates and the time required to consume a good are such that the leisure time $1 - y$ is always more than sufficient for the consumption of those commodities

[6] Since y_s is assumed fixed, we are implicitly assuming that the 'intensity' of search is constant. However, this restriction is not crucial in anything that follows. Whipple (1973) has analysed the choice of the total time spent searching during the period by assuming that y_s (in our notation) is a shift parameter in the distribution of job offers, so a higher y_s implies a more favourable distribution of offers. Alternatively, since we defined the period as that length of time which is needed to search a firm, an individual may search more intensely by choosing a shorter period. In terms of calendar time, if an individual searches two employers per week his period is equal to three days; one who searches more intensely and visits, e.g. three employers per week, has a period of two days; and so on.

[7] See Becker (1965) and Lancaster (1966) for pioneering efforts to analyse the role of time constraints on consumption. See also M. Fisher (1969, ch. 2).

which can be purchased by the individual's initial wealth plus wage income, yw.[8]

The *monetary constraints* of the consumption problem specify a budget set for each job situation that the individual may find himself at the end of search. We continue assuming that the capital and commodity markets are always in equilibrium, so there is a unique rate of discount for every future period, and unique discounted commodity prices $p(t)$ for all $t = 1, \ldots, T^*$. Take any typical job situation $\mathbf{J}_{kt}$. This job situation consists of a t-dimensional vector with typical element $(m_o - c, y_s)$, and a $(T^* - t)$-dimensional vector with typical element $(y_{kt}\, w_{kt}, y_{kt})$, where w_{kt} is the offered wage and y_{kt} the chosen hours of work. Let $\beta(t)$ be the discounting factor at time t, i.e. if there is a unique rate of discount ρ then $\beta(t) = 1/(1 + \rho)^{t-1}$. Then, if we denote by $m_{kt}(t')$ the discounted income flow in period t' under job situation $\mathbf{J}_{kt}$, we have

$$m_{kt}(t') = \begin{cases} \beta(t')(m_o - c) & (t' = 1, \ldots, t), \\ \beta(t')y_{kt}\, w_{kt}. & (t' = t + 1, \ldots, T^*). \end{cases}$$

Thus, denoting initial non-human wealth by m', the maximum amount of money that the individual can spend under $\mathbf{J}_{kt}$ is

$$M_{kt} = m' + \sum_{t'=1}^{T} m_{kt}(t').$$

The budget set for state i_{kt} is therefore defined by

$$B_{kt} = \{\mathbf{x}_{kt} \,|\, \mathbf{p}'\mathbf{x}_{kt} \leq M_{kt}\},$$

where $\mathbf{p}$ is the (column) vector of the discounted price indices $p(1), \ldots, p(T^*)$, with $p(1) \equiv 1$.

Given our restrictions on the physical constraints, the consumption problem reduces to the maximization of the expected-utility function (1) by treating each consumption $x_{kt}(t')$ and each $y_{kt}(t')$ as a separate 'commodity' for all i_{kt} and t', subject to the informational constraint (2) and the budget constraints $\mathbf{x}_{kt} \in B_{kt}$, for all i_{kt}. Further to the assumptions on the physical constraints, we shall assume that the individual is not satiated within his budget in any job situation $\mathbf{J}_{kt}$, i.e. money is always desired. Then the budget constraints hold with

[8] See the next footnote for a more formal statement.

equality in all states i_{kt},[9] so the chosen consumptions and hours of work are the unique values which maximize the expected-utility function

$$\sum_{k} \sum_{t=1}^{T} \Pr(i_{kt})\, U(\mathbf{x}_{kt}, \mathbf{y}_{kt}), \tag{1}$$

subject to the linear budget constraints

$$\mathbf{p}'\mathbf{x}_{kt} = M_{kt} \quad \text{for all } t = 1, \ldots, T \text{ and } \mathbf{J}_{kt} \in S_t,$$

and the informational constraint

$$\text{if } t > t' \text{ then } x_{kt}(t') = x_l(t') \text{ and } y_{kt}(t') = y_{kt}(t) = y_s \text{ for all } i_{kt}.$$

We shall refer to this maximization problem as the *consumption problem.*[10]

A digression: price and quantity constraints on consumption. There has been considerable discussion recently about whether neoclassical maximization theory is capable of yielding demand functions as functions of income, in the sense of realized total revenue from the sale of commodities, or whether only prices should enter as independent variables.[11] In terms of a model such as the present one, the former arises when the budget constraint is set by the total wage payments offered by the firm, and the latter when it is set by the per-hour wage rate it offers. The former is a *quantity* constraint, whereas the latter is a *price* constraint.

The discussion on price and quantity constraints has been carried out in terms of the microfoundations of Keynesian economics, so it has concentrated on the macro implications of the distinction. As we shall see in chapter 14, as far as macro analysis goes, the microeconomics of the distinction may be simplified enormously by assuming that the firm offers either a wage *rate* or no job at all. However, the distinction

[9] More formally, the restrictions on the budget and physical constraints may be stated as follows. If $(\mathbf{x}_{kt}^{*}, \mathbf{y}_{kt}^{*})$ is a preferred point in B_{kt}, there exists a point $(\mathbf{x}_{kt}', \mathbf{y}_{kt}')$ in X_{kt} which is preferred to $(\mathbf{x}_{kt}^{*}, \mathbf{y}_{kt}^{*})$ for each i_{kt}. Moreover, there exists a point $(\mathbf{x}_{kt}'', \mathbf{y}_{kt}'')$ in both B_{kt} and X_{kt} which is less preferred than $(\mathbf{x}_{kt}^{*}, \mathbf{y}_{kt}^{*})$ for each i_{kt}. Thus money is always desired and the preferred point in B_{kt} is an interior point of X_{kt}.

[10] The non-negativity constraint on hours of work does not arise in the consumption problem because each event i_{kt} implies the *acceptance* of a job at t. By acceptance of a job we mean $y(t') > 0$ for all $t' > t$, and by the informational constraint (in this context probably more appropriately called a 'searching' constraint) $y(t') = y_s > 0$ for all $t' \leq t$. See also above, p. 17.

[11] The starting point is Clower (1965).

between price and quantity constraints holds in a more general environment. As with so many other issues in economics it may be illustrated with the aid of a static utility-maximizing model under complete certainty.

Thus, let $\mathbf{x}$ be the vector of commodities, y the number of hours of work, and m the *total* wage payments received from a job. The essence of the distinction between price and quantity constraints lies in whether the individual can choose the number of hours he works or whether the firm makes an all-or-nothing offer of hours. Suppose the production function is such that the firm derives as much revenue from each hour's work as from each other hour. Then, letting w denote the per-hour wage rate, the firm which makes an all-or-nothing offer of $\bar{y}$ hours offers at the same time a total wage payment equal to $\bar{m} = w\bar{y}$. On the other hand, the firm which offers a per-hour wage rate and lets the worker choose the number of hours of work offers w per hour supplied, so if the worker supplies y^* hours his total wage payments are equal to $m^* = wy^*$.

The price constraint on consumption arises when the firm offers the worker a per-hour wage rate and lets him choose the number of hours he is willing to work. The individual's problem then is to choose $\mathbf{x}$ and y to maximize $u(\mathbf{x}, y)$ subject to $\mathbf{p}'\mathbf{x} = wy$. This problem gives unique solutions for $\mathbf{x}$ and y as functions of prices $\mathbf{p}$ and the offered wage rate w, so the constraint on consumption is a price constraint and the utility of the job offer depends solely on $\mathbf{p}$ and w, i.e. on the offered *real* wage rate.

The quantity constraint arises when the firm fixes both the number of hours and the total wage payment, and the individual must either accept the offer as it stands or reject it and search for another. Thus, suppose the firm offers a total wage payment equal to $\bar{m}$, and asks the individual to work $\bar{y}$ hours exactly. Although we may still talk of a wage 'rate' as being equal to the ratio $\bar{m}/\bar{y}$, the concept loses its former significance, for now the maximization problem is to choose $\mathbf{x}$ to maximize $u(\mathbf{x}, \bar{y})$ subject to $\mathbf{p}'\mathbf{x} = \bar{m}$. The demand functions, then, are functions of $\mathbf{p}$, $\bar{m}$ and $\bar{y}$, or if $\bar{m} = w\bar{y}$, they are functions of $\mathbf{p}$, w, *and* $\bar{y}$, i.e. demand functions are functions of prices and income, in the sense of realized hours of work, which are not necessarily equal to desired hours, given prices and the firm's wage rate.

This is the essence of the distinction in micro terms. In chapter 14 we shall argue that alternative assumptions about offered hours have important implications for macro analysis. As we would expect from the results of the standard theory of all-or-nothing demand-and-supply, if the individual can choose the number of working hours he will attach, *ceteris paribus*, a higher utility to the job offer. For suppose two firms wish to pay the same per-hour wage rate, w, and one of them offers $\bar{y}$ and the implied $w\bar{y}$, whereas the other offers w per hour supplied and lets the individual choose y. If he chooses y^*, then the utility from the first firm's job offer is either less than that from the second's or equal in the special case where $y^* = \bar{y}$. The utility from $\bar{y}$ and $w\bar{y}$ can never exceed that from y^* and wy^* because y^* maximizes by assumption utility given w. Clearly, the same theory of search holds in both cases because decisions during search depend solely on whether the individual can attach a utility number to the offered job. The difference between a 'price' and a 'quantity' offer lies in that the utility number attached to the former is not below that attached to the latter, provided per-hour wage rates are equal in both cases, and in general it will be above it. Thus the difference is purely quantitative – the searcher is more likely to accept a price offer than a quantity one.

The incorporation of consumption decisions in the structure of the model of job search

We have examined the consumption decision given job search. It remains to examine the searching decision given consumption. In the remaining part of this section we shall set up this problem.

Let V_t^* be the expected returns from an optimal search *and* consumption policy when there are $T - t$ opportunities to search remaining, and suppose the individual searched in period one and observed a wage rate w_{k1}. The maximum utility derived from this job offer will be equal to the maximum of $U_{k1} = U(\mathbf{x}_{k1}, \mathbf{y}_{k1})$, maximized with respect to $\mathbf{x}_{k1}$ and $\mathbf{y}_{k1}$, subject to $y_{k1}(1) = y_s$ and

$$\sum_{t=1}^{T^*} p(t) x_{k1}(t) = m' + m_o - c + \sum_{t=2}^{T^*} \beta(t)\, w_{k1}\, y_{k1}(t),$$

where $\mathbf{x}_{k1}$ is the consumption sequence under state i_{k1}, $\mathbf{y}_{k1}$ is the sequence of hours of work, with $y_{k1}(1) = y_s$ because in the first period the individual is searching, m' is initial wealth, $m_o - c$ unemployment compensation minus searching cost, received in period one, and $\beta(t)$ is the discount factor. (The price index $p(t)$ is already discounted, see p. 102.) Substituting the maximizing values $\mathbf{x}_{k1}^*$ and $\mathbf{y}_{k1}^*$ in U_{k1} we obtain the maximum utility U_{k1}^* obtained from the observed job offer, so the individual accepts w_{k1} if and only if $U^*_{k1} \geq V^*_1$. This gives the functional equation

$$V^*_0 = V^*_1 + \sum_{S_1} f_1(\mathbf{J})(U^*_{k1} - V^*_1). \tag{3}$$

This equation is formally identical to the recursive relation of the model without consumption choice for $t = 1$. Now, if the individual exhausted all his T opportunities without success he will have chosen some consumption sequence $x^*_l(1), \ldots, x^*_l(T-1)$ during the search process at prices $p(1), \ldots, p(T-1)$. So the maximum utility from dropping out of the labour force at the end of T unsuccessful searches, denoted by V^*_T, is the maximum of his utility function which is obtained by choosing optimal future consumption, given that his total income will be the income from unemployment benefits, minus the cost of search in T periods, and also given that he has already spent some money on consumption during search, i.e. the money left over for consumption from period T to the end of the horizon is equal to

$$m' + \sum_{t=1}^{T} \beta(t)(m_o - c) + \sum_{t=T+1}^{T^*} \beta(t)m_o - \sum_{t=1}^{T-1} p(t)x^*_l(t). \tag{4}$$

The first three terms of this expression are what we have called M_{oT} (p. 102). Hence V^*_T is the maximum of the utility function

$$U[x^*_l(1), \ldots, x^*_l(T-1), x_{oT}(T), \ldots, x_{oT}(T^*), y_{oT}(1), \ldots, y_{oT}(T^*)], \tag{5}$$

where $y_{oT}(t) = y_s$ for $t \leq T$, and $y_{oT}(t) = 0$ for $t > T$, maximized with respect to $x_{oT}(T), \ldots, x_{oT}(T^*)$, subject to a budget constraint that stipulates that total expenditure on consumption, $\sum_{t=T}^{T^*} p(t)x_{oT}(t)$, should be equal to the total income available after T, given by (4). This maximum is the indirect utility function U^*_{oT} obtained by substituting the demand functions for $x_{oT}(T), \ldots, x_{oT}(T^*)$ into (5), and it depends on the initial values $x^*_1(1), \ldots, x^*_1(T-1)$. Thus, to get V^*_T we must show how these values are determined. Once we establish that, we have the terminal condition giving V^*_T, and by recursion all the other optimal reservation values $V^*_0, \ldots, V^*_T$ employed during search.

We show this working backwards. Thus take *any* values $\bar{x}_l(1), \ldots, \bar{x}_l(T-1)$ and substitute them in (5). To simplify the notation we write the vector $x(t), \ldots, x(T^*)$ and the corresponding prices $p(t), \ldots, p(T^*)$ as $\mathbf{x}^t$ and $\mathbf{p}^t$ respectively, and the vector $y(t), \ldots, y(T^*)$ as $\mathbf{y}^t$. Moreover, we write the functional equation (3) in its equivalent form

$$V_0^* = \sum_{S_1} f_1 U_{k1}^* + (1 - a_1)V_1^*.$$

Now, the critical value $\overline{V}_{T-1}$ when past consumption takes the values $\overline{x}_I(1), \ldots, \overline{x}_I(T-1)$, is given by

$$\overline{V}_{T-1} = \sum_{S_T} f_T \operatorname*{Max}_{\mathbf{x}^T, \mathbf{y}^{T+1}} \overline{U}_{kT} + (1 - a_T) \operatorname*{Max}_{\mathbf{x}^T} \overline{U}_{oT}, \tag{6}$$

where a bar over a function denotes the value of that function when we substitute in it $\overline{x}_I(t)$ for $t = 1, \ldots, T-1$. The budget constraint is given by

$$(\mathbf{p}^T)'\mathbf{x}^T = m' + \sum_{t=1}^{T} \beta(t)(m_o - c) + \sum_{t=T+1}^{T^*} \beta(t) w_{kT} y(t) - \sum_{t=1}^{T-1} p(t)\overline{x}_I(t)$$

for the first maximization problem, and

$$(\mathbf{p}^T)'\mathbf{x}^T = m' + \sum_{t=1}^{T} \beta(t)(m_o - c) + \sum_{t=T+1}^{T^*} \beta(t) m_o - \sum_{t=1}^{T-1} p(t)\overline{x}_I(t)$$

for the second.

At period $T - 1$, and if the individual has rejected the observed offer w_{kT-1}, he must choose consumption $x_I(T-1)$ optimally. Since his expected utility under rejection for any arbitrary value $\overline{x}_I(T-1)$ and an optimal policy in the future is given by (6), his maximum expected returns, given any values for previous consumption $\overline{x}_I(1), \ldots, \overline{x}_I(T-2)$, is given by

$$\overline{V}_{T-1}^* = \operatorname*{Max}_{x_I(T-1)} \overline{V}_{T-1}.$$

The maximization is unconstrained because the budget constraints for all possible future states under rejection of w_{kT-1} are already in $\overline{V}_{T-1}$ through the first-stage maximization procedure.

Continuing working backwards we obtain

$$\overline{V}_{T-2} = \sum_{S_{T-1}} f_{T-1} \operatorname*{Max}_{\mathbf{x}^{T-1}, \mathbf{y}^T} \overline{U}_{kT-1} + (1 - a_{T-1})\overline{V}_{T-1}^*.$$

Doing the same as for period $T - 1$ we move to the next stage, and continuing relaxing and choosing optimally at each stage the relevant consumption $x_I(T - t)$, we get to the beginning, when $x_I(1)$ is relaxed from its arbitrary value $\overline{x}_I(1)$ and chosen optimally. In this way we find the optimal consumptions $x_I^*(1), \ldots, x_I^*(T-1)$, and so the critical value V_T^*, which together with the functional equation (3) gives the critical values $V_1^*, \ldots, V_T^*$ in a manner exactly analogous to the model of the last chapter.

It remains to show that the demand functions for commodities in all possible outcomes of the search process that may arise, obtained here working backwards after T stages, are the same as the demand functions obtained in a single stage from what we have called the consumption problem. It is not difficult to show that, given the informational constraint (2), and that

$$\Pr(i_{kt}) = (1 - a_1) \ldots (1 - a_{t-1}) f_t(\mathbf{J}_{kt}) \quad (t = 1, \ldots, T),$$

the demand functions obtained in the two cases are indeed the same. As an indication of the equivalence we may note here that if we substitute successively V_1^*, V_2^*, down to $V_T^* = U_{oT}^*$, into the functional equation (3), and substitute for $\Pr(i_{kt})$, we obtain the utility function (1), so the expected returns from an optimal search and consumption policy are the returns V_0 of the model of the last chapter, maximized with respect to consumption in all job situations, as we would expect. However, it is also possible to demonstrate the full equivalence from first principles. The crucial restriction is the sequential nature of choice and the informational constraint, which imply that when $x(t)$ is chosen the individual must take all decisions before t as given and maximize subject to the information signal received at t, and not those that may be received after t. The dynamic optimality principle which we have followed implies that $x(t)$ must be optimal whatever the choice before t, and this is what enabled the sequential determination of the optimal consumption during search.[12]

[12] The equivalence between the sequential and single-stage consumption problem is also demonstrated in the next chapter from first principles for a two-stage informational constraint, which is a special case of the multi-stage constraint in (2).

8

Interactions between Consumption and Job Search

The dependence of aggregate consumption expenditure on search

The outcome of search influences aggregate consumption expenditure through its influence on the budget constraints, and to a lesser extent through the influence of different levels of leisure and working hours associated with different job situations on the utility function. Moreover, search is the process which provides the individual with information about his lifetime income, so the influence of search on consumption acts both directly by determining his lifetime income and indirectly by providing information about it before the final outcome of search becomes known.

Since information is becoming available sequentially through search, the individual chooses current consumption but only intentions for the future. The intentions for period t will in general be a function from the set of information signals that will be received in period t to the set of demand functions.[1] Consider for instance the maximization of utility before any search has taken place, and the consumption decision for period one. Before search the individual chooses intentions for consumption in period one contingent on the information signal that will be received during search in that period, and then, at the end of the period, fulfils one of these intentions. The set of information signals for period one consists of two disjoint subsets, i_1 and $I(1)$, denoting respectively accepting the offer observed and rejecting it. The subset i_1 consists of all elementary events i_{k1}, one for each job offer in the acceptance set S_1, whereas $I(1)$ consists of a single information signal, unsuccessful search. The signals for i_{k1} provide complete information whereas that for $I(1)$ only incomplete information about the future course of events. Therefore the demand

[1] Thus 'intentions' here is what is known in statistical decision theory as strategy, rule of action, or decision function. See for instance Marschak and Radner (1972, pp. 45–6).

intentions for period one, as chosen before any search has taken place, are $x_{k1}(1)$ for all $\mathbf{J}_{k1} \in S_1$, and $x_I(1)$ for $\mathbf{J}_{k1} \notin S_1$. If the offer observed in period one is acceptable the actual demand functions chosen are those intentions which corresponded to the observed offer. If it is unacceptable the demand functions will be $x_I(1)$, corresponding to failure in $t = 1$.

There will be similar intentions for all other periods, and since additional information is becoming available over time (see Fig. 7.1) the number of possible demand functions will be increasing as the distance of the period from the present increases. Thus in period two the information signals correspond to i_{k1} for all $\mathbf{J}_{k1} \in S_1$, i_{k2} for all $\mathbf{J}_{k2} \in S_2$, and $I(2)$ for rejection of both offers, those for period three correspond to i_{k1}, i_{k2}, i_{k3} and $I(3)$, and so forth. So the uncertainty about the actual demand functions in any period increases as the distance of the period from the present increases.

Let now λ_{kt} be a Lagrangian multiplier associated with event i_{kt} in the maximization of utility subject to the budget constraint, before the beginning of search. The assumptions of the consumption model imply that the optimal consumption intentions are given by the unique values which maximize the Lagrangian expression

$$L = \sum_k \sum_{t=1}^{T} \Pr(i_{kt})\, U(\mathbf{x}_{kt}, \mathbf{y}_{kt}) - \sum_k \sum_{t=1}^{T} \lambda_{kt}(\mathbf{p}'\mathbf{x}_{kt} - M_{kt}), \qquad (1)$$

where $\mathbf{x}_{kt}$ is the consumption sequence for event i_{kt}, $\mathbf{y}_{kt}$ is the sequence of hours of work under i_{kt}, $\mathbf{p}$ is the vector of price indices for aggregate consumption with $p(1) \equiv 1$, and M_{kt} is the present value of the income stream under i_{kt}. Maximizing the Lagrangian (1) with respect to all $x_{kt}(t')$ and $y_{kt}(t')$, and taking into account the informational constraint (2) of chapter 7, yields the contingent demand functions for all periods in the individual's horizon. So the sequential decision-making is reduced to the choice of a single strategy at the beginning of the horizon. The effects of search on consumption may then be obtained by comparing the optimal demand functions in different states of nature. Since our main interest is in consumption and savings during and after search, we shall simplify the exposition by assuming that the hours of work are fixed and equal for all jobs $\mathbf{J}_{kt}$, so we shall drop $\mathbf{y}_{kt}$ from the notation and treat M_{kt} as exogenous.

Obtaining the effects of job search on consumption by calculating all possible demand intentions implied by the sequential informational constraint would involve a lot of complicated manipulations which are not necessary for the main result. The main result may instead be obtained by assuming that the individual chooses his current consumption on the hypothesis that the uncertainty will be eliminated before any future consumption is chosen. Thus the informational constraint is simplified to the 'two-stage' constraint

$$\text{if } t > 1 \quad \text{then} \quad x_{kt}(1) = x_I(1) \quad \text{for all } i_{kt}. \tag{2}$$

This introduces a certain 'myopia' in consumer decisions, because the individual ignores the effects of the sequential nature of information-gathering on current decisions, i.e. he assumes that the future is uncertain but not that this uncertainty may not be fully resolved before he has to face the choice of future consumption.[2] However, instead of obtaining a single strategy at the beginning of the planning horizon, we can make the two-stage assumption sequentially at the beginning of every period of search, and so obtain a sequence of 'current' consumptions which can be compared to each other to give the main influence of search on consumption. This may be interpreted as the individual's way of dealing with the excessive demands for imagination and computation required by the derivation of all intentions in all periods. This simplification is possible because of the existence of a sequence of active commodity markets.[3]

The individual maximizes the Lagrangian (1) before the outcome of search in period one becomes known, but takes his consumption decision after the outcome is known. Thus search in period one influences current consumption through its influence on the determination of the true event. We distinguish two classes of intentions, corresponding respectively to acceptance of an offer and rejection. If search results in the acceptance of $\mathbf{J}_{k1}$, the true event will be i_{k1}, and the maximum point will satisfy the conditions

$$\text{(A1)} \qquad \frac{\partial L}{\partial x_{k1}(1)} = U_1^{k1} - \lambda_{k1}\, p(1) = 0,$$

[2] This assumption is implicitly made by models of consumption under uncertainty which extend over many periods and which are more general in their treatment of uncertainty than the portfolio-type models of, e.g. Phelps (1962) and Hakansson (1970). See Lluch and Morishima (1973). It is also made by necessity in all two-period models, e.g. Leland (1968) and Sandmo (1969, 1970).

[3] The need for excessive imagination and computation by individuals in single-stage models under uncertainty, the best known one of which is the Arrow–Debreu economy, was particularly emphasized and criticized by Radner (1968, 1970). Borch (1968) also made a similar criticism.

$$\text{(A2)} \qquad \frac{\partial L}{\partial x_{k1}(t)} = U_t^{k1} - \lambda_{k1}\, p(t) = 0 \quad (t = 2, \ldots, T^*),$$

$$\text{(A3)} \qquad \sum_{t=1}^{T^*} p(t) x_{k1}(t) = M_{k1},$$

where superscripts on U denote the true event and subscripts partial derivatives. If search results in the rejection of the offer observed, the true event will be i_{kt}, $t > 1$, so taking into account the two-stage informational constraint (2), the chosen demand functions will satisfy the conditions

$$\text{(R1)} \quad \frac{\partial L}{\partial x_I(1)} = \sum_k \sum_{t=2}^{T} \Pr(i_{kt} \,|\, \mathbf{J}_{k1} \notin S_1)\, U_1^{kt} - p(1) \sum_k \sum_{t=2}^{T} \lambda_{kt} = 0,$$

$$\text{(R2)} \quad \frac{\partial L}{\partial x_{kt}(t')} = \Pr(i_{kt} \,|\, \mathbf{J}_{k1} \notin S_1)\, U_{t'}^{kt} - p(t')\lambda_{kt} = 0$$
$$(t = 2, \ldots, T,\ t' = 2, \ldots, T^*,\ \mathbf{J}_{kt} \in S_t),$$

$$\text{(R3)} \quad p(1)x_I(1) + \sum_{t'=2}^{T^*} p(t')x_{kt}(t') = M_{kt} \quad (t = 2, \ldots, T,\ \mathbf{J}_{kt} \in S_t).$$

Conditions (A1)–(A3) correspond to those that arise when there is equilibrium and certainty in all markets, whereas conditions (R1)–(R3) give current consumption and intentions for the future when the labour market is out of full equilibrium, in the sense that the individual does not know the outcome of future search. Conditions (A1)–(A3) may, of course, be put in the usual proportionality form

$$\frac{U_1^{k1}}{p(1)} = \frac{U_t^{k1}}{p(t)} = \lambda_{k1} \quad (t = 2, \ldots, T^*).$$

Conditions (R1)–(R3) may be put in a corresponding form as follows. First we simplify the notation by writing π_{kt} for the conditional probability on current rejection, $\Pr(i_{kt} \,|\, \mathbf{J}_{k1} \notin S_1)$, and $\sum_{kt}$ for the double summation sign over future events $\sum_k \sum_{t=2}^{T}$. Then summing (R2) over kt we obtain

$$\sum_{kt} \pi_{kt}\, U_{t'}^{kt} - p(t') \sum_{kt} \lambda_{kt} = 0.$$

Comparing with (R1) we have the equalities

$$\frac{\sum_{kt} \pi_{kt}\, U_1^{kt}}{p(1)} = \sum_{kt} \pi_{kt} \frac{U_{t'}^{kt}}{p(t')} = \sum_{kt} \lambda_{kt} \quad (t' = 2, \ldots, T^*),$$

i.e. the individual equates the ratio of marginal utility to price in the current period to the expected ratio of marginal utility to price in all other periods. Rearranging this condition we obtain the alternative form

$$\sum_{kt} \pi_{kt} \left(\frac{U_1^{kt}}{p(1)} - \frac{U_{t'}^{kt}}{p(t')} \right) = 0.$$

Thus each ratio $U_{t'}^{kt}/p(t')$ need not be equal to $U_1^{kt}/p(1)$ as under certainty, as long as a weighted sum of the differences in the ratios (the expected value of the differences) is equal to zero.

When current search is successful the actual outcome of search, i.e. which is the true event i_{k1} given that $\mathbf{J}_{k1} \in S_1$, affects consumption via its effect on total income, since M_{k1} is the only variable left undetermined in (A1)–(A3) when we assume acceptance. Thus the more highly-paid the job one finds, the more one spends on consumption. The interesting comparison, however, is not between consumptions when search is successful, but between consumption when search is successful and consumption when search is *un*successful, since this will show the effects of disappointed search and uncertain future on current consumption outlays. This comparison may be made by comparing the current consumption obtained from (A1)–(A3) with that obtained from (R1)–(R3).

Numerical example. Before analysing the problem formally we shall illustrate it with a simple numerical example. Suppose the individual's work horizon consists of four periods and he plans to search three times before retirement, so $T^* = 4$, $T = 3$. (See chapter 12 for the relationship between T^* and T.) Suppose further that there are only two job offers which he is willing to accept, $k = 1$ corresponding to a wage rate of 3 monetary units per period, and $k = 2$ corresponding to a wage rate of 4 units per period. Let the cost of search be $c = 1$, and the unemployment compensation be $m_o = 2$, whereas the rate of discount and initial wealth are assumed equal to zero. Then there are seven possible states of nature, i_{kt} for $k = 1, 2$ and $t = 1, 2, 3$, corresponding to acceptance of an offer during search, and i_{o3} corresponding to failure to find an acceptable offer and discouragement. The per-period and total incomes under each state are shown, respectively, in the second and third columns of table 8.1. Suppose that if the individual accepts a job in period one he plans to allocate his income equally between the four periods in his work horizon, whereas if he rejects the offer observed in period

TABLE 8.1

State: kt	Income per period: $m_{kt}(t')$	Total income: M_{kt}
11	1, 3, 3, 3	10
21	1, 4, 4, 4	13
12	1, 1, 3, 3	8
22	1, 1, 4, 4	10
13	1, 1, 1, 3	6
23	1, 1, 1, 4	7
03	1, 1, 1, 2	5

Consumption per period: $x_{kt}(t')$	Saving per period: $m_{kt}(t') - x_{kt}(t')$
2.50, 2.50, 2.50, 2.50	−1.50, 0.50, 0.50, 0.50
3.25, 3.25, 3.25, 3.25	−2.25, 0.75, 0.75, 0.75
1.80, 2.07, 2.07, 2.07	−0.80, −1.07, 0.93, 0.93
1.80, 2.73, 2.73, 2.73	−0.80, −1.73, 1.27, 1.27
1.80, 1.40, 1.40, 1.40	−0.80, −0.40, −0.40, 1.60
1.80, 1.40, 1.90, 1.90	−0.80, −0.40, −0.90, 2.10
1.80, 1.40, 0.90, 0.90	−0.80, −0.40, 0.10, 1.10

one he treats the income expected from future search as certain and chooses consumption along the same principles as under acceptance. Now, expected income under rejection of the offer observed in period one is given by the average of the last five rows of table 8.1 (to a first approximation), so, with expected income equal to 7.2, consumption under rejection, $x_r(1)$, is equal to $7.2/4 = 1.8$. Thus if search continues into the second period the individual will have already spent 1.8 on consumption, so his constraint for consumption in future periods should be adjusted according to this. Doing the adjustment, and following the same principles in the determination of consumption following the outcome of search in periods two and three as we did for period one, we obtain the consumption and saving sequences shown in the last two columns of the table. Note that the consumption sequences satisfy both the budget and the informational constraint – the saving sequences sum to zero in all possible states of nature, and consumption before the outcome of search becomes known is the same under all possible outcomes of search.

This example, despite its simplistic character, brings out the three most important features of the interaction between job search and the consumption–saving decision. First, consumption in a period during which the individual searches for a job is always higher when the individual accepts the offer observed in that period than when he rejects it. Thus, looking at consumption in period one, if the individual finds one of the two acceptable offers he will consume either 2.5 or 3.25, whereas if he does not he will consume 1.8; the same is true of other periods. Second, during unsuccessful search the individual is reducing his consumption per period. Thus if search in the first period is unsuccessful he will consume 1.8 units, and if it is also unsuccessful in the second period he will reduce his consumption to 1.4 units. Finally, savings are negative during search and positive after the termination of search. The individual borrows during search, or runs down his assets, and pays his debts by saving after the acceptance of a job. (A minor exception may arise on the last period of search if the accepted income is very low, as in the last row of the table.)

Current consumption expenditure

Let us consider the effects of searching behaviour on consumption and saving more formally. We continue assuming that hours of work do not enter the determination of the utility from a job, i.e. a job offer is characterized solely by the total wage payment it offers, and so the utility from the offer depends solely on the consumption sequence that the total wage payment makes possible. Thus if in the first period of search the individual observes a job offer $\mathbf{J}_{k1}$ he will accept it if and only if

$$U(\mathbf{x}^*_{k1}) \geq \sum_{kt} \pi_{kt}\, U(\mathbf{x}^*_{kt}), \tag{3}$$

where $\mathbf{x}^*_{k1}$ and $\mathbf{x}^*_{kt}$ denote, respectively, the utility-maximizing consumption sequence under $\mathbf{J}_{k1}$ and $\mathbf{J}_{kt}$ ($t = 2, \ldots, T$). We first show the relationship between current consumption when search is successful, $x^*_{k1}(1)$, and current consumption when search is unsuccessful, $x^*_{l}(1)$, by using the optimality conditions (A1)–(A3) and (R1)–(R3), and the condition of acceptance (3).

The problem we are analysing is unambiguously defined if both sides of (3) are quasi-concave in $\mathbf{x}$, so there exist unique demand functions $\mathbf{x}^*_{k1}$ and $\mathbf{x}^*_{kt}$. Arrow (1953) first noted that the quasi-concavity of $\sum_{kt} \pi_{kt}\, U(\mathbf{x}_{kt})$ implies that $U(\mathbf{x}_{kt})$ is a concave function of $\mathbf{x}_{kt}$, so the individual is risk averse during search, i.e. he will never choose to forego a certain consumption bundle for a fair gamble. (This is why we assumed in the last chapter that U is concave and not just quasi-concave, which implies that indifference curves must not have linear segments.) Now the concavity of U^{kt} and the linearity of the budget constraints imply that we can break up the maximization problem into two stages. Thus we define new income variables $M_{kt} - x_I(1)$ for any fixed value of current expenditure $x_I(1)$ (note that $p(1) \equiv 1$), and maximize, in the first stage, with respect to future consumption $x_{kt}(2), \ldots, x_{kt}(T^*)$, subject to $\sum_{t'=2}^{T^*} p(t')x_{kt}(t') = M_{kt} - x_I(1)$. The demand functions obtained in this stage satisfy

$$U_t^{k1} - \lambda_{k1}\, p(t) = 0 \quad (t = 2, \ldots, T^*), \tag{4}$$

$$\sum_{t=2}^{T^*} p(t)x_{k1}(t) = M_{k1} - x_{k1}(1), \tag{5}$$

for state i_{k1}, and for each i_{kt} they satisfy

$$U_{t'}^{kt} - \frac{\lambda_{kt}}{\pi_{kt}}\, p(t') = 0 \quad (t' = 2, \ldots, T^*), \tag{6}$$

$$\sum_{t'=2}^{T^*} p(t')x_{kt}(t') = M_{kt} - x_I(1). \tag{7}$$

Clearly (4) and (5) can be solved to give demand functions

$$x_{k1}^*(t) = x^t(\mathbf{p}, M_{k1} - x_{k1}(1)) \quad (t = 2, \ldots, T^*), \tag{8}$$

where **p** is the vector of future price indices normalized according to $p(1) \equiv 1$. The system (6) and (7) is formally identical, for each i_{kt}, to the system (4) and (5), so it can be solved to give intentions for the future

$$x_{kt}^*(t') = x^{t'}(\mathbf{p}, M_{kt} - x_I(1)) \quad (t' = 2, \ldots, T^*). \tag{9}$$

One interesting feature of these intentions is that given current consumption they are independent of the probabilities π_{kt} and the incomes expected in other states, i.e. once current consumption is chosen, the individual assumes that he will be able to choose future consumption under income certainty. This is a direct consequence of the two-stage informational constraint. Now substituting (8) and (9) into U^{k1} and U^{kt} respectively we obtain the *semi-indirect* utility functions[4]

[4] The semi-indirect utility function was also used, in a similar context, by Lluch and Morishima (1973, pp. 177–83) and, in a related context, by Arrow and Hahn (1971, p. 144). Lluch and Morishima used it to obtain current demand functions under uncertainty when future demands are stochastic, so the formal structure of their model is similar to the one in the text, although the origins and interpretations of the models are different. When the number of future states is finite the Lluch–Morishima two-stage results become equivalent to the single-stage results obtained from (R1)–(R3).

$$\hat{U}^{k1} = U[x_{k1}(1), \mathbf{p}, M_{k1} - x_{k1}(1)], \tag{10}$$

$$\hat{U}^{kt} = U[x_I(1), \mathbf{p}, M_{kt} - x_I(1)]. \tag{11}$$

In the second stage the individual maximizes (10) with respect to $x_{k1}(1)$, giving the condition on current consumption implicit in (A1)–(A3), as

$$\frac{\partial \hat{U}^{k1}}{\partial x_{k1}(1)} = U_1^{k1} - U_3^{k1} = 0, \tag{12}$$

where subscripts 1 and 3 denote, respectively, differentiation with respect to the first and third arguments of $\hat{U}^{k1}$. If search is unsuccessful the individual maximizes the expected value

$$\hat{U} = \sum_{kt} \pi_{kt} \hat{U}^{kt}$$

with respect to $x_I(1)$, giving the condition on current consumption implicit in (R1)–(R3) as

$$\frac{\partial \hat{U}}{\partial x_I(1)} = \sum_{kt} \pi_{kt}(U_1^{kt} - U_3^{kt}) = 0. \tag{13}$$

To demonstrate the latter equivalence (which also demonstrates that the Lluch–Morishima two-stage approach is equivalent to the single-stage approach of (R1)–(R3), and that the equivalence pointed out in the last chapter, p. 108, is indeed true with a two-stage informational constraint) we note that (6) and (7) imply that $U_3^{kt} = \lambda_{kt}/\pi_{kt}$, so, substituting in (13) we obtain

$$\sum_{kt} \pi_{kt} U_1^{kt} - \sum_{kt} \lambda_{kt} = 0.$$

This condition is precisely (R1) since $p(1) \equiv 1$, so the consumption sequence implicit in (R1)–(R3) is identical to that obtained in the two-stage approach in (6), (7) and (13).

Now using the condition $\partial U^{kt}/\partial M_{kt} = U_3^{kt} = \lambda_{kt}/\pi_{kt}$, we may write (6) in vector notation as

$$[U_{t'}^{kt}] - U_3^{kt}\,\mathbf{p} = 0 \quad (t' = 2, \ldots, T^*).$$

Differentiating with respect to M_{kt} and keeping $x_I(1)$ fixed we obtain

$$[U_{t'\tau}^{kt}]\left[\frac{\partial x_{kt}(\tau)}{\partial M_{kt}}\right] - U_{33}^{kt}\,\mathbf{p} = 0 \quad (t', \tau = 2, \ldots, T^*),$$

where $[U^{kt}_{t'\tau}]$ is the matrix of second-order partial derivatives of U^{kt} with respect to future consumptions. Pre-multiplying by the row vector $[\partial x_{kt}(\tau)/\partial M_{kt}]'$ and noting that, for fixed $x_l(1)$, (7) implies Engel's aggregation

$$\left[\frac{\partial x_{kt}(\tau)}{\partial M_{kt}}\right]' \mathbf{p} = 1,$$

we obtain

$$\left[\frac{\partial x_{kt}(\tau)}{\partial M_{kt}}\right]' [U^{kt}_{t'\tau}] \left[\frac{\partial x_{kt}(\tau)}{\partial M_{kt}}\right] = U^{kt}_{33}. \tag{14}$$

Thus since U^{kt} is a concave function of $x_{kt}(2), \ldots, x_{kt}(T^*)$ for all $x_l(1)$, the left-hand side of (14) is negative because the matrix of second-order partials is negative definite, and so the semi-indirect utility function (11) is concave in income for all $x_l(1)$ and $\mathbf{p}$. Therefore there exists a positive quantity ρ measured in the same units as M_{kt} and depending on $\mathbf{p}$, $x_l(1)$ and the probability distribution π_{kt} such that

$$\hat{U} = \sum_{kt} \pi_{kt}\, U[x_l(1), \mathbf{p}, M_{kt} - x_l(1)]$$
$$= U[x_l(1), \mathbf{p}, \overline{M} - \rho - x_l(1)], \tag{15}$$

where $\overline{M}$ is the expected value of income earned from job offers which may be accepted in the future, i.e. $\overline{M} = \sum_{kt} \pi_{kt} M_{kt}$. The quantity ρ is what Pratt (1964) calls the risk premium, defined to be that amount of money which leaves the individual indifferent between earning $\overline{M} - \rho$ with certainty and earning M_{kt} with probability π_{kt}. The risk premium increases with the aversion to risk-bearing and with the uncertainty of the random variable M_{kt}. Arrow (1965) and Pratt further postulate that the risk premium of a 'reasonable' individual should decline as his wealth increases.

Now let $x^*_{k1}(1)$ and $x^*_l(1)$ be the values which respectively maximize the semi-indirect utility functions $\hat{U}^{k1}$ and $\hat{U}$. Let ρ^* be the value of the risk premium which is obtained when we substitute $x^*_l(1)$ in (15). Then we can write $x^*_{k1}(1)$ as a function of income M_{k1} and prices $\mathbf{p}$, and $x^*_l(1)$ as a function of the certainty-equivalent of expected income, $\overline{M} - \rho^*$, and prices $\mathbf{p}$. Substituting these in the semi-indirect utility functions and using (15) we can write the acceptance constraint (3) as

$$U^*(M_{k1}, \mathbf{p}) \geq U^*(\overline{M} - \rho^*, \mathbf{p}),$$

where U^* denotes the indirect utility function. Since the indirect utility function is increasing in income it follows immediately that the condition of acceptance of the job offer observed in period one becomes

$$M_{k1} \geq \overline{M} - \rho^*, \tag{16}$$

i.e. a job offer is accepted if and only if the present value of the income stream it promises is at least as high as the certainty-equivalent of the expected streams from continued search.

Current consumption under rejection of the offer, $x_I^*(1)$, is clearly independent of the offer observed in period one, whereas current consumption under acceptance, $x_{k1}^*(1)$, will in general be higher the higher the income received from the job offer. Thus, even if there is an income level M_{k1} which makes $x_{k1}^*(1)$ equal to $x_I^*(1)$, the latter will not be true for a different income level. The result that interests us most, however, is whether there are *any* acceptable job offers which imply that $x_{k1}^*(1)$ will not be greater than $x_I^*(1)$. To answer this question we need only consider the lowest acceptable income level, since if $x_{k1}^*(1)$ exceeds $x_I^*(1)$ when M_{k1} is at the lowest possible level, it will exceed it at all other acceptable income levels. But by the acceptance condition (16) the lowest acceptable income level is equal to the certainty-equivalent $\overline{M} - \rho^*$. Thus the question becomes: if $M_{k1} = \overline{M} - \rho^*$, is it possible that $x_{k1}^*(1) \leq x_I^*(1)$?

To answer this question we shall restate the optimality condition satisfied by $x_I^*(1)$ by using (15). Thus, the continuity of U implies that for any $x_I(1)$ it is possible to find a risk premium such that (15) is true, so the value $x_I^*(1)$ which maximizes the expected value of $\hat{U}^{kt}$ also maximizes the right-hand side of (15).[5] Condition (13) is therefore equivalent to

$$\frac{\partial \hat{U}}{\partial x_I(1)} = U_1^{kt} - U_3^{kt} - U_3^{kt} \frac{\partial \rho}{\partial x_I(1)} = 0. \tag{17}$$

Writing $M_{k1} = \overline{M} - \rho^*$ in (12) we obtain, for the optimality of $x_{k1}^*(1)$,

$$U_1[x_{k1}^*(1), \mathbf{p}, \overline{M} - \rho^* - x_{k1}^*(1)] \\ - U_3[x_{k1}^*(1), \mathbf{p}, \overline{M} - \rho^* - x_{k1}^*(1)] = 0, \tag{12'}$$

[5] The analysis that follows is a simple alternative way of obtaining the results of those who analyse the dependence of consumption on income uncertainty, e.g. Leland (1968) and Sandmo (1970).

whereas the optimality of $x_I^*(1)$ implies, from (17),

$$U_1[x_I^*(1), \mathbf{p}, \overline{M} - \rho^* - x_I^*(1)] \\ - U_3[x_I^*(1), \mathbf{p}, \overline{M} - \rho^* - x_I^*(1)] \\ = U_3[x_I^*(1), \mathbf{p}, \overline{M} - \rho^* - x_I^*(1)]\frac{\partial \rho}{\partial x_I(1)}. \quad (17')$$

Thus, if the individual receives an income which is equal to the certainty-equivalent of continued search, he will consume the same amount in the current period as he would have done if he rejected the offer only in the special case where risk attitudes, as measured by the risk premium, are unaffected by current consumption. In this case $\partial\rho/\partial x_I(1) = 0$, so (17′) becomes formally identical to (12′) and $x_{k1}^*(1)$ equal to $x_I^*(1)$. This is obviously a restrictive case, both because by its definition in (15) the risk premium depends on current consumption, and also because as pointed out by several authors[6] risk attitudes are likely to vary as consumption and savings vary. Nevertheless the assumption is required in analyses where uncertainty is dealt with by discounting the uncertain variables and treating the resulting values as certain, the best known examples of which are Keynes (1930, pp. 142–4) and Hicks (1946, pp. 135–7).

Now (15) does not impose any restrictions on the sign of $\partial\rho/\partial x_I(1)$, nor do such intuitively appealing restrictions as decreasing risk premium with respect to *total* wealth go any further. For instance, justification of a negative sign could rest with the argument that, *ceteris paribus*, an increase in current consumption makes an individual 'better off', so he is more tolerant of small risks on future consumption. Current and future consumption are treated then as substitutes. On the other hand, a positive sign may be justified by the argument that an increase in current consumption, prices and incomes constant, implies a reduction in the funds available for future consumption (i.e. savings) so the individual becomes more averse to future risks. In this case current and future consumption are complementary. Suppose the latter is true, so $\partial\rho/\partial x_I(1)$ is positive.[7]

6 See for instance Pratt (1964), Arrow (1965) and Sandmo (1969, 1970).

7 This corresponds to one part of Sandmo's (1970) 'decreasing temporal risk aversion', the other part being equivalent to $\partial\rho/\partial x_{kt}(t') < 0$ for all $t' = 2, \ldots, T^*$, and hence $\partial\rho/\partial M < 0$. The latter restriction is clearly not needed for the analysis here, although on intuitive grounds it may be more 'reasonable' than the former.

Then (17′) implies

$$U_1[x_I^*(1), \mathbf{p}, \overline{M} - \rho^* - x_I^*(1)] \\ - U_3[x_I^*(1), \mathbf{p}, \overline{M} - \rho^* - x_I^*(1)] > 0. \quad (18)$$

Comparing with (12′) and using the second-order condition

$$\frac{\partial^2 U}{\partial x(1)^2} < 0 \quad \text{for all } x_{k1}(1) \text{ and } x_I(1),$$

we obtain the result

$$x_{k1}^*(1) > x_I^*(1). \quad (19)$$

Thus, current consumption when search stops exceeds current consumption when search continues, even if the income paid by the job accepted is below the expected value (and equal to the certainty-equivalent) of the incomes paid by offers which may be accepted in the future. Clearly, if M_{k1} exceeds $\overline{M} - \rho^*$ the inequality in (19) becomes stronger, so since the reservation income level is equal to the certainty-equivalent $\overline{M} - \rho^*$, current consumption under acceptance is always greater than current consumption under rejection.

If risk aversion decreases as current consumption increases, condition (17′) implies that the inequality sign in (18) is reversed, so $x_I^*(1) > x_{k1}^*(1)$. This condition, however, although it implies that when the accepted income level is equal to the certainty-equivalent, $\overline{M} - \rho^*$, $x_{k1}^*(1)$ falls below $x_I^*(1)$, does not necessarilty imply that if M_{k1} is equal to $\overline{M}$, (19) is false, i.e. that uncertainty alone induces the individual to spend more now. This implication needs a high absolute value of $\partial\rho/\partial x_I(1)$ which is unlikely to arise ((17′) implies that it must be below one). Nevertheless, complementarity between current and future consumption is more appealing than substitutability and supported by a wide range of 'habit persistence' and 'ratchet effect' hypotheses.[8]

Thus, we have shown that since the lowest acceptable income level is equal to the certainty-equivalent from continued search, the 'reasonable' individual who treats current and future consumption as complements will definitely spend more when he accepts a job than

[8] Sandmo (1969, 1970) postulated that 'decreasing temporal risk aversion' is the natural extension of the Arrow–Pratt 'decreasing absolute risk aversion' to temporal situations and demonstrated how some of Arrow's (1965) results extend in a natural way.

when he continues searching. On the other hand, the individual who treats current and future consumption as substitutes may reduce his current consumption by accepting a job at the low end of the 'acceptable' income scale. In the latter case the individual accepts the offer because the higher consumption during search compensates him for the reduction in consumption after the end of search.

To conclude the analysis of current consumption under acceptance and rejection we illustrate the main result obtained with the aid of a simple diagram (Fig. 8.1). The vertical axis measures the difference $U_1 - U_3$ which is zero in equilibrium under acceptance and under rejection when current consumption does not affect the risk premium. The curve labelled $M_{k1} = \overline{M} - \rho^*$ shows the relationship between that difference and the current consumption level $x(1)$ when the individual's income is equal to the certainty-equivalent $\overline{M} - \rho^*$. The maximizing value under rejection therefore is equal to $x^*(1)$ when current consumption does not influence the risk premium, is less than $x^*(1)$ when it affects it positively so (18) is true, and greater than x^* when it affects it negatively so the sign of (18) is reversed. The distance oA (or oB) is equal to $U_3 \; \partial\rho/\partial x_I(1)$ so it is higher the higher the marginal utility of future income, and the higher the sensitivity of the risk premium to current consumption. When

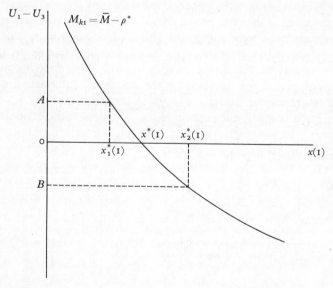

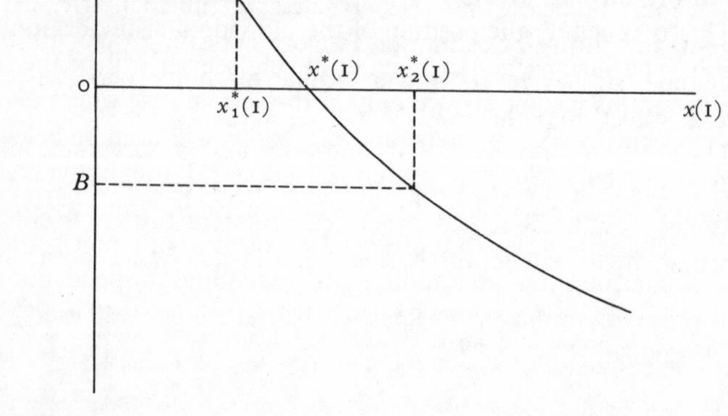

Fig. 8.1

$M_{k1} = \overline{M} - \rho^*$ current consumption under acceptance is equal to $x^*(1)$, but if $M_{k1} > \overline{M} - \rho^*$ current consumption under acceptance is given by the intersection of the horizontal axis with a curve which lies to the right of the one drawn for $\overline{M} - \rho^*$. Thus, even when current and future consumption are substitutes, current consumption under acceptance will be greater than current consumption under rejection when M_{k1} is high enough to push the curve to the right such that its intersection with the horizontal axis lies beyond $x_2^*(1)$.

Savings and future consumption expenditure

Suppose the individual is told that the typical element in his income stream will be $m_o - c$ in the first T periods, and m_o in the remaining $T^* - T$ periods. Then if the utility function is well behaved this individual will maximize his utility by dissaving in the first T periods, and saving in the remaining $T^* - T$ periods to repay his debts.[9] Suppose now that this individual is told that in the first period he will definitely receive $m_o - c$, as before, but from the second period onwards he will either receive the original stream, or a revised stream whose typical element is greater than that of the original stream at every period in his horizon. If the second stream is promised with some probability above zero, the von Neumann–Morgenstern axioms imply that this individual will increase his consumption *in the current period*, and before he is told which of the two streams he will finally receive. Thus the net dissaving in the current period will increase by the additional information about the future income stream.

This is precisely the position of the individual at the beginning of search. The income he is receiving during search will be the *typical* element in his income stream only in the special case where search is unsuccessful in all T periods (and if $c > 0$ it will even be below that typical element). Since if search is successful the individual will definitely be earning more than m_o per period – otherwise he will not be willing to accept the offer – the existence of a non-zero probability of success in search induces the individual to spend more than he is receiving in the current period. Thus during search there will be net dissaving.

[9] By 'well behaved' we mean the broad class of the Fisher–Hicks utility function. For modern work in this area see Modigliani and Brumberg (1954) and Freidman (1957).

Now if the individual searches in the first period but fails to find an acceptable offer, he will face a similar consumption and saving decision in the second period as in the first. There are at least two factors, however, which will induce lower consumption, and hence lower dissaving, in the second period if the offer observed is not accepted. First, the net wealth position of the individual will be worse at the beginning of the second period than at the beginning of the first, because of first period's dissaving. A fall in initial wealth will reduce planned consumption in all periods, so even if everything else concerning the choice of $x_I(1)$ and $x_I(2)$ is the same, the dissaving in the first period implies that $x_I(2)$ will be lower than $x_I(1)$. Second, the finiteness of the work horizon implies that if a search opportunity is lost there is one period less left during which the individual can earn the higher income. Thus, if search in the first period is unsuccessful, the individual will receive $m_o - c$ in the first two periods, but he may receive a higher income in the third period onwards. But if search is unsuccessful in the second period as well, the third period's income will also be $m_o - c$, so, if expectations do not change for the better in the meantime, the present value of the income stream expected from successful search will go down. Moreover, if search in one more period turns out to be unsuccessful, the probability that search will be unsuccessful in all periods increases, so the expected income stream falls further. Thus planned consumption is reduced in all periods, and with it $x_I(2)$ is reduced further below $x_I(1)$.

Changes in the initial wealth at the beginning of search, in the rate of discount, and in expectations for the future outcome of search make only a quantitative difference to these results. The effects of the first and the last changes are similar. An increase in initial wealth, or an increase in the expected value of the income stream, will induce, in the first place, an increase in planned consumption expenditure in all periods in the work horizon. Thus dissaving during search will be even higher. In the second place, when the individual becomes more wealthy he becomes more tolerant of small risks, so if he is forced to choose some of his consumption under uncertainty, he will increase it further and reduce the (precautionary) demand for saving.[10] Thus an increased net wealth posi-

[10] This result is conditional on the Arrow–Pratt–Sandmo 'reasonable' standards of behaviour. In our notation $\partial \rho / \partial M < 0$ and $\partial \rho / \partial x_I(1) > 0$.

tion increases consumption during search, and so it also increases dissaving, by easing the budget constraint and reducing the individual's aversion to risk.

An increase in the rate of discount – which in our notation corresponds to a fall in the discounting factor $\beta(t)$ – presents more difficulties usually, but in our model the analysis of its effects is straightforward. Since the individual plans to dissave in the current period, and probably some other periods in the near future, and save after accepting a permanent job, a fall in $\beta(t)$ reduces the present value of his income stream by a greater amount than the present value of his consumption stream, so the net present value of his saving stream falls from zero to negative.[11] Thus there will be a negative income effect on consumption in all periods.

But if $\beta(t)$ falls, the prices of future consumption goods relative to their price in the current period falls, so, in our notation, since we took $p(1) \equiv 1$, a fall in $\beta(t)$, associated with a rise in the rate of discount, reduces all future prices $p(2), \ldots, p(T^*)$. Thus there will be a substitution of expenditure away from current consumption and towards future consumption. The substitution effect on current consumption will therefore be in the same direction as the income effect. If the rate of interest rises, current consumption expenditure during search, and so current dissaving, will certainly fall.

Summary and conclusion

If an individual is currently searching for a job, his lifetime income stream will depend on the outcome of search. If not all firms offer the same wage rate, the present value of the income stream of the individual will be a random variable which depends on the wage offers available, on the policy of the individual during search, and on the sequence of offers which the individual happens to observe. The optimal job search policy imposes some restrictions on the uncertainty over the lifetime income which enable the derivation of a distribution function giving the probability that the individual should expect to receive some lifetime income level. Given this distribution over lifetime income, the choice of consumption and savings reduces to the

[11] This is a typical case of what Hicks (1946, p. 234) has called an individual who 'plans to be a borrower'.

standard problem of choosing a consumption sequence to maximize the expected value of a von Neumann–Morgenstern utility function.

The job searcher who behaves according to these principles should spend more than he is earning during search, and save after the acceptance of a job to repay his debts. During unsuccessful search he should be reducing his consumption from one period to the next, whereas if and when he finds an acceptable job offer he should increase his consumption, but not to the full extent of the increase in income. The time path of income and consumption for an individual who spends t periods searching and who accepts a job at t paying m_{kt} per period is shown in Fig. 8.2. The income stream takes a step upwards in the period of the successful termination of search, with the typical income before that equal to $m_o - c$ and after that equal to $m_{kt} > m_o - c$. The consumption sequence also takes a similar upward shift in the same period, but it shows less fluctuation than the income stream. Although savings act to counterbalance the fluctuations in income, consumption and *current* income should be correlated, to some extent, because of the similarity of the movement at t. Thus, the theory of search may provide the rationale for the simultaneous correlation of consumption to current and permanent income in a rational and voluntary world, a conclusion not implied by the

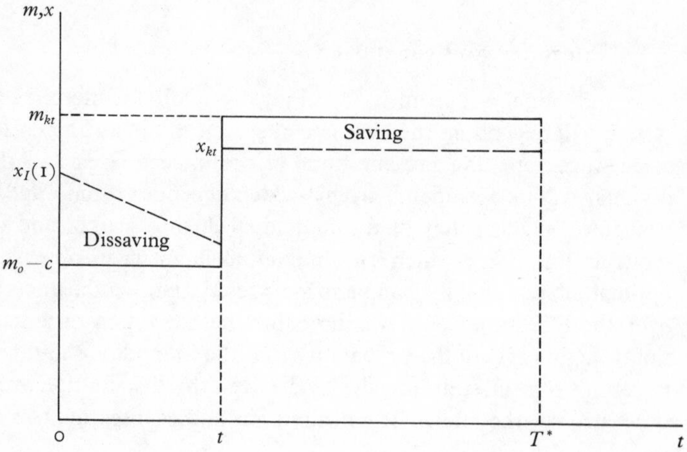

Fig. 8.2

standard utility-maximizing model under certainty but frequently observed in practice.[12]

[12] As is well known, Friedman (1957), and to a lesser extent Modigliani and Brumberg (1954) and others who analysed consumption within the standard utility-maximizing framework, argued that consumption should not be correlated directly with current income at all. The inclusion of uncertainty, in a general form, does not appear to modify this result, so it is the nature of the search process which is the crucial element for the result in the text, and not simply the introduction of uncertainty. Frequent tests of Friedman's theory showed that although consumption is certainly correlated with permanent income, it is also correlated with current income, to an extent not consistent with the theory. See for instance Mayer (1972).

9

Job Search: Dynamic Properties – I

It is apparent from the analysis of the last three chapters that job search performs two major interrelated functions. In the first place, it is the process whereby labour is allocated to a number of alternative uses; in the second, it is the process which produces income for the individual. The first function is related to the adjustment process in the labour market, whereas the second provides the link between commodity markets and the labour market during that adjustment. In this and the next two chapters we shall concentrate on the first function of search, just as we concentrated on the second in the last two chapters. Later on we shall bring the analysis together and consider the interactions between markets and the functioning of the complete economic system over time.

The dynamic path of the reservation utility levels

In the model of search without savings we considered an individual faced with job offers $\mathbf{J}_1, \ldots, \mathbf{J}_T$, and choosing optimally a sequence of acceptance sets $S_1, \ldots, S_T$. The individual accepts the first offer observed which belongs to the acceptance set of the period in which it is observed and terminates the search. The most important result obtained in chapter 6 is that the acceptance set for some period t is uniquely determined by a 'reservation utility level' V_t, such that the individual accepts any job offer $\mathbf{J}_t$ which yields utility at least equal to V_t. So, to consider the dynamic properties of the acceptance policy, we need only consider the dynamic properties of the path of reservation utility levels, $V_1, \ldots, V_T$.

Successive reservation levels were shown to satisfy a simple recursive relation, given by

$$V_{t-1} = a_t W_t + (1 - a_t)V_t \quad (t = 1, \ldots, T), \qquad (1)$$

where a_t is the probability of accepting the offer observed at t, equal to $\sum_{S_t} f_t(\mathbf{J})$, and W_t is the expected utility from successful search in period t, equal to $(1/a_t) \sum_{S_t} f_t U(\mathbf{J})$. The terminal value of the sequence, V_T, is given by the utility from unsuccessful search in all T periods, $U(\mathbf{J}_{oT})$. In this section we shall consider the dynamic path of the V_ts implied by this functional equation system, and in the following we shall consider the role of savings during the process.

The functional equation (1) may be written more explicitly as

$$V_{t-1} - V_t = \sum_{S_t} f_t(U - V_t) \quad (t = 1, \ldots, T). \tag{1'}$$

Since S_t includes all job offers which yield utility above V_t, it follows immediately that if S_t is not empty, V_{t-1} will exceed V_t. On the other hand, if S_t is empty, $V_{t-1} = V_t$. But if S_t is empty the individual will not search in period t, because search is costly and there are no job offers which he may accept, even if he was able to find them. So the reservation utility level of the disappointed searcher will definitely fall over time. When no search takes place the reservation utility level remains constant.

Now if the individual completes T searches without success, his reservation utility level will fall down to the utility from dropping out of the labour market, $U(\mathbf{J}_{oT})$. So he will terminate the search, and not search again, unless some unexpected change in labour market conditions pushes the returns from search above his current-utility level, $U(\mathbf{J}_{oT})$. His reservation utility level after period T will therefore remain fixed at $U(\mathbf{J}_{oT}) = V_T$. On the other hand if the individual accepts a job offer in some period t and terminates the search, he will increase his reservation level up to the utility from the new job, $U(\mathbf{J}_t)$, since he will not leave the job unless the returns from search rise above the utility from the job. As long as the returns from search are below $U(\mathbf{J}_t)$, the reservation level of the individual remains fixed at $U(\mathbf{J}_t)$.

Thus when the individual's current utility level falls below his reservation level he will search. During unsuccessful search he reduces successively his reservation level. If he finds a job which yields utility above the reservation level he accepts it and terminates the search, raising his reservation level to the utility from the new job. If he does not, the successive revision in the reservation level eventually leads to the point where the utility from his current situation no longer falls below the reservation level. When that occurs he terminates the search and keeps his reservation utility level fixed at the utility from dropping out, V_T. Thus if no search is taking place the reservation level is constant; if it is taking place unsuccessfully it is declining; and if it results in success it rises.[1]

This result holds in the framework of the general model so it is true both in stationary and non-stationary market conditions. In fact, there is a large number of factors that may give rise to this result independently, and in practice one or more of these factors will be interacting to produce a fast decline in the reservation levels during search. Before considering these factors we shall consider the relative speed of decline of the reservation values and also illustrate the dynamic path diagrammatically.

The path of reservation levels (or the acceptance policy) is said to be *concave* at some period t if

$$\tfrac{1}{2}(V_{t-1} + V_{t+1}) < V_t, \tag{2}$$

and convex if the inequality sign is reversed. It follows that reservation values decline at an increasing rate when the path is concave, and a decreasing rate when it is convex.

In the appendix to this chapter we show that if the distributions of job offers $f_1, \ldots, f_T$ are identical, or if they improve over time (e.g. if they shift successively to the right), then the path of the reservation levels is always concave. On the other hand if they deteriorate over time the path may be either convex or concave, depending on the extent of the deterioration. In general, if the distributions shift sufficiently to the left the path may be convex, whereas if they are close to each other it is more likely to be concave.

Now, if the individual can choose the order in which he searches prospective employers, and given that search is costly, there will be good reasons for supposing that the distributions of job offers relevant for the job-searching decision will be deteriorating during unsuccessful search.[2] So the relative speed of decline of the reservation values will depend on the extent of the deterioration. Under certain plausible conditions, when for instance there are one or two employers whom he considers very superior to all others, the deterioration in

[1] This is the kind of behaviour attributed by psychologists, and some economists, to 'aspiration' levels. The restrictions on behaviour obtained in the text are usually assumed in an *ad hoc* fashion in the psychology-oriented literature. See for instance Simon (1959, pp. 262–5), and Holt (1970).

[2] See below, chapter 10.

the distributions may be more rapid at first than later. So the reservation values decrease at a decreasing rate at first, and if the individual is still unemployed after the first few periods of search, they may decrease at a constant or slowly changing rate.[3]

The optimal acceptance policy for a search horizon T may be illustrated diagrammatically (Fig. 9.1). The horizontal axis measures time and the vertical axis utility units (this is permissible because of the von Neumann–Morgenstern axioms satisfied by U). oT^* is equal to the work horizon and oT equal to the search horizon, so T may lie anywhere between zero and T^*.[4] The curve CT^* gives, for each t, the utility level achieved when the individual has searched unsuccessfully in periods $1, \ldots, t$ and terminated the search at t, dropping out of the labour market. Thus oC is equal to the returns from no search, $U(\mathbf{J}_o)$, and at T^* the curve meets the horizontal axis, by our assumption that the utility from unsuccessful search in all periods in the work horizon is the origin of the utility scale. The vertical difference between the point of the curve at $t - 1$, and that at t, measures the cost of search at t (in utility units) when the individual remains unemployed. When the cost of search is positive CT^* must be forward falling, but it may take any shape depending on the nature of the cost of search and the shape of the utility function. If there is decreasing

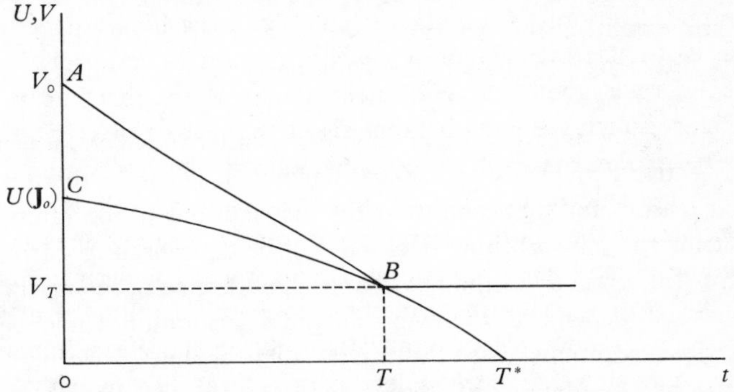

Fig. 9.1

[3] The usual assumption in the literature is that the distributions are identical, so on the assumptions of this model the reservation values must be declining at an increasing rate. The limited empirical evidence on the matter suggests that the reservation values decline at a decreasing rate. See Holt (1970, pp. 96–101).

[4] Just *where* it lies is the topic of chapter 12.

marginal utility (or, in this case, increasing marginal utility-cost) the curve will be concave to the origin, and we may take this as more reasonable *a priori*.

As we argued above, an acceptance policy $S_1, \ldots, S_T$ may be described uniquely by the path of the reservation values $V_1, \ldots, V_T$. Since V_T is equal to the utility from unsuccessful search in all periods in the search horizon, $U(\mathbf{J}_{oT})$, the path of the V_ts must start from some value V_0 on the vertical axis and terminate on the curve CT^* at the point where $t = T$. V_0 must lie above C, otherwise the individual would not search. The optimal policy path is then given by a curve like AB. Clearly, there will be a different path for each possible T. But for any T, the path must be forward falling in periods $1, \ldots, T$ if the individual plans to search in all periods until he finds an acceptable job. If search stops temporarily at some $t < T$, the policy path must be horizontal at that t, since V_t remains constant if no search takes place at t. Similarly, CT^* must contain a linear segment at that t if no search costs are incurred. For this reason, if search stops permanently at T, the reservation level remains constant at V_T, and so does the current utility level, until such time as some unexpected change takes place and induces the individual to re-estimate the returns from search and his reservation utility level.

In periods before T, when the path is falling, it may fall at a decreasing or increasing rate, depending on whether the distributions of offers deteriorate over time or not. The most likely shape of the path is the one that is more convex at t closer to zero than t closer to T, so reservation values fall more rapidly at first than later.

Before moving on to the analysis of the factors that give rise to this particular shape of the dynamic path of the reservation utility levels, it should be emphasized that this result, as well as the other properties of the optimal search policy, are in terms of a reservation *utility* level, and not a reservation job, or wage. The derivation of an optimal search policy in terms of a reservation utility level is, of course, a considerable generalization of the more traditional job search model which deals solely with wages. The model restores the flexibility of the neoclassical equilibrium choice framework to a process of job search which retains the basic features of the processes explored by Stigler (1962), McCall (1970), Phelps *et al.* (1970) and others, so further analysis may shed light on such problems as participation, wage differentials, work–leisure trade-offs, and the other features of the traditional model which the search model has suppressed.[5] But it is also important to note that this generalization of the search model implies that the strong results obtained by the search literature hold only under special assumptions, usually that utility is linear so returns and costs can be treated separately, and that non-wage components of job offers are unimportant, so *wages* have to be bid up to attract more employees.[6] In the sequel we shall analyse some of the most important new problems that the generalization opens up, but a large number of them will be left for future research.

To return to the dynamic path of the reservation utility levels, it was agrued by Kasper (1967), Holt (1970), Gronau (1971) and Salop (1973*a*), and demonstrated empirically by Kasper and others,[7] that optimizing behaviour during job search implies that the searcher should reduce his reservation *wage rate* during unsuccessful search. Although this result needs stronger restrictions on the utility function and the costs of search than the corresponding result on reservation utility levels proved here, it can be shown that in most cases the two results will coincide, especially if the cost of search is not too high and the remaining periods in the work horizon not too few. Let ω_0 be the reservation wage before the beginning of search, and ω_1 the same at the end of the first period. Then by definition

$$V_0 = U(\omega_0, \ldots, \omega_0),$$

$$V_1 = U(m_o - c, \omega_1, \ldots, \omega_1).$$

From the functional equation relating V_0 and V_1 we have

$$U(\omega_0, \ldots, \omega_0) - U(m_o - c, \omega_1, \ldots, \omega_1) = \sum_{S_1} f_1(U - V_1). \quad (3)$$

The right-hand side may be described as the expected lifetime 'bonus' from the jobs accepted in the first period, and it is always positive. Now ω_0 is greater than $m_o - c$, otherwise the individual would not search, so even if ω_1 is equal to ω_0, the left-hand side will always be positive. But the right-hand side is a *lifetime* bonus, whereas the difference in the left-hand side is merely the cost of search in period one (in utility units), plus the utility value of the difference between

[5] Labour economists are especially critical of this loss of flexibility for the analysis of traditional labour problems within an information-search model. See Corina (1972, ch. 5) for a critical survey.

[6] The latter assumption is particularly important for the rationalization of the inflation–unemployment trade-off within a search model. See below, chapter 14.

[7] The brief empirical literature on this topic is reviewed by Holt (1970, pp. 96–101).

ω_0 and m_o. Thus if the cost of search is not too high, and if there are enough periods in the work horizon left, equation (3) will not be satisfied unless ω_0 exceeds ω_1, i.e. unless the reservation wage rate as well as the reservation utility level fall over time.

Nevertheless, the generalized search model yields the result in terms of utilities, and it is in these terms that we must talk when we talk of the optimal search policy. If one is interested in the properties of the reservation wage, one should bear in mind (3).

The role of savings during search

It may be obvious by now, and it will become more obvious later on, that the analysis of job search as an adjustment process is more conveniently carried out with the aid of the recursive relation system obtained in the model without savings. On the other hand, it is also obvious from the analysis of the last two chapters that the role of savings during and after search – i.e. the possibility of deviations between current income and current consumption expenditure – is more conveniently analysed by considering the individual as maximizing an expected utility function which depends on the search policy in all periods in the search horizon. The two procedures, of course, give identical results, since they are merely two different methods (dynamic programming and the maximization calculus) used to analyse the same problem. We shall conclude this chapter with an investigation of the role of savings during the search process, by considering the single-stage approach of the last two chapters. Once this is achieved the analysis of the interaction between the job searching and the consumption–saving decision will be complete, so we shall be able to concentrate more closely on the properties of search as the adjustment process in a decentralized labour market by considering the recursive solution to the problem.

In the model without savings the utility from a job offer was taken to be defined over a T^*-dimensional vector $\mathbf{J}$, referred to as the lifetime job. If a wage offer w_k was observed and accepted in period t, this vector consisted of a t-dimensional subvector with typical element $(m_o - c, y_s)$, and a $(T^* - t)$-dimensional subvector with typical element $(w_k y, y)$, where y_s stands for the time spent searching in a period, and y the time spent working after the acceptance of the offer. Thus, without savings, the *timing* of income receipts affects the utility from a job, since the individual can consume an amount at most equal to $m_0 - c$ per period before the acceptance of an offer, and an amount equal to $w_k y$ per period after the acceptance of the offer.

In the model with savings, the utility from a job was taken to be the indirect utility function, obtained by substituting the demand functions from commodities and the supply functions of hours into the 'direct' utility function. Leaving to the side the choice of hours, the indirect utility function depends on the present value of the lifetime income stream that a particular job offer makes possible, and the vector of commodity prices. Thus the timing of income receipts is irrelevant: if the individual observes and accepts w_k in period t his utility will be determined by prices $p(1), \ldots, p(T^*)$, and M_{kt}, where

$$M_{kt} = m' + \sum_{t'=1}^{T^*} m_{kt}(t'),$$

$$m_{kt}(t') \begin{cases} = \beta(t')(m_0 - c) & (t' = 1, \ldots, t), \\ = \beta(t')w_k y & (t' = t+1, \ldots, T^*), \end{cases}$$

and where m' is initial wealth (positive, negative, or zero), and $\beta(t')$ is the discounting factor for period t'.

Savings therefore shift the emphasis from current income to wealth, and the utility from a job offer $\mathbf{J}_{kt}$ may now be written as $U(\mathbf{p}, M_{kt})$ instead of the more general $U(\mathbf{J}_{kt})$. But since the former is an indirect utility function, its use in the sequential model carries with it a problem which normally arises in temporal situations under uncertainty. In particular, the use of an indirect utility function to obtain the optimal decision in a dynamic model where the uncertainty persists over time is likely to give rise to a contradiction of the von Neumann–Morgenstern assumptions, and so to suboptimal decision-making under expected-utility maximization.[8] Consider for instance the acceptance decision in period one. If the individual observes $\mathbf{J}_{k1}$ he will accept it when the utility from the offer, $U(\mathbf{J}_{k1})$, is at least equal to the utility from continued search, V_1. Since the former depends solely on the characteristics of the offered job, the effects of different market conditions on the acceptance decision depend wholly on their effects on V_1. So if any of these conditions change, the analysis will have to deal first with the effects of this change on V_1.

In the model without savings, V_1 could be put in expected-value form, with the probability distribution over the different states of

[8] See Markowitz (1959, chs. 10–11), Mossin (1969), and Spence and Zeckhauser (1972).

nature given by the distribution of offers and the optimal acceptance policy.[9] The strong separability properties of the expected-value operation may therefore be used to obtain some strong results about the effects of changes in labour market conditions, comparable to those obtained by the portfolio selection literature under similar conditions. Once we allow savings, however, and treat the utility over a job as indirect, this separability property of the Vs is lost. Writing $U(\mathbf{x}_{kt})$ for the direct utility function, the consumption sequence for all $t > 1$ has at least its first element, $x_l(1)$, chosen under uncertainty about the lifetime job. So the choice of $x_l(1)$ depends on the whole distribution over the lifetime job situation, and not just on a particular income level.[10] Putting the demand functions for commodities into the utility function, the utility $U(\mathbf{J}_{k1})$, over $\mathbf{J}_{k1}$, may be written as $U(\mathbf{p}, M_{k1})$, since consumption under $\mathbf{J}_{k1}$ is chosen under complete certainty. But the utilities over all other $\mathbf{J}_{kt}$s, $t > 1$, depend on $\mathbf{p}$, M_{kt}, and also on the distribution over all income levels, which is the same as the distribution over states of nature and which we denoted by π. So V_1 becomes

$$V_1 = \underset{\mathbf{x}_{kt}}{\text{Max}} \sum_{kt} \pi_{kt} U(\mathbf{x}_{kt}) \equiv \sum_{kt} \pi_{kt} U(\mathbf{p}, M_{kt}, \pi).$$

This clearly violates the strong separability properties of the von Neumann–Morgenstern axioms.

The main difficulty with having the utility function depend on the probability distribution in a general fashion is that now we cannot use the properties of separability to obtain strong comparative static results of the effects of changes in labour market conditions. The structure of the optimal search policy described in the model of chapter 6 is, of course, still valid, as we demonstrated in chapter 7. Thus in the analysis of the effects of saving decisions on the optimal search policy we must do away with the separability restriction. But the latter restriction will be used again later, to obtain the effects of other changes – correct qualitatively but only to a first approximation quantitatively – where savings assume peripheral interest and the lack of separability makes the problem very messy.

When the timing of income receipts and consumption expenditure may not coincide, the wealth constraint during search assumes pri-

[9] See above, pp. 90–1.

[10] See the optimality conditions (R1)–(R3) which give the optimal $x_l(1)$, obtained in the last chapter.

mary importance. The form of the constraint employed in the consumption problem, that the present value of consumption expenditure should be equal to the present value of the income stream, implies that the individual is willing to borrow any amount of money, provided he does not run the risk of bankruptcy in any possible job situation that may arise. Since when the maximum number of searches planned is T, the worst that can happen to him is to search T periods and not find a job (state i_{oT}), he should not spend as much as the net income that will be available after T unsuccessful searches, M_{oT}, on consumption before he terminates search. If the expenditure during search exceeds M_{oT} the individual runs the risk of being bankrupt at some future period in his horizon, and this risk must be avoided. So if search terminates at a period after t, we require

$$\sum_{t'=1}^{t} p(t')x_I(t') < M_{oT}$$

as a no-bankruptcy condition.

Now suppose an individual accepted a wage rate w_k in period t, and another individual accepted the same wage rate in period $t + 1$. The total wealth of the first individual will then be given by

$$M_{kt} = m' + \sum_{t'=1}^{t} \beta(t')(m_o - c) + \sum_{t'=t+1}^{T^*} \beta(t')w_k y,$$

and that of the second will be

$$M_{kt+1} = m' + \sum_{t'=1}^{t+1} \beta(t')(m_o - c) + \sum_{t'=t+2}^{T^*} \beta(t')w_k y.$$

If these individuals have the same initial wealth, m', then the wealth of the first individual will exceed that of the second, because $w_k y$ exceeds m_o when w_k is acceptable. If it did not, the individual would not accept w_k, since he could derive more utility by terminating the search and receiving m_o as unemployment compensation. Thus, even if the direct cost of search, c, is zero, the quickest an individual finds a given job offer the better off he is. The existence of savings may therefore justify putting more emphasis on the *accumulated foregone earnings* among the costs of search than on the direct costs c.[11]

[11] This, in fact, is the most common assumption in the literature, although the consumption–saving decision is not made explicit. See e.g. Mortensen (1970*a*, pp. 174–5).

Thus although savings do not change the structure and basic properties of the optimal job search policy, they do have an effect on the emphasis placed on each element in the policy. In particular wealth constraints become more important. Since the wealth constraint becomes more stringent as search proceeds unsuccessfully, the individual will lower his reservation utility level more quickly during unsuccessful search so as to increase his chances of finding an acceptable wage offer quickly.

This may be shown formally by comparing the reservation utility level when savings and borrowing are identically equal to zero in all periods and the same when savings are chosen optimally to maximize the utility from consumption. In the former case the reservation utility level at time t is given by

$$V_t = \sum_{kt'} \pi_{kt'} U(\mathbf{J}_{kt'}) \quad (\mathbf{J}_{kt'} \in S_{t'},\ t' > t,\ t = 0, 1, \ldots, T),$$

where $\pi_{kt'}$ is the probability of observing and accepting job offer $\mathbf{J}_k$ in period t' given that the searcher has reached period t' unsuccessfully. Since we do not allow savings, the individual consumes everything he receives at the time of payment, so U depends on the vector $\mathbf{J}_{kt'}$. If the searcher can borrow and repay his debts from future savings the reservation utility level at t is given by

$$V_t^* = \operatorname*{Max}_{\mathbf{x}_{kt'}, \mathbf{y}_{kt'}} \sum_{kt'} \pi_{kt'} U(\mathbf{x}_{kt'}, \mathbf{y}_{kt'}),$$

where the expected utility function is maximized subject to the budget and informational constraints for each job situation $\mathbf{J}_{kt'}$.[12] Thus savings are chosen in such a way as to maximize the reservation utility level in all periods that the individual contemplates search, and so the reservation utility level with savings cannot be lower, and in general it will be higher, than that without savings.

Now to show that the reservation utility level will decline faster when the individual can borrow and repay later, we must show that the difference $V_{t-1} - V_t$ is less than the difference $V_{t-1}^* - V_t^*$. To show this, consider the role of savings in the typical case where the individual's income is low during search but higher afterwards. Savings in this case will be negative during search but positive when the individual accepts a job, so their function is to transfer purchasing power from the future to the present. Thus the individual will bene-

[12] See above, chapter 8.

fit more from the right to save the more purchasing power he expects to have for transfer, i.e. the greater the value of lifetime wealth he expects to receive from his job. But as search proceeds unsuccessfully the individual revises upwards the total number of periods he expects to spend searching, and so the purchasing power he expects to have for transfer declines. In addition borrowing is usually heavy in the first few periods of search[13] so when the ability to save in the future declines, the individual will tend to dissave even lower amounts as search proceeds unsuccessfully. Thus the right to borrow during search will be used more extensively at the beginning of search, so the reservation utility level V_{t-1} will increase more than V_t when that right is conferred (see also below, p. 155).

Thus if we consider the sequence of reservation values $V_0, V_1, \ldots, V_T$, obtained without allowing savings, and the sequence $V_0^*, V_1^*, \ldots, V_T^*$, obtained by allowing the individual to choose his consumption sequence optimally by saving or dissaving, we shall observe the following differences. First, V_t may be expressed as the sum of the utility from a number of different job situations, each weighted by its probability of occurrence. The corresponding value in the sequence with savings, V_t^*, does not satisfy such strong separability properties. Second, each V_t^* will be greater than the corresponding value obtained without savings, V_t, because the individual will choose to save that amount which maximizes the utility from search. The two values will be equal only in the special case where optimal savings are equal to zero in all periods in the horizon, a situation which is inconsistent with any notion of 'reasonable' behaviour. Third, during unsuccessful search the individual will borrow on the basis of his expected future earning capacity, and since the expected future earning capacity declines as search proceeds unsuccessfully, the reservation utility level will be reduced faster to increase the chances of finding an acceptable job quickly. Thus, in Fig. 9.2, if the optimal policy curve without savings is *AB*, the existence of the possibility to save implies that the path of reservation values shifts up, from *AB* to *A'B'*.

Thus the possibility of saving during search does not alter the structure of the optimal job search policy, but has an effect on the dynamic path of the reservation utility levels. In particular, the existence of savings puts more emphasis on wealth constraints, and through this leads to a faster reduction in the reservation utility levels during unsuccessful search. Having obtained this, we shall

13 See above, chapter 8.

again push the saving decision to the background, and talk of a job offer **J** in general terms, as we did in chapter 6. As it will become obvious later on, the separability of V_t which results from the expected-value formulation of the model of chapter 6, although lost when we allow savings, does not lead to any contradictions or paradoxes when we analyse search as an adjustment process. On the contrary it has a number of strong and reasonable implications which should prove especially useful in the analysis of the functioning of labour markets.

Mathematical appendix

The result follows directly if we make use of the properties of Lebesgue–Stieltjes integrals. Thus writing F_t for the cumulative of f_t the functional equation (1′) may be written as

$$V_{t-1} = V_t + \int_{S_t} (U - V_t)\, \mathrm{d}F_t. \tag{A.1}$$

Condition (2) says that the optimal policy is concave at t if

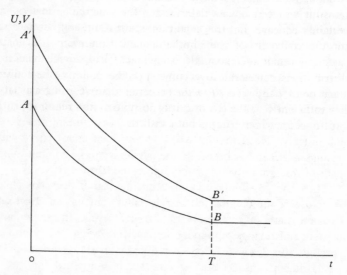

$$V_{t-1} - V_t \leq V_t - V_{t+1}.$$

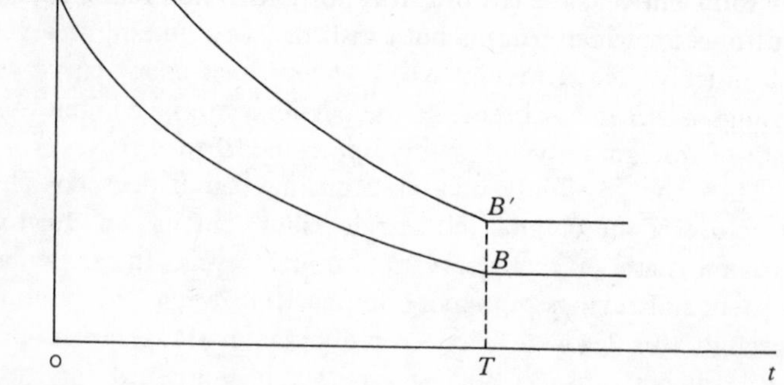

Fig. 9.2

Substituting from (A.1) we obtain

$$\int_{S_t} (U - V_t)\, dF_t \leq \int_{S_{t+1}} (U - V_{t+1})\, dF_{t+1}. \qquad (A.2)$$

Writing $\int_{S_t} dF_{t+1} = a^*_{t+1}$, (A.2) may be rearranged to give

$$\int_{S_t} U\,(dF_t - dF_{t+1}) \leq a_t V_t - a^*_{t+1} V_{t+1} + $$
$$+ \int_{U=V_{t+1}}^{U=V_t} (U - V_{t+1})\, dF_{t+1}, \qquad (A.3)$$

where $a_t = \int_{S_t} dF_t$. Integrating the left-hand side of (A.3) by parts and rearranging we obtain

$$\int_{S_t} (F_{t+1} - F_t)\, dU \leq \int_{U=V_{t+1}}^{U=V_t} (U - V_{t+1})\, dF_{t+1} + $$
$$+ a^*_{t+1} (V_t - V_{t+1}). \qquad (A.4)$$

Now by the property of declining reservation utility values, the right-hand side is always positive, so if

$$F_t \geq F_{t+1} \quad \text{for all } \mathbf{J} \in S_t, \qquad (A.5)$$

condition (A.4) is always satisfied. Condition (A.5) implies that F_{t+1} is not 'worse'[14] than F_t for any utility function U, so if the distributions of job offers do not deteriorate over time the optimal policy is certainly concave. But this condition is sufficient, and not necessary, for the concavity of the optimal policy. Condition (A.4) may be satisfied even if the inequality sign in (A.5) is reversed, i.e. if the distributions deteriorate over time. For the policy to be convex at some point t, however, F_t *must* be better than F_{t+1}. Clearly, if f_{t+1} lies sufficiently to the left of f_t it is possible to find reasonable utility functions for which (A.4) is not satisfied.

[14] On stochastic-dominance criteria. See Hadar and Russell (1969), Hanoch and Levy (1969), and Rothschild and Stiglitz (1970).

10

Job Search: Dynamic Properties – II

The framework of the model of job search is general in two main respects. First, the distribution of job offers in any period t need not satisfy any strong restrictions, and it need not bear any special relationship to the distributions ruling in other periods. Second, the utility function is unrestricted and it is taken to be defined over the *lifetime* job. The first generalization is the most important one, since many factors which are likely to influence job-searching behaviour may be shown to lead to shifts in the distributions of job offers in one or more periods, so their effects on the optimal policy may be obtained by comparing the optimal policy derived with the original sequence of distributions on the one hand, and the new sequence on the other. The second generalization is important for two reasons. First, it enables the derivation of the implications of given patterns of tastes for the optimal policy. When there is imperfect information the most relevant feature of tastes is that related to risk behaviour, so the role of risk behaviour during search becomes clearer. Second, the use of a lifetime job, including hours of work and the costs of search, should enable the derivation of the role of work–leisure trade-offs during and after search, and also the role of the cost of search in the process. The next three chapters will be concerned with the analysis and applications of the model along these lines. In this chapter we shall be mainly concerned with the analysis of the effects of a number of changes on the reservation values $V_0, \ldots, V_T$ which, as we have seen, specify completely the acceptance policy. The implications of the various effects obtained here for the functioning of the labour market during adjustment will be discussed in chapters 11 and 12.

Risk behaviour

The total returns from search is a sum of the utility from a number of possible job situations weighted by the probability of occurrence of each job situation (see equation (6) of chapter 6). In a sequential formulation the individual is capable of influencing the probability of occurrence of each state, and by choice of an optimal policy we mean choice of that configuration of the probabilities which maximizes the expected returns from search. The individual could choose to forego all uncertainties by accepting the first job offer that comes along, but the existence of a distribution of offers in every period make it optimal to bear some uncertainty in return for a better job which the random workings of the system may sooner or later reveal. Thus attitudes towards uncertainty-bearing will in general influence the optimal search policy.

Consider the optimal acceptance policy for a fixed search horizon T. The reservation value for period $T - 1$ is given by

$$V_{T-1} = a_T W_T + (1 - a_T) V_T,$$

so it is a gamble with two outcomes, success and failure. The returns from success, W_T, is itself an expected-utility value, given by $(1/a_T) \sum_{S_t} f_t U$, whereas the returns from failure, V_T, is riskless, and equal to $U(\mathbf{J}_{oT})$. So an increase in the individual's risk aversion reduces W_T, and it also reduces V_{T-1}, partly because of the fall in W_T, but also because V_{T-1} is itself a gamble for fixed W_T and so falls when risk aversion increases.[1]

Similarly, the reservation value for period $T - 2$,

$$V_{T-2} = a_{T-1} W_{T-1} + (1 - a_{T-1}) V_{T-1},$$

falls when risk aversion increases, partly because it is a gamble for fixed W_{T-1} and V_{T-1}, and partly because both W_{T-1} and V_{T-1} fall. Thus we would expect risk aversion to reduce all reservation values $V_1, \ldots, V_T$, and also the total expected returns from search, V_0. In Fig. 10.1, an increase in risk aversion leads to a shift in the optimal policy path from AB to $A'B'$. The shift in periods near the beginning of search is likely to be greater because of the greater uncertainty about the outcome of search in the first few stages of search.

Changes in the distributions of job offers

Consider an individual who expects to search a sequence of distributions $f_1, \ldots, f_T$, and who chooses the reservation values $V_1, \ldots, V_T$ to maximize his expected returns from search. Let now the distribu-

[1] This is definitionally true. See Rothschild and Stiglitz (1970, 1971).

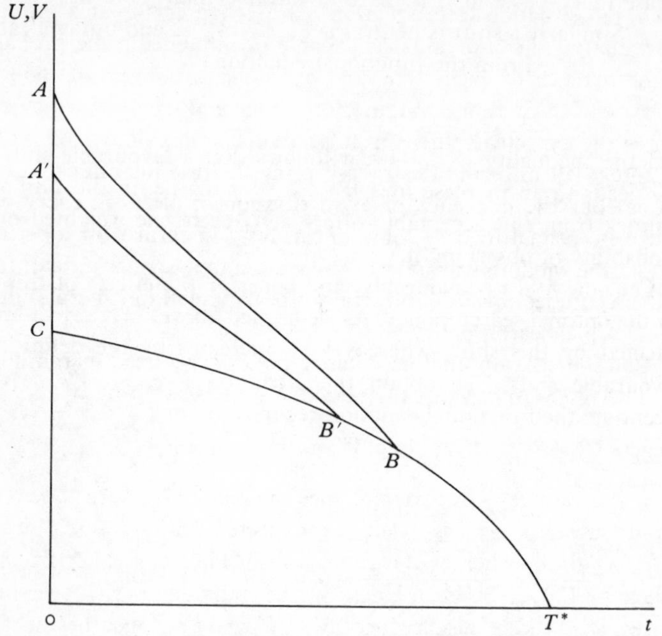

Fig. 10.1

tion f_t, expected in period t, shift to some other distribution f_t', all other distributions remaining the same. We want to know the effect of this shift on searching behaviour and the causes of such a shift.

Let the reservation values implied by the new sequence of distributions, $f_1, \ldots, f_t', \ldots, f_T$, be denoted by $V_1', \ldots, V_T'$. The effects of the shift in f_t on searching behaviour may be obtained by comparing the old reservation utility levels with the new ones.

It follows immediately from the functional equation system (1) or (1′) of chapter 9 that none of the reservation values from period t onwards, $V_t, \ldots, V_T$, are affected by the shift in f_t, since f_t does not enter their determination. But the reservation value V_{t-1} for period $t-1$ depends directly on f_t, so it changes when f_t changes, whereas all other values $V_0, \ldots, V_{t-2}$, prior to $t - 1$, depend on V_{t-1} by the backward nature of the recursive relation linking them, so they also change when V_{t-1} changes. Thus the effect of the shift in f_t on reservation values prior to $t - 1$ may be obtained via its effect on V_{t-1}.

We define a *favourable* shift in f_t as a shift which leads to an increase in V_{t-1}, i.e. if f_t' is more favourable than f_t we have $V_{t-1}' > V_{t-1}$. Similarly a shift is neutral if $V_{t-1}' = V_{t-1}$, and unfavourable if $V_{t-1}' < V_{t-1}$. From the functional equation

$$V_{t-1} = a_t W_t + (1 - a_t)V_t,$$

and the inequality $W_t > V_t$, it follows that a favourable shift in f_t also leads to an increase in $a_t W_t = \sum_{S_t} f_t U$, i.e. in the sum of the utilities from the acceptable offers at t, each one weighted by the probability of observing it.

Let now f_t shift favourably, and consider the effects of this shift on the optimal search policy. As we argued above, $V_t, \ldots, V_T$ are not affected by this shift, whereas V_{t-1} increases by the definition of favourable shifts. To obtain the effect on $V_0, \ldots, V_{t-2}$ we differentiate the functional equation recursively for $t-1, t-2, \ldots, 1$, to get

$$\frac{\partial V_{t-2}}{\partial V_{t-1}} = 1 - a_{t-1} > 0,$$

$$\frac{\partial V_{t-3}}{\partial V_{t-1}} = \frac{\partial V_{t-3}}{\partial V_{t-2}} \frac{\partial V_{t-2}}{\partial V_{t-1}} = (1 - a_{t-2})(1 - a_{t-1}) > 0,$$

$$\ldots$$

Thus if the distribution of job offers in some period t shifts favourably, all reservation utility levels prior to t increase. Moreover, the rate of increase is greater for periods closer to t than periods which come much before t.

There is an intuitive explanation for this kind of behaviour. Since when the distribution of job offers at t improves, the expected returns from search at t increase, an individual who responds to such a change by increasing his reservation levels before t may be viewed as planning to 'protect' himself from hiding away at some marginal job which may be observed before t, and so not enjoying the extra advantage from searching at t. But if the offer observed before t is a good one, it may be worth taking and sacrificing the extra advantage from searching at t. Since the closer a period is to t the less costly it will be to wait until t to accept an offer, the individual is less willing to accept offers observed just before t than offers observed a long time before it. So he increases the reservation value at periods closer to t by a greater amount than those at more distant periods. But if he reached t and he was still unsuccessful in finding an acceptable job, he should return to his previous reservation standards, since as far as search after t is concerned nothing is gained or lost by the

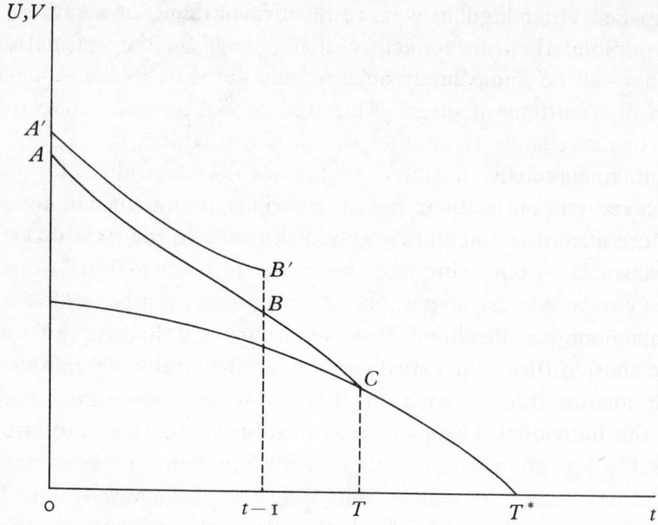

Fig. 10.2

changes that took place before t. Diagrammatically a favourable shift in f_t has the effect of shifting the optimal policy path from ABC to $A'B'BC$ (Fig. 10.2).

An unfavourable shift in f_t produces exactly opposite effects to those of a favourable one. Thus, the reservation values for periods after t remain fixed, whereas V_{t-1}, and with it the expected returns from search at t, fall. By the recursive relation all other reservation values prior to t also fall, and the closer a period is to t the greater the rate of decline in its reservation value will be. The individual will now be keen to *avoid* searching at t, not encourage it, so he will reduce his reservation levels prior to t to increase the probability of finding an acceptable offer before he reaches t.[2]

The structure of the sequential search model is such that almost all endogenous and exogenous changes which are of potential interest in the analysis of problems related to job search, except those changes which depend on risk attitudes and the structure of tastes, may be represented by shifts in the sequence of the distributions of job offers. If the type of shift that a particular change produces can be

[2] Simultaneous shifts in the distributions of some, or all, periods have similar, but more pronounced effects. When more than one distribution shifts, each one of the distributions may be taken in turn and analysed along the lines of the above analysis.

classified unambiguously as either favourable, neutral, or unfavourable, then the effect of that change on the optimal search policy can be immediately obtained via the shift in the sequence of the distributions of offers. Thus the crucial question concerning a particular change is whether the shift it produces in $f_1, \ldots, f_T$ can be unambiguously classified.

Some types of shifts in the distributions of offers can undoubtedly be classified unambiguously – e.g. a shift of f_t to the right is certainly favourable – but there are other less restrictive shifts which are likely to be relevant in practice and which may not be capable of unambiguous classification.[3] However, it appears that the shifts which are most difficult to classify as either favourable or unfavourable are mainly those related to changes in the *information* available to the individual. Complete classification of changes in information need prior knowledge of the utility function, so tastes and risk attitudes become of central importance in the analysis of a process of job search when the information flows are constantly changing.[4] Most other changes in the distributions of offers appear to be capable of classification one way or another without additional restrictions on the utility function. We shall examine three types of shifts which are of potential interest, paying particular attention to their causes and effects.

1. *Additive shifts.* The changes in labour market conditions traditionally analysed in equilibrium economics may be approximated in the search model by additive (horizontal) shifts in the distributions of job offers. For instance, the expression 'increase in the wage rate' is now replaced by the expression 'the distribution of job offers shifts uniformly to the right'. The full list of factors which may cause additive shifts in the distribution of job offers may be obtained directly from the derivation of the distributions of job offers in chapter 6. Recall that f_t was defined over the lifetime job from acceptance at t, given by a t-dimensional subvector with typical

[3] The similarity of the classification of shifts here and in the stochastic-dominance literature implies that the progress of the latter in analysing various types of shifts should be of great help in the analysis of shifts here. See Hadar and Russell (1969), Hanoch and Levy (1969), and Rothschild and Stiglitz (1970), and below, pp. 148–53.

[4] See Marschak and Radner (1972, ch. 2) for the problems involved in classifying different information flows. There is as yet no theoretical work on the problem of different information networks in labour markets. For some empirical work see Rees (1966) and Reid (1972).

element $(m_o - c, y_s)$ and a $(T^* - t)$-dimensional vector with typical element (wy, y). Recall also that the probability $f_t(\mathbf{J})$ of being offered some particular job offer **J**, was the product of observing **J** and that of being recruited at the job. So the following changes lead to a rightward shift in some distribution f_t (changes in the opposite direction lead to leftward shifts): (1) an increase in the per-hour wage rate offered by all firms, (2) a fall in the recruitment standards of firms, (3) a fall in the cost of search, (4) an increase in unemployment benefits, and (5) and increase in the periods remaining in the work horizon.

Additive shifts may be analysed by introducing an additive shift parameter θ in the distributions of offers, such that a given job offer **J** depends on θ with $d\mathbf{J}/d\theta = 1$. So if a single distribution f_t shifts to the right, we may differentiate V_{t-1}, from the functional equation, with respect to θ to obtain

$$\frac{\partial V_{t-1}}{\partial \theta} = \sum_{S_t} f_t \; U'(\mathbf{J}) > 0,$$

where $U'(\mathbf{J})$ is the 'marginal utility' of a job and it is always positive. It follows that a rightward shift in a distribution f_t is always favourable, whereas a leftward shift is always unfavourable. So the effects of any of the changes mentioned in the last paragraph on searching behaviour may be obtained directly by employing the general method of the analysis of favourable shifts developed above. We shall have occasion to use this method in this respect in this and later chapters.

2. *Multiplicative shifts.* Multiplicative shifts in the distributions of job offers represent changes in the spread of the distributions, their means remaining fixed. The shape of a distribution f_t, in particular whether it is more or less concentrated, as opposed to more or less skewed, depends primarily on the information available to individuals and firms, but also on their willingness to act on less than perfect information. If no one was willing to act on less than perfect information, search would be stimulated to such an extent that the distribution of offers would collapse to a single point. So the following changes may be approximated by an inward multiplicative shift (or a fall in the spread of the distribution; outward shifts are produced by changes in the opposite direction): (1) an increase in the information that searchers have about potential employers, (2) an increase in the 'intensity' of search, in the sense of greater search horizon and higher reservation values, and (3) an increase in the information that

firms have about each other's wage offers, and an increase in the uniformity of the policy followed in setting wage offers. The first change will induce more searchers to visit the high-wage firms, and fewer to visit the low-wage ones, so the former may reduce their wages and the latter will definitely raise them. The second change will lead to more searchers turning down low offers, and so to an increase in the wages of low-wage firms, whereas the last change will induce firms to move closer to the 'average' in setting wages, since if firms are not very dissimilar the profit-maximizing wage of different firms will also not be very dissimilar if they are aware of each other's policy.[5]

Let θ be a multiplicative shift parameter in f_t, then we may write

$$\mathbf{J}_t(\theta) = \mathbf{J}_t + \theta(\mathbf{J}_t - \bar{\mathbf{J}}_t),$$

where $\mathbf{J}_t$ is the original job offer, evaluated at $\theta = 0$, $\bar{\mathbf{J}}_t$ is the expected value of job offers at t, and $\mathbf{J}_t(\theta)$ is the offer which is expected with the same probability as $\mathbf{J}_t$ was before the shift in f_t. A fall in the spread of f_t is represented by a fall in θ. Differentiating V_{t-1} with respect to θ and noting that $\mathrm{d}\mathbf{J}_t(\theta)/\mathrm{d}\theta = \mathbf{J}_t - \bar{\mathbf{J}}_t$, we obtain

$$\frac{\partial V_{t-1}}{\partial \theta} = \sum_{S_t} f_t \; U'(\mathbf{J})\,(\mathbf{J} - \bar{\mathbf{J}}_t). \tag{1}$$

Clearly, this cannot be signed without knowledge of $U'(\mathbf{J})$ for different $\mathbf{J}$, so a change in the spread of a distribution cannot be unambiguously classified without knowledge of the utility function.

Suppose S_t included all job offers in f_t, i.e. the individual planned to accept whatever job he was offered at t. Then (1) would be positive if the utility function was convex and negative if it was concave, since $\sum_{S_t} f_t U$ would now be an expected utility value.[6] So a risk lover would lose by an inward shift in f_t, whereas a risk averter would gain – the shift in f_t would be unfavourable for the former and favourable for the latter. This result, however, does not carry over to the sequential search model because a searcher would not in general be willing to accept whatever job he was offered. (If he were, there would be no search because he would have accepted the offer observed in period one!)

[5] However, wage variability will still persist. See chapter 13.

[6] Rothschild and Stiglitz (1970) proved that expected utility rises when the distribution shifts outwards and U is convex, and falls when U is concave.

Since S_t contains only job offers which yield utility above a critical value V_t, which is not affected by the shift in f_t, $\partial V_{t-1}/\partial\theta$ can never fall below $\partial E(U)/\partial\theta$, where $E(U)$ is the expected value of U with respect to f_t. This follows directly from the fact that the former contains only the top terms contained in the latter, and most of the excluded terms are negative, since $\mathbf{J} - \bar{\mathbf{J}}_t$ for relatively unattractive $\mathbf{J}$ is negative. Hence if $\partial E(U)/\partial\theta$ is positive or zero, $\partial V_{t-1}/\partial\theta$ is certainly positive, so for convex or linear utility functions the effect of a fall in θ will be to reduce the expected returns from search. But if the utility function is concave and the individual is willing to accept some jobs below the average, $\bar{\mathbf{J}}_t$, the summation in the right-hand side of (1) will contain some negative terms. These terms, however, will be small, because offers for which the difference $\mathbf{J} - \bar{\mathbf{J}}_t$ is large (in absolute value) will be rejected. So in general we would expect $\partial V_{t-1}/\partial\theta$ to be positive even if the utility function is concave, although it is more likely to be positive if some measure of concavity, such as the absolute risk aversion coefficient, $-U''/U'$, is small.[7]

So an inward multiplicative shift in a distribution f_t will be regarded as unfavourable by most individuals, although some 'very' risk-averse individuals may treat it as favourable. The reason for this is that the fall in the spread of f_t diminishes the chances of finding a very good offer in that period. The simultaneous reduction in the chances of being offered a very poor offer does not compensate because poor offers were unacceptable in the first place.

3. *Generalized discrete-probability shifts.* If the set of job offers is finite and the probability of observing each offer a discrete number between zero and one, then any arbitrary change in the distribution of job offers – additive and multiplicative shifts not excluded – may be represented by compensated variations in the probabilities of offers. The changes must be compensated because the sum of all probabilities must be equal to unity. This method[8] is more realistic than the method of simultaneous shifts in all offers in an environment where job offers are chosen by optimizing atomistic entrepreneurs, because an entrepreneur may change his job offer in isolation, with all others keeping theirs fixed. For instance, if the total number of outstanding job offers

[7] But see below, pp. 152–3.

[8] The method was originally used in comparative-static analysis by B. Reddy and M. Morishima. See Reddy (1971), Lluch and Morishima (1973, pp. 177–83), and Allingham and Morishima (1973, pp. 260–70).

is n, and there is a probability n_i/n that offer i will be observed, and n_k/n that offer k will be observed, then if an entrepreneur changes his offer from i to k the respective probabilities change to $(n_i - 1)/n$ and $(n_k + 1)/n$. The effects of this kind of change in the distribution of job offers can only be captured by what we have called the method of generalized discrete-probability shifts.

From the point of view of the searcher this change in the probabilities will have different effects on his policy depending on whether the offer is acceptable or unacceptable before and after the change. Thus we may distinguish three kinds of exclusive and exhaustive probability changes: (1) a change in the probabilities of unacceptable offers, those of acceptable offers remaining unchanged, (2) a change in the probabilities of unacceptable offers compensated by changes in the probabilities of acceptable offers, and (3) a change in the probabilities of acceptable offers, those of unacceptable ones remaining unchanged.

By the definition of the expected returns from search, the acceptance sets, and therefore every other characteristic of the search process, remain unaffected after a change of the first kind. Thus consider the effects of changes of the second and third kinds. There are two general kinds of shifts that may take place, which may be thought of, respectively, as examples of additive and multiplicative shifts. First, a fall in the probability of some offer, with an equal increase in the probability of some other offer, corresponding to an additive shift of the distribution of offers. If the change takes place at period t and we let Δf_t^i denote the fall in the probability of offer i, and Δf_t^k the increase in that of offer k, with $\Delta f_t^i + \Delta f_t^k = 0$ and $U(\mathbf{J}_i) < U(\mathbf{J}_k)$, the change in the expected returns from search when $\mathbf{J}_i$ is unacceptable and $\mathbf{J}_k$ acceptable will be

$$\Delta V_{t-1} = \Delta f_t^k[U(\mathbf{J}_k) - V_t] > 0,$$
$$\Delta V_{t'} = (1 - a_{t'+1}) \dots (1 - a_{t-1}) \Delta V_{t-1} \quad (t' = 0, 1, \dots, t-2).$$

In the case where both $\mathbf{J}_i$ and $\mathbf{J}_k$ are acceptable we obtain

$$\Delta V_{t-1} = \Delta f_t^k [U(\mathbf{J}_k) - U(\mathbf{J}_i)],$$

which is again positive but less than the increase in the previous case, because $U(\mathbf{J}_i) \geq V_t$, by the condition of acceptance of $\mathbf{J}_i$. So the rightward compensated change in some probabilities is, like the uniform additive shift, always favourable. The advantage of considering this type of change, however, is that now we have a *quantitative* measure of the change in the returns from search. This method should therefore prove particularly useful in econometric work, but (to this author's knowledge) it has not yet been used to that end.

A change in probabilities which is an important special case of a multiplicative shift takes place when, in the case of a shrinkage of the distribution, the probability of the mean offer increases, and all other probabilities fall in an equal proportion. The effect of this kind of change on behaviour depends crucially on whether the mean offer is acceptable or not. Let $\Delta \bar{f}_t$ be the increase in the probability of the mean offer, and Δf_t^k the decrease in all other probabilities. Then by simple manipulation we obtain $\Delta f_t^k = \alpha f_t^k$, where $\alpha = -\Delta \bar{f}_t / (1 - \bar{f}_t)$. If the mean offer at t is unacceptable then the change in V_{t-1} is

$$\begin{aligned} \Delta V_{t-1} &= \sum_k \Delta f_t^k \, (U - V_t) \\ &= \alpha \sum_k f_t^k \, (U - V_t) \\ &= \alpha (V_{t-1} - V_t) < 0. \end{aligned} \tag{2}$$

So if the mean offer is not acceptable this type of multiplicative shift in f_t is always unfavourable. Moreover, the expected returns from search at $t - 1$ fall by the same proportion as the difference between the expected returns at $t - 1$ and the expected returns at t, and the factor of proportionality is the same as that by which the probabilities of acceptable offers fell. Since V_t remains fixed, the difference $V_{t-1} - V_t$ also falls by the same proportion α.

If the mean offer at t is acceptable, V_{t-1} changes by

$$\begin{aligned} \Delta V_{t-1} &= \Delta \bar{f}_t [U(\bar{\mathbf{J}}_t) - V_t] + \sum_k \Delta f_t^k \, (U - V_t) \\ &= -\alpha (1 - \bar{f}_t) \, [U(\bar{\mathbf{J}}_t) - V_t] + \alpha \sum_k f_t^k (U - V_t) \\ &= \alpha (V_{t-1} - V_t) - \alpha [U(\bar{\mathbf{J}}_t) - V_t] \\ &= \alpha [V_{t-1} - U(\bar{\mathbf{J}}_t)]. \end{aligned} \tag{3}$$

Thus the effect of this type of multiplicative shift in a distribution f_t is more clear-cut than the effect of a uniform multiplicative shift. If $\bar{\mathbf{J}}_t$, the mean job offer at t, yields utility above the reservation value at period $t - 1$, i.e. if $\bar{\mathbf{J}}_t$ is acceptable both at t and $t - 1$, then the reservation value at $t - 1$ increases, whereas if $\bar{\mathbf{J}}_t$ is unacceptable at $t - 1$ it decreases. This is the kind of strong result that the analysis of uniform multiplicative shifts with the use of parameter changes was incapable of yielding.

The analysis, of course, extends to multiplicative changes about any value, and also to other kinds of changes. If the job offer whose probability increases is unacceptable, then a result similar to that in (2) holds, whereas if the offer is acceptable a result similar to that in (3) holds. The details of the analysis are omitted since the method is the same as for the cases discussed.

Classification of the influences on the optimal acceptance policy

As we have seen in the last chapter the optimally acting individual should choose a reservation utility level V_t for every period in his horizon, and search for a job if the utility from his current state in the labour market falls below this level. During unsuccessful search, reservation standards fall over time, whereas if no search takes place they remain constant. We also hinted in the last chapter that there is a large number of factors that contribute to this result. We now come to a more detailed examination of these factors.

The factors influencing the optimal acceptance policy fall into two main classes: those which are specific to the individual and those which affect all individuals. The factors affecting all individuals are those which produce changes in the distributions of job offers ruling in the market, such as changes in the recruitment standards of firms or changes in their wage offers. The factors which are specific to the individual include the length of his horizon, the order in which he searches firms, the number of unsuccessful searches he has already made and hence the total searching costs which he has incurred, and so on. This group of factors influences the individual's policy even when the distributions of job offers are fixed and identical in all periods. We shall call the sequence of distributions which results from the policy of firms and is the same for all individuals the *objective* sequence, and the sequence which results when we allow for the effects of the factors specific to the individual the *subjective* sequence. The factors which bring about variations in the objective sequence are called *exogenous* and those which bring about variations in the subjective sequence for a given objective sequence *endogenous*.

The change in the reservation utility levels over time may be decomposed into two parts. First, that change which takes place even if the subjective sequence of distributions consists of identical distributions, and second the additional change induced by the variations in the distributions between one period and the next. The first part of the change is clearly due to endogenous factors, since if the subjective distributions are identical any factors acting on the objective distributions will not have an effect on the policy. The second part may be due either to endogenous or exogenous factors, since differences in the subjective distributions may arise even when the objective distributions are fixed, but they also arise when the objective distributions change.

Suppose the subjective distributions of job offers are identical in all periods, and denote the common distribution by f. Then, substituting in the basic functional equation we obtain,

$$V_{t-1} - V_t = \sum_{S_t} f(U - V_t) > 0 \quad (t = 1, \ldots, T).$$

So the first part of the decomposition of the change in the reservation utility levels is certainly negative, i.e. when the distributions of offers are identical the reservation utility level certainly falls over time. The most important factor operating when the distributions are identical is the finiteness of the work horizon.[9] Since the individual can search only a finite number of times in his lifetime, if a period elapses and he is still unemployed, the chances that he will never find a job increase, so he responds by lowering his reservation utility level.

Consider now variations in the distributions of offers. If a distribution f_t shifts unfavourably, all reservation values prior to t decline, but those closer to t decline at a greater rate than the more distant ones. Hence an unfavourable shift in f_t reinforces the decline in the reservation values prior to t; conversely a favourable shift diminishes it. Since the reservation values must decline whatever the sequence of distributions searched, it follows that the finite work horizon is the strongest influence on the optimal path of reservation values. Any additional influence, either exogenous or endogenous, that leads to a deterioration in some distribution f_t reinforces the downward pressure on the path in periods before t, whereas any influence that leads to an improvement in the distribution diminishes it. It follows that a reallocation of the distributions in a random sequence $f_1, \ldots, f_T$ which brings the more favourable ones forward in time reinforces the downward pressure on the path. For instance, if f_{t+1} is more favourable than f_t and we swap their positions in the sequence $f_1, \ldots, f_T$, the

[9] The finiteness of the horizon was emphasized by Gronau (1971). Karlin (1962) proved the same result in a related context.

distribution at time $t + 1$ will take an unfavourable shift whereas that at t will take a corresponding favourable shift. Hence V_t will fall, whereas V_{t-1} will rise, since the upward pressure from the favourable shift at t will outweigh the downward pressure from the unfavourable shift at $t + 1$, if only because $t - 1$ is closer to t than $t + 1$. So the difference $V_{t-1} - V_t$ will definitely increase. It follows that the reservation utility levels will be falling at the fastest possible rate when the sequence of distributions searched deteriorates over time. As we have seen in chapter 9, under these conditions the optimal path is likely to be convex, i.e. the reservation values are likely to decline at a decreasing rate.

The effects of endogenous and exogenous changes on the optimal policy may be obtained in this way. If we are interested in the effects of some particular change we should check whether that change leads to an improvement in the distributions of offers or a deterioration. If it leads to an improvement the particular change in question will diminish the downward pressure on the reservation path, and increase its concavity. (As we showed in the last chapter if the distributions are identical the path is always concave.) But if it leads to a deterioration of the distributions it will reinforce the downward pressure on the path and diminish its concavity, possibly making it convex.[10] We shall consider two factors here, the cost of searching and non-random search. Both of these may be said to be endogenous, since they affect the policy of the individual without affecting the objective distributions of offers. In chapter 12 we shall consider variations in exogenous factors over the cycle in more detail.

1. The *cost of searching* leads to successive unfavourable shifts in the distributions of job offers. If an individual plans to search sequentially at every period in his search horizon until he finds an acceptable job, a job observed at t involves less searching cost than one observed

[10] By using this method it is possible to see more clearly why the possibility of borrowing during search reinforces the downward movement of the path of reservation utility levels (see above, p. 139). Since, when there are perfect capital markets the individual is interested in the discounted present value of the stream of income earnings, the distribution of offers in period t is partly defined over the discounted sum of m_0 for t periods and m for $T^* - t$ periods, where m_0 is unemployment compensation minus the monetary cost of search and m is the per-period payment from an observed job offer. But the distribution in period $t + 1$ is defined over the discounted sum of m_0 for $t + 1$ periods, and m for $T^* - (t + 1)$ periods, so even if all jobs are identical in periods t and $t + 1$, the distribution in period $t + 1$ will be less preferred than that in t, because $m > m_0$ for all acceptable jobs. Thus, when there is borrowing, the distributions over the lifetime job deteriorate over time because the lifetime wealth position deteriorates.

at $t + 1$, so, *ceteris paribus*, f_t will be more favourable than f_{t+1}. Since the greatest cost is borne when searching is unsuccessful in all periods in the search horizon, the returns with zero opportunities remaining, V_T, and the distribution f_T, ruling at T, are the worst affected by the existence of a positive searching cost. The existence of such costs, therefore, leads to a faster reduction in the reservation values and induces a decline at a decreasing rate.

2. *Systematic* (non-random) *search* arises when we acknowledge that the individual has some information about the job he is likely to be offered by each prospective employer, so he may not be indifferent about the order in which he searches employers.[11] Thus, suppose the individual has T prospective employers to search, and if he visits the tth employer he expects to be offered a job out of the distribution f_t. Once the order in which the individual plans to search the T employers is chosen, the systematic search model becomes formally identical to the random search model of chapter 6. The random search model took any sequence of distributions $f_1, \ldots, f_T$ and derived an optimal policy; the systematic search model assumes that the distributions are ordered such that the expected returns from an optimal policy, V_0, are maximized.

Now, suppose the T employers are allocated randomly to the T time periods required to search them, and the resulting sequence of distributions is $f_1, \ldots, f_T$, with implied reservation values $V_0, \ldots, V_T$. Let f_t be the distribution allocated to period t, and f_{t+1} the one allocated to period $t + 1$, and suppose f_{t+1} is more favourable than f_t. Then if the individual swaps the positions of these distributions the expected returns from search will increase, since the upward pressure on V_0 resulting from the replacement of f_t by f_{t+1} at position t will outweigh the downward pressure from the replacement of f_{t+1} by f_t at position $t + 1$, because period t is closer to the beginning of search than period $t + 1$. It follows that the expected returns from search are maximized when it is no longer possible to swap the positions of any pair of distributions and bring the more favourable one forward in the sequence. So if the individual searches systematically, the distributions of offers will be deteriorating over time.

Thus systematic search implies that reservation values are revised downwards more rapidly than otherwise, and they will tend to be

[11] See Holt (1970) and Salop (1973*a*).

reduced at a decreasing rate.[12] The individual may be viewed as trying to maximize the returns from search by visiting the more attractive employers and enquiring for a job when he first starts the search. This implies that the probability of finding an acceptable job quickly increases, but also that if no job is found in the first few stages of search, the prospect of continuing the search looks much less promising now that the 'good' employers have already been searched. The searcher responds to this by lowering his reservation standards more quickly. Under the additional reasonable hypothesis that the individual usually singles out one or two employers as the best ones from his point of view, being largely indifferent about the others, the reservation values will decline more rapidly in the first few stages of search than later.

Summary

In this and the last chapter we considered the dynamic path of the reservation utility levels during unsuccessful search and analysed the effects of a number of important variables on the optimal path. The reservation utility levels were shown to behave like the 'aspiration' levels of satisficing theory, in that they were reduced during unsuccessful search but increased when search ended in success. The possibility of borrowing on the basis of future earning prospects was shown to lead to higher reservation utility levels during search, but risk aversion exerted a depressing influence on them as the individual attempted to reduce the uncertainty about his future job by accepting low-paying jobs.

Reservation utility levels fall during unsuccessful search for a number of reasons. The most important appears to be the finiteness of the work horizon and the foregone earnings suffered during unsuccessful search. Borrowing during search also induces a downward movement in reservation levels: as search proceeds unsuccessfully the lifetime wealth situation deteriorates because there is now less time to work for a wage, and if there was heavy borrowing in the first few

[12] It is interesting to note that if the distributions are randomly allocated, and then re-allocated systematically, some $V_{t-1} - V_t$ may actually decline, especially if t is large and the systematically allocated f_t is inferior to the randomly allocated one (this is easily shown by a method similar to that of the appendix to chapter 9).

stages of search the net wealth position will be deteriorating faster. Thus the reservation utility level is lowered to increase the chances of finding an acceptable job. Any additional influence that leads to a deterioration of the prospects of finding a good job induces a faster decline in reservation levels, whereas an improvement in the prospects induces a slower decline. The cost of searching and non-random search were identified as two influences which produce a deterioration of the prospects, and many others can no doubt be found.

The cost of searching leads to a deterioration in the prospect of finding a good job as search proceeds unsuccessfully, because the individual is interested in the utility from his *lifetime* job. A given job offer observed at time t produces a worse lifetime job than the same offer observed in period $t - 1$, because the former will involve the payment of a searching cost at t, not arising in the latter. Systematic search implies that the individual will visit the more promising employers when he first starts the search, so if he fails to find an acceptable job with these, the prospect of finding one from the less promising ones in the future will be worse than if he searched employers randomly.

11

Unemployment and On-the-job Search

Up to the present the model of job search has considered an unemployed worker looking for work, paying particular attention to the dynamic process involved when this worker is *unsuccessful* in his search for a job. It has paid little attention to the factors that led the worker into unemployment and job-searching in the first place, and also to what happens after the acceptance of a job and the termination of search. Thus, in a sense, we have dealt with the problem of 'deaths' during search, but not 'births'. The study of births, however, is as important in the analysis of the dynamic adjustment of a decentralized labour market as that of deaths, since the stock of searchers at any point of time will be determined by last period's stock *plus* the difference between current births and deaths. As we saw in chapter 5, variations in the stock of searchers cause changes in firm policy, which in turn may cause changes in job-searching behaviour giving rise to a circular policy interaction, so the dynamic analysis of the market requires an analysis of changes in the *stock* of searchers, i.e. an analysis of both flows into and flows out of the pool of active searchers.[1]

But before we complete the analysis by considering the question of the birth of a searcher, we pause and make a short digression into the more empirically-oriented aspect of the problem, namely the problem of unemployment (voluntary and involuntary) and on-the-job search. Thus this chapter contributes little to the theoretical framework of adjustment, and it may be skipped without loss of continuity. But the questions it tackles have cropped up, and have been deliberately avoided, at several points in the previous argument, so it may clear up a few obscure points. These questions have also occupied a large part of the related literature, and they are relevant to what is sometimes referred to as 'manpower' policies, an issue which lacks firm theoretical analysis.

[1] I owe this point to Professor J. Black.

The duration of search

Consider an individual who plans to search sequentially a maximum of T firms according to the acceptance policy $S_1, \ldots, S_T$, and suppose he observes the sequence of job offers $\mathbf{J}_1, \ldots, \mathbf{J}_t$, such that

$$\mathbf{J}_{t'} \notin S_{t'} \quad (t' = 1, \ldots, t - 1),$$
$$\mathbf{J}_t \in S_t. \tag{1}$$

This means that he will reject all offers observed in periods 1, ..., $t - 1$, accept the offer observed at t, and terminate the search, beginning his new job at period $t + 1$. Thus under these conditions the individual expects to spend t periods searching, foregoing any possible wage payments during these periods and incurring a searching cost of c per period. The probability of observing a sequence such as (1) is given by

$$P(t) = (1 - a_1) \ldots (1 - a_{t-1})a_t,$$

where a_t is the probability of accepting the offer observed at t. So if the individual is currently unemployed he expects his unemployment to last t periods with probability $P(t)$.

In general, searchers may be classified into three categories as far as their status during search is concerned. First, there is the *involuntary* searcher, who is searching because he has been dismissed by his former employer despite his willingness to continue working at the same job. Such a dismissal, as we have seen, may take place when the firm employing the worker raises its recruitment standard, so the involuntary searcher is a symptom of what we have called the fixwage system. Under involuntary unemployment and searching, however, we may also include the searcher who, although he may have become unemployed and started the search quite voluntarily, was not recruited by some firm he has searched later on and whose offer he was willing to accept. Once again, such refusal to recruit someone who is willing to work at the offered wage rate is a symptom of the fixwage system, since it will only arise in cases where the searcher's efficiency falls below the firm's recruitment standard. Clearly, the involuntary searcher is always unemployed during search.

Second, there is the *voluntary* searcher who is currently unemployed. His unemployment may be described as frictional, because he prefers to be unemployed, instead of accepting one of the offers he has already observed, in the hope of finding a better offer in the future. The unemployed searcher included in this category may be either a new entrant to the labour market, looking for his first job, or an older worker who was not satisfied with his previous job and so he quit to look for another. A worker who is not satisfied with his current job, however, may not be willing to take the risk of quitting to search for another job. Instead, he may prefer to search whilst holding his current job, and quit only if and when he finds a better job. This searcher forms the last of our three categories, the voluntary searcher who is searching *on-the-job*.

Although our basic model of job search was developed for an individual who is currently unemployed, this assumption was not crucial in any of the results obtained. The current status of the searcher influences the optimal search policy only to the extent that it determines the first component of what we have been calling the lifetime job.[2] But since the results obtained are independent of the particular elements making up the vector of a lifetime job, it is immaterial whether, e.g., the first t elements of a lifetime job $\mathbf{J}_t$ consist of unemployment compensation, or wage payments from a job which the searcher is trying to change. So the same theory of job search holds for both unemployed and on-the-job searchers.

Thus the properties of the duration of search are independent of the status of the individual during search and the cause of that status, apart from the indirect influence through the optimal search policy. Nevertheless, most authors of job search models assume that the searcher is voluntarily unemployed and searching, so they interpret the expected value of $P(t)$ as the expected length of frictional unemployment when individuals are behaving optimally.[3] This interpretation, however, requires two further assumptions. First, that firms follow a flexwage policy, so no involuntary unemployment during search arises. Second, that those individuals who wish to change their jobs find it optimal to quit to search for another job, and not search on-the-job. As we shall see below, the model of job search does not imply that these assumptions are necessarily correct, so the empirical content of a theory of *frictional* unemployment, based on the theory of job search, is questionable.[4] (The combined firm-worker model, however, may serve as a theory of involuntary unemployment, if, as we

[2] See pp. 83–4.

[3] See for instance Reder (1969) and the contributions to Phelps *et al.* (1970).

[4] See chapter 14 for the first assumption, and this chapter, pp. 167–73 for the second.

shall argue below, on-the-job search is more common than voluntary quits.)

The duration of search, however, is of considerable interest for other reasons. First, involuntary unemployment is common today, perhaps more common than normally assumed because of the success of those made involuntarily unemployed in finding alternative jobs quickly, although certainly not as common as before the war. Understanding the factors that influence the duration of search should contribute towards the understanding of the factors that influence the duration of unemployment of redundant workers and the problems involved in their placement in new jobs.[5] Second, the distribution $P(t)$ which is defined over the periods of termination of search is of crucial importance to firms contemplating an optimal recruitment policy, since it determines, to a large extent, the number of searchers remaining out of a given initial entry of new searchers into the market. For instance, suppose n new searchers enter the market in period one. Then, if a firm is contemplating recruiting some new workers, it should expect on average a proportion $P(t)$ of these searchers to leave the pool of searchers at every period t. Hence, from the n searchers entering at period one a number equal to

$$n - nP(1) - \ldots - nP(t) = n(1 - a_1) \ldots (1 - a_t)$$

would on average be searching in period $t + 1$.

Thus the distribution over termination periods, $P(t)$, is relevant both for the worker (and the government as the enactor of manpower policy) because it gives the duration of unemployment of redundant employees, and also for the firm because it gives the proportion of searchers who are still searching t periods after their entry into the market. Before investigating the trade-off between quitting to search and on-the-job search, we shall review the main features of the distribution $P(t)$, most of which have already been given in a number of occasions in the discussion of job search in previous chapters.

If the individual plans a maximum of T searches, $P(t)$ can take on $T + 1$ values – T values for successful termination of search in periods

[5] There is increasing awareness, both in the United States and Britain, that what are termed 'manpower' policies, i.e. policies designed to place redundant employees in new jobs, depend on the factors that influence the duration of unemployment of the employees. The pioneering study in Britain is Fowler (1968). See also MacKay (1972a), MacKay and Reid (1972), and Cripps and Tarling (1974).

1, . . ., T, and a single value for failure in all T searches. The probability of success in each period is given by

$$\begin{aligned} P(1) &= a_1 \\ P(2) &= (1 - a_1)a_2, \\ &\dots \\ P(T) &= (1 - a_1)\dots(1 - a_{T-1})a_T. \end{aligned}$$

The probability of failure in all T searches is given by

$$P'(T) = (1 - a_1)\dots(1 - a_T).$$

Thus the probabilities $P(t)$ depend on the distributions of job offers up to period t, and also on the individual's acceptance policy in all periods up to t. Since the acceptance policy in periods 1, . . ., t also depends on the distributions of offers in periods after t, and on the acceptance policy in those periods, each $P(t)$ depends on the distribution of offers and the acceptance policy in all periods in the search horizon.

The dependence on the optimal policy is the easier one to analyse. Since each probability a_t is defined by $\sum_{S_t} f_t(\mathbf{J})$, where S_t includes all job offers which yield utility above the reservation value V_t, an increase in V_t reduces a_t, whereas a fall in V_t increases it. An increase in a_t will, in its turn, cause an increase in $P(t)$ and a fall in all probabilities $P(t')$ for $t' = t + 1, \dots, T$. That is, the probability that search will terminate at t increases, whereas the probability that it will terminate after t falls. However, it is more convenient to obtain the effects of changes in $a_1, \dots, a_T$ through their effects on the 'no death' probability $P'(t)$, defined by

$$P'(t) = (1 - a_1)\dots(1 - a_t).$$

$P'(t)$ gives the probability that the individual will still be searching after t periods if he follows an optimal policy. (When $t = T$ this probability coincides with the probability of terminating the search unsuccessfully, defined above.) Clearly, when a_t rises, all probabilities $P'(t), \dots, P'(T)$ fall, whereas $P'(1), \dots, P'(t - 1)$ remain the same, so the probability that the individual will reach period t without success is the same, but the chances that he will continue searching after t goes down. Under these conditions search will on average take fewer periods than before.

However, it is important to consider the cause of the change in a_t before analysing its effect, because a_t depends on both the distribution of offers and the optimal acceptance policy at t, and as we have repeatedly seen the acceptance policy at t is not independent of the acceptance policy in other periods before t. Thus, if the increase in a_t is due to a fall in V_t, with the distribution at t remaining fixed, there will also be effects on $V_0, V_1, \ldots, V_{t-1}$ and so on the probabilities $a_1, \ldots, a_{t-1}$. These will in turn have repercussions on the duration of search, and so must be taken into account when analysing the effects of the change in V_t on duration. But there is no difficulty in taking into account these interdependencies when the change in a_t is due to a change in the reservation utility level. Since an increase in V_t will cause an increase in all reservation values prior to t, and a decline in V_t will cause a fall in them, any change in a_t caused by a change in V_t must be assumed as taking place simultaneously with a change in $a_1, \ldots, a_{t-1}$ in the same direction. So when one or more reservation values decrease, all probabilities a_t up to the period(s) of the change increase, causing a fall in the probability of continuing the search, $P'(t)$, in all periods in the search horizon; i.e. when one or more reservation utility levels fall, the probability that the individual will still be searching t periods after the beginning of search falls, for all $t = 1, \ldots, T$. The duration of search under these circumstances declines. This has the implication, for instance, that risk averters who normally choose a lower reservation level, are less likely to spend a long time searching.

The dependence of the duration of search on the distributions of job offers is a bit more difficult to analyse. In chapter 10 we defined a distribution f_t as more favourable than another distribution f_t' if by putting f_t at place t in the sequence of distributions searched yields a higher V_{t-1} (and hence by recursion higher $V_0, \ldots, V_{t-2}$) than that obtained by putting f_t' at place t. Unfortunately even those shifts in f_t which can be classified unambiguously as either favourable or unfavourable do not produce unambiguous changes in a_t. For instance, f_t may be more favourable than f_t' because it contains some exceptionally good offers, although the probability of observing an acceptable offer from f_t may be less than the probability of observing an acceptable offer from f_t'.

However, such problems clearly arise when the shift in the distribution is not of a simple type. A simple additive shift will certainly produce a change in V_{t-1} and a_t in the same direction – a rightward shift in f_t will increase the reservation values prior to t and the probability of accepting the offer at t, whereas a leftward shift will reduce them. If the former occurs (conversely for the latter) all probabilities of acceptance $a_1, \ldots, a_{t-1}$, prior to t, will fall, because of the increase in $V_1, \ldots, V_{t-1}$. So the probability of continuing the search after any period prior to t increases. But a_t goes up as well when f_t shifts to the right, so there are two opposing influences on the probability of continuing the search after t, the upward pressure from the rise in $P'(t - 1)$, the probability of reaching t without success, and the downward pressure from the increase in a_t, the probability of stopping at t. In the case of an additive shift we may assume that a 'reasonable' individual will not over-react to the change in f_t so as to cancel the beneficial effects from the increase in a_t by raising his reservation values to a large extent prior to t. Then, when f_t improves, the probability of continuing the search until t increases whereas that of continuing it after t falls. The effect on the expected duration of search will therefore be downward if t lies before the expected termination period and upward if it lies after it. Since changes which take place near the current period are more strongly felt than more distant ones, a simultaneous improvement in all distributions will result in a fall in all continuation probabilities $P'(1), \ldots, P'(T)$, and so in a fall in the expected duration of search.[6]

Now if the individual has some information about prospective employers and searches the more favourable ones before the others, the distributions of offers will be deteriorating over time.[7] So, given the state of the market and the individual's search policy, non-random search implies that the probability of observing an acceptable job offer, a_t, declines with t. The probability of continuing the search after period t will therefore fall very rapidly at first, but level off if the individual is unlucky enough to have searched the better prospects without success. Put differently, the more time one has already spent searching, the more likely one is to continue searching.[8]

The searcher, of course, will respond to the deterioration in the distributions of job offers by lowering his reservation utility levels more rapidly, so the probability of finding an acceptable offer will increase to some extent. But the adjustment in the optimal acceptance

[6] If the improvement in f_t has a 'perverse' effect on a_t, i.e. it reduces a_t, the duration of search will certainly increase by the improvement in f_t, since $a_1, \ldots, a_t$ will all fall. We shall not consider this possibility any further because it is unlikely to arise in the cases we shall be analysing.

[7] See above, pp. 156–7.

[8] This was demonstrated to be empirically correct in Britain by Fowler (1968). For more recent evidence see *Department of Employment Gazette*, February 1973, esp. pp. 112–14.

policy is made to counteract the effects of non-random search to some extent, but not reverse them. When the individual has some information about the market and he is searching non-randomly we would expect him to find an acceptable job very quickly after the beginning of search. If he is unlucky enough to be unsuccessful after the first few stages of search his search is likely to be prolonged.[9]

The distributions of job offers will also depend, to a large extent, on the pressure of supply-and-demand in the labour market. Flexwage firms will respond to a change in market conditions by varying their wage offers, whereas fixwage firms will respond by varying their recruitment standard. Both changes will produce shifts in the distributions of offers used by the individual during search, so the effects of changes in labour market conditions on the duration of search may be obtained via their effects on the distributions of offers – during a boom the distributions shift to the right and during a depression to the left. Their effects on duration, therefore, are the same as those analysed above for additive shifts.

Now the probability of being offered a particular job in any period t was defined as the product of two other probabilities, that of observing the offer, and that of being recruited at the observed offer. So if one wishes to consider the factors which determine the duration of search of some particular individual one should look at the chances that this individual has of observing a particular wage offer, his chances of being recruited at that offer, and his policy during search. If market conditions are stationary, then *on average* variations in the period spent searching by different individuals can arise when the individuals' efficiency, measured by their production coefficient q, or their policy followed during search, are different. Thus, the higher the individual's efficiency the more likely he is to find a job quickly, and the higher the reservation level he chooses the more likely he is to spend a longer time searching. The latter implies, as we have seen, that risk averters are likely to spend a shorter period searching than risk lovers. The former implies that if a firm is uncertain of the searcher's efficiency, and attempts to estimate it by observing some personal and other characteristics of the searcher, the duration of search will depend to a large extent on the searcher's personal characteristics.[10]

[9] See, in addition to the references in the last footnote, MacKay (1972*a*) and MacKay and Reid (1972).

[10] The hypothesis that firms observe personal and other characteristics, e.g. education, to deduce a prospective employee's efficiency was put forward by Spence (1973). The hypothesis that the duration of search depends on personal characteristics was put forward in Britain and tested by MacKay and Reid (1972) and Cripps and Tarling (1974).

For instance, if old age is considered a serious handicap in production, the old are likely to spend a longer period searching for a job than the young, especially when firms follow a fixwage policy and choose a recruitment standard. Similarly, if an employer is suspicious of a worker who has been unable to find work for some time, prolonged search is likely to lead to a fall in the probability of being recruited quickly, a factor which may reinforce the pattern expected to arise when the individual is searching non-randomly.[11]

Quitting and on-the-job search

Suppose a firm is currently operating near the maximum of its capacity, but as a result of a fall in the demand for its output it decides to cut its demand for labour. The fixwage firm will respond to this by raising its recruitment standard, so it will dismiss the less efficient of its employees. These employees will then be made 'involuntarily' unemployed. Most of them will probably search for a new job, so the properties and duration of their unemployment become identical to those of search in general analysed in the last section. Search and unemployment in this case become indistinguishable – we can talk about them interchangeably without loss of generality.[12]

But if the firm is operating in a flexwage environment it will respond to a fall in the demand for its product by lowering the wage rates it pays to its employees. If, as a result of this wage cut, some of the firm's employees decide to search for another job, then the correspondence between search and unemployment is not as clear-cut. The question is whether the dissatisfied employee should give up his job to search whilst unemployed, or whether he should search on-the-job and give up his current job only after he has found a better one. Given that choosing to become unemployed reduces utility temporarily below that obtained from the current job, the individual will

[11] Other similar hypotheses may be advanced and tested within this framework. Although the empirical literature has not worked within an optimizing individual model it has identified a number of characteristics of the duration of search. For instance, the old search longer before finding a job, and the chances of finding a job deteriorate during search. For Britain the literature is still in its infancy. See the work of Fowler, MacKay, Reid, and Cripps and Tarling already referred to. The problem with identifying the determinants of duration, of course, is that the model is probabilistic, so chance plays a central role in determining actual duration. One should normally require a large number of observations to eliminate the chance element by averaging.

[12] This appears to be the practice of MacKay and Reid in the papers quoted in the last section. Since their sample consisted of employees declared redundant in the West Midlands in 1966, this is consistent with the model.

choose to quit only if on-the-job search is less efficient than search whilst unemployed, or alternatively if it is more costly.

If we can find reasonable assumptions which imply that individuals will always quit to search, then the length of search and the properties of that length may be identified with frictional unemployment, so the theory of search in a flexwage world may be used to obtain testable hypotheses about that category of unemployment. On-the-job search is a rather elusive concept for an empirical analysis of the labour market, so most authors of search models attempt to find assumptions that will justify quitting before search, and usually employ such assumptions explicitly.[13]

An assumption to the extent that on-the-job search is inefficient will also have other implications for labour market analysis, in particular about the place of temporary employment. Thus, suppose an individual is currently unemployed, and he searches and observes a job offer **J**. In general he can do one of four things: (1) reject **J** and do not search again, remaining unemployed, (2) reject **J** and search again, (3) accept **J** and terminate the search, and (4) accept **J** but continue the search for a better job. The first option is related to the choice of search horizon and to what we shall call later 'discouragement'. It will be considered in some detail in chapter 12, so further consideration of this issue is postponed. The second and third alternatives are those considered in the basic model of chapter 6, and they undoubtedly form the basis of any model of search, theoretical and empirical.[14] The fourth option, which will be considered here, implies that **J** is accepted *temporarily*, i.e. until a better job is found. Although this option did not find a place in the search model of chapter 6, if on-the-job search is not inefficient and changing jobs not too costly, temporary acceptance *will* take place, when the individual is currently unemployed and the observed job offer, although better than the state of unemployment, is not good enough to be accepted as a permanent job.

[13] Although most descriptive analyses of search assume fixwage, mostly implicitly, all theoretical models deal with flexwage. In this they all follow the precedent of Stigler (1962) and Phelps *et al.* (1970).

[14] i.e., the most important decision during search, with regard to both the properties of adjustment of a decentralized labour market and the empirical theory of unemployment and search, is whether to accept an offer and terminate search or reject the offer and continue searching. The other options are related more to specific aspects of the problem, e.g. the question of discouragement is related more to the 'secondary' labour force, and that of on-the-job search to temporary employment.

The most explicit statement of the assumption that on-the-job search is inefficient, so the individual will normally choose to be unemployed during search, was put forward by Alchian and described as 'critical' in the analysis of information costs and resource unemployment. Alchian (1970, p. 29) argues that 'gathering and disseminating information about goods or about oneself is in some circumstances more efficiently done while the good or person is not employed', and the reason for this is attributed to the fact that if unemployed the person can specialize in search and so search more efficiently.[15] The notion of 'efficiency' in search is not made explicit, nor do the models using this assumption explain the reasons (within their models) for the greater 'efficiency' if the searcher is unemployed. Thus most effort in the literature is devoted to the study of the changes in the *number* of those who choose temporary unemployment instead of temporary employment, without explaining why this number should ever be positive on supply considerations alone.[16]

The assumption that the worker will quit to search if he is no longer satisfied with his own job has been criticized by Tobin (1972) and others on empirical grounds. For instance, Stein (1960) found that 55 per cent of all job changes in the United States in 1955 occurred without unemployment in-between, and Tobin argued that Alchian's assumption is inconsistent with the observation that at 5–6 per cent unemployment rate about 40 per cent of accessions in manufacturing are rehires rather than new hires. Moreover, about 3 per cent of the employed labour force are temporarily employed in part-time jobs, so presumably searching on-the-job.[17]

Thus it appears that the evidence contradicts the assumption of efficiency in information-gathering whilst unemployed, or at best it

[15] Alchian emphasizes that the specialization is not in seeking 'jobs' but in seeking 'job information' (p. 30), so the implication is that the individual specializes in search as an information-gathering activity and not as a job-seeking activity. In general, however, the latter function of search is more important than the former, and indeed the former is lost in the formal models contained in Phelps *et al.* alongside Alchian's paper and elsewhere, although the efficiency assumption is retained.

[16] Inter-firm movements of labour are treated by some models, e.g. Holt (1970) and Mortensen (1970*a*), but these same models also adopt Alchian's efficiency assumption to explain movements via the unemployment pool.

[17] More recently Parsons (1973) has provided more evidence for this, and also provided an extension of the standard information-search model to explain temporary acceptance of jobs and quitting only when a new job is found. Thus, in 1961 only 15 per cent of the unemployed were voluntary quitters, whereas 80 per cent of quitters experienced no interim unemployment. This further points to the observation above that the properties of search are more relevant to 'involuntary' unemployment than frictional.

suggests that it is not correct in all cases. To find the factors which might induce a worker to give up his job to search for another, we shall consider Alchian's argument that differences in the efficiency of information-gathering are reflected in differences in search costs, i.e. the unemployed may obtain information about jobs more cheaply than the employed, and this difference in costs is high enough to induce rejection of temporary employment.

Let V_0 be the returns from search when the worker quits to search whilst unemployed, and V_0' the returns from searching on-the-job. Clearly, the worker will quit if V_0 exceeds V_0', and he will search on-the-job if V_0 is less than V_0'. Now V_0 may be written as the sum of the utility from successful search, weighted by the probability of success, plus the utility from unsuccessful search, weighted by the probability of failure.[18] V_0' may also be written as a similar sum, but whereas in the former case the utility from failure is equal to the utility from T unsuccessful searches and dropping out of the labour market altogether, in the latter case the utility from failure is equal to the utility that the searcher derives from his current job (provided, of course, that he can keep his current job for as long as he wishes) minus the cost of T unsuccessful searches. If the current job is better than the state of unemployment, as will in general be the case if the firm is to get any worker at all to work for it at the job, the utility from failure of on-the-job search is higher than the utility from failure of search after quitting. Thus workers will *always* prefer to search on-the-job if (1) the expected utility from success after on-the-job search is not less than the expected utility from success after quitting and searching whilst unemployed, and (2) the probability of failure of employed searchers is not greater than that of unemployed searchers. These, however, are sufficient conditions, and not necessary – if they are satisfied, workers will always search on-the-job, if they are not some workers may quit to search but some may still prefer to search on-the-job.

Let $\mathbf{J}_c$ be the individual's current job (or alternatively the job which he is considering for temporary acceptance) and $\mathbf{J}_o$ the state of unemployment. Then, if the individual is searching on-the-job his state during search is described by the pair $(w_c y - c, y + y_s)$, where w_c is the per-hour wage from his current job, y the hours of work, c the cost of searching one firm, and y_s the time needed to

[18] See above, p. 90.

search one firm. On the other hand, if the individual is unemployed during search his state is described by the pair $(m_o - c, y_s)$, where m_o is unemployment compensation. Suppose the individual expects to observe the same sequence of job offers whether he is employed or unemployed during search. Then the expected utility from successful search will be greater if he searches on-the-job if and only if supplying y hours per period in addition to y_s, for an additional return of $w_c y - m_o$, increases utility for all future job situations that the individual may find himself in. If this condition is not satisfied, we may say that on-the-job search is *more costly*. That is, if an individual who is 'working' y_s hours for a 'return' of $m_o - c$ finds it uneconomical to supply any additional hours for a return of $w_c y - m_o$, then on-the-job search is more costly for this individual.[19] The expected lifetime utility from successful search then is higher if the individual is unemployed during search, so the worker is faced with a choice between two gambles: (1) search on-the-job, and receive lower expected returns from successful search but higher returns from unsuccessful search, (2) quit to search, and receive higher expected returns from success but lower returns from failure. Thus when on-the-job search is more costly we may use the choice between these two gambles to obtain some properties of the trade-off between quitting and on-the-job search.

Consider first the role of risk aversion in this choice problem. Since by quitting the individual reduces his returns from failure and increases his expected returns from success, the uncertainty when the worker quits to search is greater than when he searches on-the-job. So risk averters are less likely to quit to search for another job, and more likely to accept temporary employment and continue searching for a better job on-the-job. In contrast, more risk-tolerant individuals will find it more attractive to quit and search, and remain unemployed until they find a job which they find good enough to keep on a permanent basis.

Similarly, wealthy individuals will find it more attractive to quit and refuse temporary employment, preferring to search whilst unemployed. When the individual is more wealthy he evaluates leisure more highly per unit of money received, so the (subjective) cost of on-the-job search is higher. Also, the state of unemployment is not as

[19] Thus, 'differential search costs' here is taken to mean 'differential *subjective* search costs'. Alchian does not make explicit the sense in which he talks of 'costs'.

unattractive when the individual is wealthy; so an increase in non-wage wealth increases the expected returns from on-the-job search to a less extent than the expected returns from unemployed search. Thus quitting to search whilst unemployed becomes a more attractive prospect.

The effects of other changes may also be obtained in a similar manner. In general, any factor which increases the cost differential also increases the chances that the worker will quit to search, whereas any factor which reduces the probability of terminating the search successfully increases the attractiveness of on-the-job search. Also, the more undesirable the state of unemployment is, given the individual's current condition, the more likely he is to want to minimize the risk of ending up unemployed, so the more attractive acceptance of a temporary employment becomes.

The cost-explanation of the trade-off between quitting and on-the-job search, however, may not be sufficient to capture the whole range of factors that enter the choice between these two alternatives. For instance, unemployed workers have much more time to search for a job, and they are likely to press prospective employers harder to recruit them. Our assumption that the 'intensity' of search is the same for both employed and unemployed searchers is not very realistic when analysing the choice between quitting and on-the-job search and is likely to bias our results against quitting to search more intensely. Also, employers, but more so government legislation and trade unions, are likely to discriminate in favour of unemployed searchers when new jobs become available, on grounds of social justice and fairness.[20] These and other factors lead to what may be called a greater *efficiency* is search when the person is unemployed.

Greater efficiency may be assumed to lead to more favourable distributions of job offers encountered during search. Thus the returns from successful search are higher when the person is unemployed and the probability of success is also higher. The effects of differences in the efficiency of search, therefore, may be obtained in exactly the same way as the effects of differential costs. In general, any factor which increases the efficiency of searching whilst unemployed increases the attractiveness of quitting to search.

Thus we have identified two reasons that may lead to quitting

[20] Conversely, employers' recruitment standards may be higher for unemployed searchers, because employed searchers have more up-to-date information about their efficiency to convey to prospective employers.

and searching whilst unemployed. The first is that the subjective cost of search is higher if searching takes place on-the-job, and the second is that the efficiency of search is higher if searching takes place whilst unemployed. This implies that some may find it optimal to quit to search for a new job, and refuse temporary employment and continuation of search, when the chance arises. However, it does not imply that *all* will quit to search. For some, the risk of remaining unemployed for long periods may make on-the-job search more attractive despite the higher cost and inefficiency involved. Thus Tobin's (1972) and Parsons' (1973) evidence does not contradict Alchian's efficiency and differential-cost assumption. On the contrary, the fact that *some* voluntary quitting and searching takes place confirms the assumption, since if it were not true none would quit to search. But the risk of remaining unemployed for long periods appears to be too high for most workers to take, so most search on-the-job and quit after finding a new job.

12
Participation and Job Search

We now come to the final part of our job-searching story, namely the flow of new searchers into the market, or what we have called in the last chapter the question of the birth of a searcher.

If we classify searchers by cause of origin we shall find three types. First, new entrants into the labour force, second involuntary searchers who have been laid off by their former employers and are currently searching for a new job, and finally voluntary searchers who are dissatisfied with their current job and are looking for a new one. The analysis of the first type is related to the wider issue of labour-force participation and discouragement, and is analysed here under the assumption that population is constant. The second and third types are related to changes in firm policy, in that the second type is a symptom of the fixwage world and arises when firms raise their recruitment standards, dismissing their less efficient employees, whereas the third type arises mainly in the flexwage system when the firm's wage relative to the average in the market falls and its workers decide to search for a new job. As we have seen in the last chapter, most workers will remain employed and search on-the-job, quitting if and when they find a better job. Layoffs and quits are considered in the second section of this chapter.

Participation and discouragement: the problem

An individual will participate in the labour market if the returns from search exceed the lifetime utility obtained from not entering the labour market at all, and remaining unemployed for life. He will terminate his participation if the returns from subsequent search fall down to the utility from dropping out of the labour market. Since the expected returns from search decline over time, whereas when the individual stops searching his utility remains fixed at its current level, if he decides to terminate his participation he will not enter the market again, unless there is some change in market conditions which raises the returns from search above the current utility level. When the individual terminates his participation we say that he is 'discouraged' by his experience in search.[1] Thus the question of participation is related to the magnitude of the expected returns from search, V_0, and the factors that influence it, and that of discouragement is related to the choice of search horizon, i.e. when should the worker terminate the search if he is unsuccessful at every attempt. An individual will participate if V_0 exceeds the utility from non-participation, $U(\mathbf{J}_o)$, for at least one search horizon $T > 0$, and he will be discouraged if the optimal search horizon is smaller than the work horizon T^* and he fails to find an acceptable job before T.[2]

By search horizon we mean the maximum number of times (periods) that the individual chooses to search sequentially if he fails to find an acceptable job in the meantime. The search horizon influences the optimal acceptance policy by completely specifying the terminal condition of the functional equation system giving the optimal reservation utility levels $V_1, \ldots, V_{T-1}$, since if we know T we can automatically obtain the utility from failure in all T searches, which serves as terminal condition. So it also influences the expected returns from search V_0, which is obtained from the same functional equation system, and since the individual is free to choose his search horizon he will choose that horizon which maximizes the expected returns from search. Let V_0^T denote the expected returns from search when the search horizon is T and the individual is following an optimal acceptance policy. If we consider successively $T = 1, 2, \ldots, T^*$, and also the returns from no search at all, V_0^0, we should obtain a sequence

[1] Thus our use of 'discouragement' is consistent with the use made of it in the descriptive and more empirically-oriented literature. See for instance Mincer (1965) and Bowen and Finegan (1969, esp. pp. 24–5). But as Bowen and Finegan stress, the method used to formalize and estimate it – as the substitution effect of a supply-of-hours equation – is not really the most appropriate one. The present model may therefore offer a better foundation for that phenomenon, which has been observed several times in practice but never formalized within a search model which takes into account the issues involved explicitly.

[2] The following have been observed in practice. Primary males, age 25–50, exhibit 100 per cent participation rate, and no discouragement. Varying participation rates and discouragement is observed in the following groups, for whom there is a viable alternative to work: young males and females, with schooling as an alternative; 'primary' females, with housework as alternative; old men and women, with retirement as alternative. Thus when we talk of this source of labour we mean mainly these last three types, often referred to as the secondary labour force. The standard reference for the empirical analysis of participation is Bowen and Finegan (1969). Some work on Britain is contained in Corry and Roberts (1970) and Bowers (1970), and an important case study in MacKay (1972*a*).

$V_0^0, V_0^1, \ldots, V_0^{T^*}$, whose terms would all be finite, because the utility from all possible job situations is finite. Thus the sequence of maximum returns contains at least one element which is as high as any other element. The searcher should choose the search horizon T which yields that maximum return.

Now clearly, $V_0^0 = U(\mathbf{J}_o)$, the returns from no search at all (the utility from non-participation if the individual is unemployed, and that from the current job if he is employed). Also,

$$V_0^{T^*} \leq V_0^{T^*-1} \qquad (1)$$

always, because search at T^* is costly but has no returns, even if the individual finds a good offer, since he will not be able to take it before retirement. So it is never optimal to continue searching after $T^* - 1$.

We have seen in chapter 6, equation (6), that given the optimal acceptance policy the returns from search may be expressed as the weighted sum of expected utility values W_t ($t = 1, \ldots, T$), each one giving the expected utility from successful termination of search in each of the periods in the search horizon, and also $U(\mathbf{J}_{oT})$ giving the utility from unsuccessful search in all periods. Thus it appears to be impossible to order all V_0^Ts completely without restricting further either the utility function, or the probability distribution over the possible termination periods, or both.[3] In addition, the problem is made more complex by the dependence of both the utility numbers W_t and the probabilities $P(t)$ on the optimal acceptance policy.

However, it is one of the most powerful implications of sequential search that we can get round this stochastic-ordering problem, and order the V_0^Ts without having to restrict either the utility function or the distributions of offers. This property of the model has the additional implication that the optimal T and acceptance policy may be chosen simultaneously without having to compute the acceptance policy for all possible Ts, so economizing considerably on computational requirement.

These results may be obtained using the diagram introduced in chapter 9, and reproduced here as Fig. 12.1. The curve CT^* gives, for each t, the utility obtained when the individual searches unsuccessfully in periods 1, ..., t and then terminates the search and remains unemployed. The curve AB gives the path of the reservation values when the search horizon is T. Clearly, $0C$ is equal to the

[3] See Hadar and Russell (1969), Hanoch and Levy (1969), and Rothschild and Stiglitz (1970).

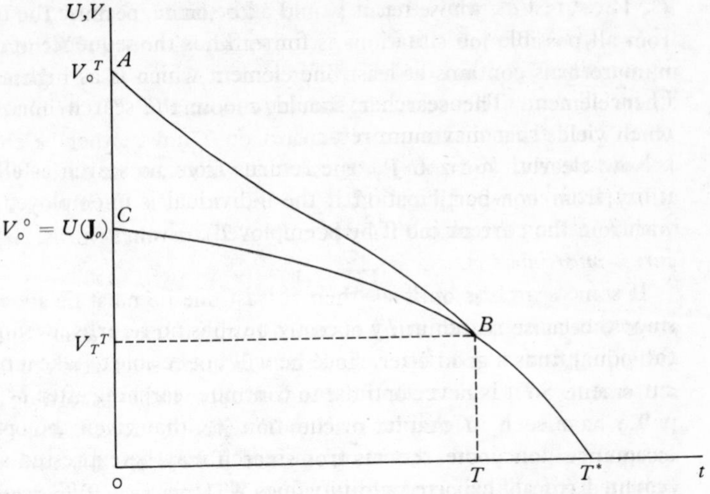

Fig. 12.1

returns from non-participation, V_0°, whereas $0A$ is equal to the total expected returns from search with horizon T, V_0^T. For each search horizon T the terminal value of the reservation utility levels is given by the relevant point on CT^*. For reference purposes AB may be referred to as a 'policy curve', whereas CT^* as the 'failure curve'.

Now consider the optimal policy $V_0', V_1', \ldots, V_{T'}'$, implied by some other search horizon T'. (For notational convenience we shall drop the superscript T, using a prime on a symbol when it refers to the optimal policy with horizon T', and no prime if it refers to T.) Let $V_t = V_t'$ for some $t \leq \min(T, T')$. Then by the recursive relation system

$$V_{t-1} = V_t + \sum_{S_t} f_t (U - V_t) = V_t' + \sum_{S_t'} f_t (U - V_t') = V_{t-1}',$$

since when $V_t = V_t'$ the acceptance sets S_t and S_t' coincide. Thus, if $V_t = V_t'$, by recursion all other values $V_0, V_1, \ldots, V_{t-1}$ must also coincide, respectively, with $V_0', V_1', \ldots, V_{t-1}'$.

Now let V_t increase above V_t'. Then, since $V_0, V_1, \ldots, V_{t-1}$ are monotonic functions of V_t,[4] the whole sequence of reservation values $V_0, V_1, \ldots, V_{t-1}$ rises above the corresponding sequence with horizon

[4] Recall that $\partial V_{t'}/\partial V_t = (1 - a_{t'+1}) \ldots (1 - a_t)$, where $a_{t'} = \Sigma_{S_{t'}} f_{t'}$, $t' = 0, 1, \ldots, t-1$.

T'. These results imply that if $V_t = V'_t$ for some $t \leq \min(T, T')$ then $V_{t'} = V'_{t'}$ for all $t' \leq t$; if $V_t > V'_t$ for some $t \leq \min(T, T')$ then $V_{t'} > V'_{t'}$ for all $t' \leq t$; and if $V_t < V'_t$ for some $t \leq \min(T, T')$ then $V_{t'} < V'_{t'}$ for all $t' \leq t$. Hence by considering $t = \min(T, T')$, we obtain the result that the policy curve with horizon T must either be entirely below that with horizon T', or coincide with it, or be entirely above it, respectively when $V_T < V'_T$, $V_T = V'_T$, or $V_T > V'_T$ (if $T \leq T'$, and with T' taking the place of T when $T' \leq T$). In other words, *no policy curves must intersect.*

If some search is optimal, then at least one V_0^T must lie above V_0^0, since the latter is the utility obtained from no search at all. Suppose the policy curve with that T as search horizon intersects the failure curve at $t = T'$ (Fig. 12.2). If the individual searches according to the policy implied by T and he reaches T' without success, it is clearly optimal to terminate the search, since if he stops his utility will remain fixed at the current-utility level BT', whereas if he continues he will travel down the policy path BD, below the failure curve CT^*. But a policy curve obtained with horizon T' will coincide with AB at all $t \leq T'$, because $V'_{T'} = V_{T'}$, so the effective search horizon for ABD is T' – the acceptance policy after T' is irrelevant for search.[5]

Thus the optimal policy curve must lie entirely above the failure curve CT^*. But since policy curves must not intersect, and the optimal search horizon is that which yields returns V_0 which are above those obtained by any other horizon, it is almost trivial to obtain the property satisfied by the optimal curve. Clearly, the greatest $T \leq T^*$ whose policy curve lies entirely above the failure curve is also the optimal T, since any curve with horizon $T' < T$ must lie entirely below that with horizon T (since that with T' starts off at $U(\mathbf{J}_{oT'}) < V^T_{T'}$ by assumption) and any policy curve with horizon $T'' > T$ has at least one segment below the failure curve.

The optimal search horizon may therefore be chosen in the following simple manner. Start from the last period in the work horizon T^* and consider each period in turn working backwards. T^* must be rejected because of equation (1). If for any search horizon T, a V_t ($t < T$) is obtained which is less than the corresponding $U(\mathbf{J}_{ot})$, then

[5] The individual may, of course, employ T as his search horizon and not T', with no difference whatsoever to the optimal acceptance policy. But T is meaningless as search horizon for an operational theory of the labour market, because it does not tell us for how long the individual will be searching if he is unsuccessful in search, i.e. when he will be discouraged.

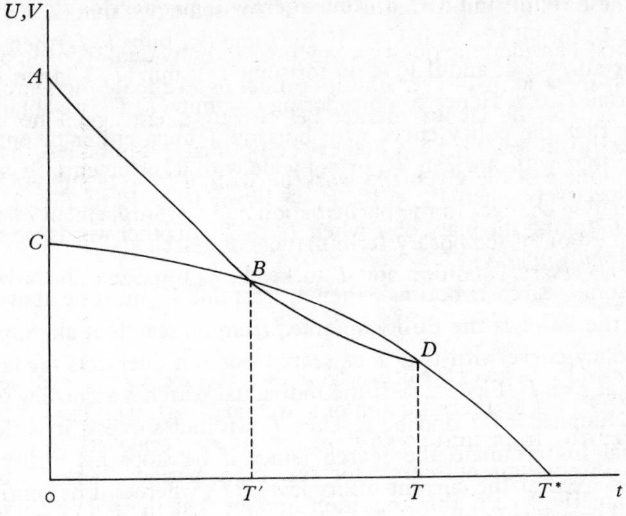

Fig. 12.2

T must be rejected and $T - 1$ considered instead. The first T for which all V_ts lie above the corresponding $U(\mathbf{J}_{ot})$s is the optimal T. If no T is found for which this requirement is satisfied, the optimal policy is non-participation, i.e. $T = 0$.

If the optimal search horizon is chosen in this manner, only the acceptance policy for the optimal T will have to be formulated in its entirety, and not for any other T. This can be seen directly if we recall that the optimal acceptance policy, for any T, was also obtained working backwards, starting from T. If a T is suboptimal the searcher will be informed of this before he derives all $V_T, V_{T-1}, \ldots, V_0$ for this T, since he need only calculate the critical values up to the first t for which $V_t \leq U(\mathbf{J}_{ot})$. Some V_ts, of course, will have to be calculated for suboptimal Ts as well, but in practice if a T is not optimal, it will be at those periods which are close to T that the individual will find that the optimality condition is violated, so the calculation of suboptimal V_ts will be minimal.[6]

[6] This follows directly from the diagram. If *ABD* (Fig. 12.2) does not fall below CT^* at periods close to T it is unlikely to do so at periods near zero, given that it must be forward falling, and that CT^* is likely to be concave.

Participation and discouragement: properties

We first consider the question whether an individual who chooses to search for a job will ever find it optimal to terminate the search and drop out of the labour market before retirement age if he is unsuccessful in search, i.e. whether the optimal T can be less than the maximum possible given the work horizon, $T^* - 1$. Subsequently, we analyse changes in the participation and discouragement rate, and the question of temporary terminations of search.

A necessary condition for T to be the optimal search horizon is

$$V_{T-1} > U(\mathbf{J}_{oT-1}),$$

where $U(\mathbf{J}_{oT-1})$ gives the utility from unsuccessful search in all periods $1, \ldots, T-1$ and termination of search at $T-1$, whereas V_{T-1} gives the returns from unsuccessful search in all periods $1, \ldots, T-1$ but continuation of search for one more period. In terms of the diagram (Fig. 12.1) this condition implies that the policy curve AB does not lie below CT^* in the neighbourhood of B. In view of the shape of AB and CT^*, if this condition is satisfied AB is likely to lie entirely above CT^* at all $t = 1, \ldots, T$. Using the functional equation (5) of chapter 6, and the terminal condition $V_T = U(\mathbf{J}_{oT})$, this condition may be written as

$$a_T W_T + (1 - a_T)\, U(\mathbf{J}_{oT}) > U(\mathbf{J}_{oT-1}), \tag{2}$$

where a_T denotes the probability of accepting the offer observed at T and W_T the expected utility from acceptance. Condition (2) implies that the individual must prefer the gamble with outcomes W_T and $U(\mathbf{J}_{oT})$ with probability of occurrence, repectively, a_T and $1 - a_T$, to the certainty of $U(\mathbf{J}_{oT-1})$. Now $U(\mathbf{J}_{oT-1})$ exceeds $U(\mathbf{J}_{oT})$ by the cost of search at T (in utility units), so condition (2) is not necessarily satisfied for all utility functions and distributions of offers. Since (2) is necessary for the optimality of T, if there is a T which does not satisfy (2), then that T cannot serve as optimal search horizon, in that the individual will search at most until period $T - 1$.

Thus if the utility cost of search is positive the optimal search horizon is not necessarily equal to the maximum number of periods the individual can search in his work horizon. However, a positive cost of search is not sufficient for discouragement, but necessary. It is not sufficient because the cost of search may be positive and yet (2) may be satisfied for $T = T^* - 1$. It is necessary because if the cost of search is zero the optimal search horizon is certainly equal to $T^* - 1$. Putting a zero cost of search in (2) we obtain $U(\mathbf{J}_{oT}) = U(\mathbf{J}_{oT-1})$, and since $W_T \geq U(\mathbf{J}_{oT})$ by its definition, (2) is satisfied for all utility functions and distributions of offers (except when S_T is empty, in which case search will stop *temporarily* at T). The left-hand side of (2) is equal to V_{T-1} obtained with horizon T, and the right-hand side to V_{T-1} obtained with horizon $T - 1$, so, since the former exceeds the latter, the expected returns from search with horizon T exceed those with horizon $T - 1$. Hence it is always optimal to choose T instead of $T - 1$, provided $T \neq T^*$, i.e. search will continue either until an acceptable job is found or until the age of retirement.

Thus a worker who chooses to participate in the labour market will be discouraged and drop out of the labour force before retirement age only if the 'psychic' and/or monetary cost of search is positive. An increase in the cost of search will increase the chances of early termination of search, whereas if costs fall to zero there will be no discouragement. The effect of variations in searching costs on discouragement may be seen more directly by writing (2) as

$$a_T[W_T - U(\mathbf{J}_{oT})] > U(\mathbf{J}_{oT-1}) - U(\mathbf{J}_{oT}). \qquad (2)$$

This says that the individual will search at T if the expected marginal revenue exceeds the marginal cost in that period (both in utility units). An increase in searching costs will therefore increase the changes of discouragement.

In Fig. 12.3, when the cost of search is zero the failure curve becomes a straight line, CB, since the only factor that produced a downward pressure on CT^* (Fig. 12.1) was the cost of search. Since searching costs are only one, certainly not very important, factor inducing a decline in reservation values, policy curves are still forward falling when the searching cost is zero. Thus all policy curves must lie entirely above CB, so AB, the curve with horizon $T^* - 1$, is the optimal one, i.e. there is participation but no discouragement.

Now suppose there is a positive searching cost and the individual's policy is as in Fig. 12.1. The comparative-static analysis of participation and discouragement may be conducted by considering shifts of the curves in this diagram. Any factor which induces an upward shift in the policy curve AB, especially in the neighbourhood of B, leads to an increase in the chances of participation and an increase in the length of time needed before discouragement. However, this does not necessarily lead to a fall in the chances of discouragement, because

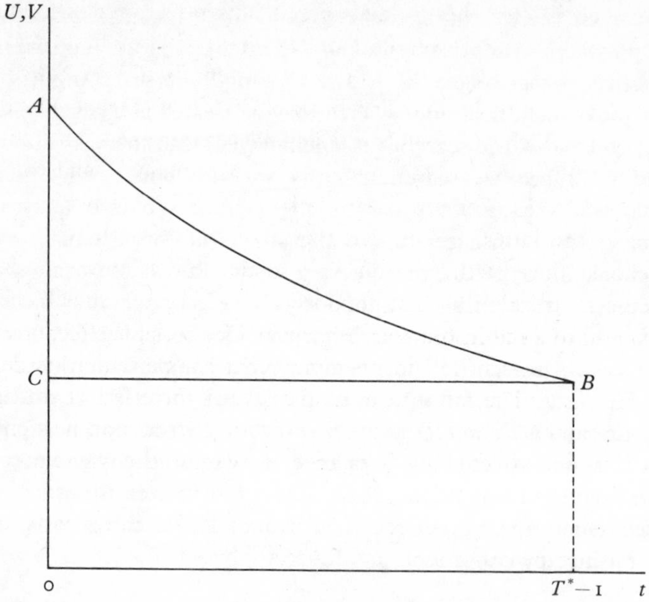

Fig. 12.3

when AB shifts up, the individual's reservation values rise, and, depending on the cause of the shfit, the chances of success in any single period may diminish (see below). So, although when AB shifts up the individual is *potentially* less likely to be discouraged, the probability of actually being discouraged, $P'(T) = (1 - a_1) \dots (1 - a_T)$, may rise. On the other hand, when the failure curve CT^* shifts up the chances of participation diminish, whereas the chances of discouragement will definitely increase, because T falls and the probability of success in any period before T remains the same. Considering this kind of individual behaviour as 'typical', any factor that leads to an upward shift in AB increases the participation rate and the willingness of people to remain in the market for longer periods, even though their experience during search may be disappointing; an upward shift in CT^* reduces the participation rate and increases the discouragement rate.

The factors which lead to shifts in AB and CT^* were examined in some detail in chapter 10. Recalling, AB shifts up when wage offers increase, when firms' recruitment standards fall, and when the individual's risk tolerance increases. On the other hand CT^* shifts up when there is an increase in non-wage income, including unemployment compensation, and when there is an increase in the relative attractiveness of leisure. Changes in searching costs and unemployment insurance (which may be treated as a negative searching cost when the searcher is unemployed) lead to shifts in both *AB* and CT^* because searching costs are also borne when search is successful, i.e. they are part of the lifetime job whether search is successful or unsuccessful, so the effects of their changes are ambiguous in terms of the diagram alone. But as we argued above, increases in searching costs (and so decreases in unemployment benefits) lead to a fall in the search horizon. One possible effect of a rise in the cost of search (fall in unemployment compensation) is depicted in Fig. 12.4. The fall in searching costs has the effect of shifting *AB* to *A′B′* and CT^* to *CD*. (Note that the utility from non-participation, *OC*, is not affected by a change in searching costs, whereas the total returns from search, *OA*, fall, because searching costs enter the lifetime job which gives V_0. Also *AB* and CT^* fall by the same amount at *T*, since by definition $V_T = U(\mathbf{J}_{0T})$.)

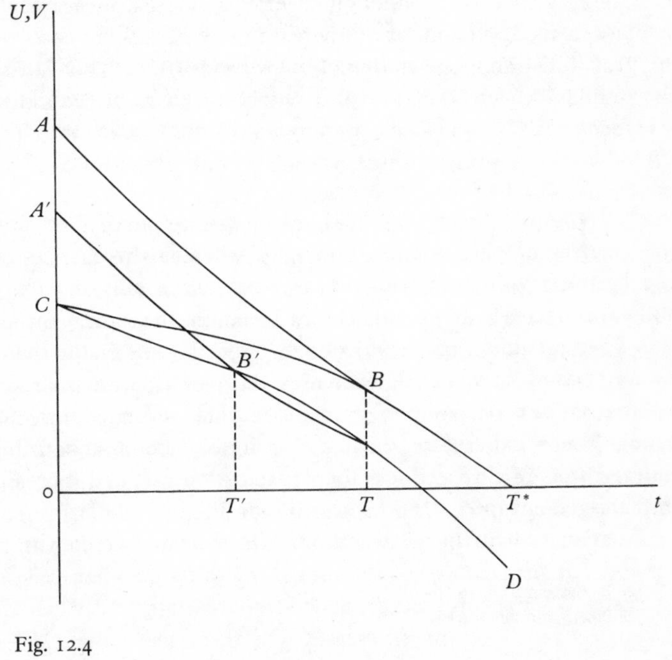

Fig. 12.4

Thus, the following changes will increase the total participation rate in the market: an increase in wage offers, a fall in recruitment standards, an increase in risk tolerance, a fall in non-wage income, a fall in the attractiveness of leisure, a fall in the cost of searching, and an increase in unemployment compensation to active searchers. These include the most important factors identified in the literature, but also some neglected ones.[7]

Changes in the aggregate discouragement rate are more difficult to analyse because of the simultaneous change in the probability of finding a job, and the search horizon, observed when *AB* shifts. However, an upward shift in CT^*, with *AB* remaining fixed, will definitely increase the discouragement rate, because it reduces the search horizon and leaves the probability of success unchanged. Thus an increase in non-wage income or in the relative attractiveness of leisure increases the discouragement rate. Moreover, increases in wage offers and decreases in recruitment standards, although they increase reservation wages, lead to an *increase* in the probability of finding a job, so they both lead to a decrease in the discouragement rate. This leaves risk aversion, the cost of searching, and unemployment compensation, which have ambiguous effects on discouragement. An increase in risk aversion, or an increase in net searching costs reduce the probability that the individual will be still without a job after a few periods' search, but they also reduce the periods the individual will spend searching before dropping out of the labour force. The net effect on the aggregate discouragement rate observed is therefore an empirical issue.

The various hypotheses about participation that feature in empirical labour market analyses may be shown to be hypotheses about shifts in one of the two curves *AB* and CT^*. Thus the 'discouraged-worker hypothesis' asserts that as unemployment increases and wages decline the chances of finding a job decline, so potential entrants to the labour market are discouraged from entering, and employees declared redundant or long-standing unemployed searchers are induced to leave it.[8] In terms of our model, the discouraged-worker hypothesis simply states two of the factors that shift the policy curve *AB* downwards (admittedly the most important ones): reduction in firms' wage offers and reduction in the prob-

[7] See Bowen and Finegan (1969), in particular ch. 2.
[8] See Bowen and Finegan (1969, pp. 24–5).

ability of being offered a job. As we have seen, these particular causes of the shift lead unambiguously to a fall in the participation and an increase in the discouragement rate.

The 'additional-worker hypothesis' asserts that as husbands become unemployed and family income falls, wives are induced to look for a job to boost family income.[9] Now if our 'individual' stands for 'wife', husband's income is a non-wage income to the wife. Thus when the husband becomes unemployed, the wife's non-wage income falls and the attractiveness of her leisure decreases, because the husband can now stay at home and do the housework. These two factors, as we have seen, lead unambiguously to a downward shift in the failure curve CT^*, so wives' participation rates will increase, and their discouragement rates will decline. It follows that the 'discouraged-worker hypothesis' is a hypothesis about shifts in the policy curve AB, whereas the 'additional-worker hypothesis' is a hypothesis about shifts in the failure curve CT^*.

In contrast to permanent terminations of search before retirement age, *temporary* terminations may be observed even if the cost of searching is zero. Thus consider any sequence of distributions f_1, $\ldots, f_T$ and let the distributions for late periods shift favourably, those for the current and near-future periods remaining fixed. This change will lead to an increase in the reservation values for *all* periods prior to the expected boom, so, given that in early periods the distributions of offers are fixed, there will now be less offers available which the individual would be willing to take. Search will *not* take place in the current and near-future periods when the improvement in the more distant distributions is such that there are no job offers which the individual would be willing to accept currently, i.e. when the acceptance sets for small t become empty.

Thus the only necessary condition for temporary terminations of search is that conditions in the labour market be considered more favourable in the more remote future than in the nearer one. (Once again this condition is not sufficient.) The higher the cost of searching, however, the more common will temporary terminations be. To show this (and also derive a more explicit condition on temporary terminations), suppose the individual is told that he is to incur the cost of searching at *every* period before acceptance of an offer, whether he searches or not. Let $V'_0, \ldots, V'_T$ be the reservation values derived

[9] See Bowen and Finegan (1969, pp. 21–2).

under this constraint. Relax this constraint subsequently and suppose that only the cost of those periods during which search actually takes place has to be borne. Let $V_0, \ldots, V_T$ be the new reservation values. Since the searching cost at period t is part of the lifetime job obtained from acceptance at any period from t onwards, if the cost of searching is not borne at t, the distributions of job offers in periods $t + 1, \ldots, T$ *improve*, and the utility from unsuccessful termination, $U(\mathbf{J}_{ot'})$, also increases by a corresponding amount at all $t' = t, \ldots, T$. Thus if search terminates temporarily at t there will be a new terminal reservation value $V_T > V'_T$, and also new values $V_t, \ldots, V_{T-1}$ exceeding the respective values $V'_t, \ldots, V'_{T-1}$. The utility evaluation of the cost of search at t may therefore be measured by the difference $V_t - V'_t$.

But if search does not take place at t, the new reservation value V_{t-1}, for $t - 1$, will be equal to V_t. Moreover, if V_{t-1} exceeds V'_{t-1}, then the total returns from search when no search takes place at t, V_0, will also exceed the returns when search takes place at every period, V'_0. Hence the individual will not search at t if and only if

$$V_{t-1} = V_t > V'_{t-1}.$$

Substituting V'_{t-1} from the functional equation (5) of chapter 6 and rearranging we obtain

$$V_t - V'_t > a'_t(W'_t - V'_t), \tag{3}$$

where the primes denote the values obtained under the constraint that the searching cost be borne in all periods in the search horizon. Since the left-hand side measures the addition to total searching costs, and the right-hand side the addition to total returns, from search at t, this appears to be one way of stating the familiar condition that search will take place at t only if the marginal cost does not exceed the expected marginal returns at that period, and it is a generalization of condition (2′) to all periods in the search horizon.

However, it is important to see this condition within the context of the sequential model. Since when one chooses the search horizon T optimally, search can only stop *temporarily* at any period before T, condition (3) does not say that search will continue until the returns from one more period's search fall below the costs from that period. Condition (3) presumes resumption of search after t, so it is important to regard it simply as the condition on temporary terminations – given an optimal policy before and after t, search will stop temporarily at *t* only if the costs from search at *t* exceed the additional returns from search at that period.

Thus if the cost of search increases, temporary terminations will be more common. If the individual can get a part-time job or other temporary employment during a temporary termination of search, then the returns from that employment must be taken into account in the evaluation of the cost of search. There is in fact some evidence that, for primary males at least, the slumps we have been experiencing since the war have not been serious enough to induce abandonment of search, even on a temporary basis, but when temporary employment was available such termination did take place.[10] For women and old males, on the other hand, the utility evaluation of the cost of search is sufficiently high to induce temporary and some permanent terminations of search even during mild slumps.[11]

Layoffs and quits

Up to now we considered changes in the stock of searchers coming from outside the labour force, i.e. 'births' of searchers through increases in the participation rate and 'deaths' of searchers through the discouragement of potential entrants and long-standing unemployed searchers. As we have seen, such changes are primarily features of the secondary labour force, since primary males normally exhibit 100 per cent participation rate and no discouragement. Thus the birth of primary searchers must be sought from within the labour market, i.e. from layoffs and quits from existing jobs.

Layoffs, as we have seen, are a feature of the fixwage system. The fixwage firm keeps its wages more or less fixed, and chooses a recruitment standard for the current period, given current conditions and its expectations for the future. The behaviour of the recruitment standard – which is in the form of a minimum efficiency level required from potential employees – is formally similar to the behaviour of reservation wages.[12] If conditions are as predicted, recruitment standards will never rise over time. But if conditions change, e.g. if prices fall or the supply of labour increases, the firm may respond by raising

[10] See MacKay's (1972*b*) study of car workers during the 1966 slump and the 1967–8 recovery.

[11] See footnote 2 of this chapter.

[12] See chapter 4.

its recruitment standards. Thus when conditions are as predicted no worker will ever be laid off, since when the recruitment standard does not rise from t to $t + 1$ those taken on at t will certainly qualify in $t + 1$. But if some change takes place which has the effect of raising firms' recruitment standards, some of those who previously qualified for a job with the firm may now be too inefficient to qualify. When recruitment standards, rise, those whose contribution to production falls below the new minimum requirement are dismissed, so every time conditions change such that some firms may find it optimal to raise their recruitment standards there will be a number of layoffs of each firm's less efficient employees.[13] Such increases in recruitment standards occur in a trade slump, when prices decline and it becomes easier to find new employees because of the increase in the aggregate unemployment rate, and when vacancies and labour's reservation wages fall.[14]

Thus during trade slumps there will be a supply of new searchers, put into the unemployment pool by fixwage firms. Some of these workers, may, of course, decide to leave the labour force, either temporarily or on a more permanent basis, and not search for a new job. This kind of behaviour, however, will be more typical of the secondary labour force, for whom there are more attractive alternatives available when the prospects of finding a new job are very low. Primary males are likely to embark on search for a new job when they are made redundant, or if they expect the slump to be short-lived they may take a lower-grade, temporary job until recovery, and search when the prospects for a new job improve. Layoffs are an important source of new searchers in practice, something which reflects the fact that most firms hesitate to change their wages as often as their prices.

However, some wage changes do take place, and it is mainly in

[13] In chapter 3 we argued that the firm does not take on employees on a temporary basis until more efficient men can be found, either because of turnover costs or because of long-term employment contracts. These same constraints may also reduce the number of layoffs when recruitment standards rise, or they may lead to a lag between the time of the raising of the recruitment standard and the time of the layoffs.

[14] Since prices are flexible in our system, a trade slump leads to a fall in prices. If prices were rigid the slump would be manifested in other ways (e.g. unsold stocks of goods) but its effects would be the same. Since the firm dismisses its less efficient employees it is mainly unskilled, or less efficient skilled, workers that are more prone to redundancy in a slump and who are more easy to re-employ in the recovery. On this, see Reder (1955) and Oi (1962). On the characteristics of those made redundant in the West Midlands in 1966 see MacKay (1972*a*).

response to these that workers quit to search for a new job, or to join another firm after on-the-job search.[15] In a wholly flexwage world there will, of course, be no layoffs, since the firm will be willing to employ any worker, as long as he is willing to accept a suitably chosen wage offer. Thus all movement of workers between firms will be the result of voluntary quitting.[16] As we have seen in the last chapter most workers will choose to search on-the-job and quit only if and when they find a better job. Some, however, may quit before finding a new job, to search more vigorously whilst unemployed. In the remaining part of this chapter we shall consider the choice between remaining in the job already held or searching for another, without specifying whether one who chooses to search quits or searches on-the-job, and whether, in the latter case, he ever manages to find a new job to take, or whether he keeps his current job after all. Since our primary interest at this point is in the flow of new searchers into the market this simplification is not restrictive.

Suppose the worker is currently employed at a job $\mathbf{J}_c$, which yields him utility $U(\mathbf{J}_c)$. Let again V_0 denote the expected returns from search, but now write V_0 as the expected utility from all possible job situations that searching may yield,[17] i.e.

$$V_0 = \sum_{t=1}^{T} \sum_{k} \Pr(i_{kt})\, U(\mathbf{J}_{kt}) \quad \text{for all } \mathbf{J}_{kt} \in S_t,$$

where i_{kt} is the event 'accept job $\mathbf{J}_k$ in period t', $\Pr(i_{kt})$ is the probability of occurrence of that event, equal to $(1 - a_1) \ldots (1 - a_{t-1}) f_t(\mathbf{J}_k)$ for each acceptable job $\mathbf{J}_k$, and $\mathbf{J}_{kt}$ is the lifetime job that results from acceptance of $\mathbf{J}_k$ in period t. The individual will remain in his current job and not search for another as long as $U(\mathbf{J}_c) \geq V_0$. If some change takes place which results in the violation of this condition then he will search for another job.

Let w_c be the wage rate that the individual is currently receiving from his job, $\mathbf{w}_c^+$ be the vector of all wage rates over and above w_c, and p be the general level of prices. Since V_0 is defined over acceptable

[15] Quits may, of course, also arise in a fixwage system. For instance, if recruitment standards decline a worker may realize that it is now easier to qualify for a better job, so he may search some firms to see if there are any vacancies. But quitting will be less frequent when own wages in relation to others are fixed than when wages change.

[16] Such is the case in the flexwage models of Phelps *et al.* (1970). See for instance the paper by Mortensen in that volume, p. 172.

[17] See above, chapter 7.

offers, changes in unacceptable offers do not affect behaviour. When the individual is currently earning w_c and is seeking a new job he may choose a high reservation wage at the start of search, but he will gradually lower it towards w_c if search proceeds unsuccessfully. Thus V_0 depends on p, w_c and $\mathbf{w}_c^+$, whereas the utility from the current job, $U(\mathbf{J}_c)$, depends on p and w_c.

It is clear from the discussion of chapter 7 that the individual is free of money illusion, so the utility from the current job is homogeneous of degree zero in p and w_c. Similarly, the expected utility V_0 is homogeneous in p, w_c and $\mathbf{w}_c^+$, provided the set of states of nature does not change by proportional changes in w_c and $\mathbf{w}_c^+$. However, given that proportional changes in w_c and $\mathbf{w}_c^+$ cause changes in the shape of the wage distribution, this proviso will not be usually met. An equi-proportional increase in all wage rates leads to an increase in the spread of the distribution, and so it leads to a change in V_0 over and above the increase caused by the rightward shift in the distribution. If the individual is not 'very' risk averse he will benefit from the increase in the spread of the distribution, so V_0 will increase.[18] Thus V_0 will not in general be homogeneous in p, w_c and $\mathbf{w}_c^+$, although it is an expected utility function which depends on prices and wage rates. However, if the individual is risk averse, the change in V_0 caused by the change in the shape of the wage distribution will be very small compared to the change caused by the horizontal shift.

Let D denote the difference

$$D = U(p, w_c) - V_0(p, w_c, \mathbf{w}_c^+).$$

Clearly, if $D \geq 0$ the worker will remain employed at his current job, being satisfied with the terms of employment, but if $D < 0$ he will join the pool of active searchers. In considering voluntary additions to the stock of searchers we must therefore assume $D \geq 0$, and examine the factors that may reverse the sign of D.

The most important changes that may reverse the sign of D are those which influence the position of the own wage rate in relation to other wage rates. Any change which does not alter the relative position of w_c will have only a minor effect on D, if at all. Thus, an increase in the general price level may reduce D to some extent because when the marginal utility of real income is diminishing the utility from the current job may be affected to a greater extent than

[18] See above, chapter 10.

the utility from the better jobs; but a price increase may also increase the individual's aversion to risk by reducing the real value of his wealth, and so reduce the expected returns from search. Overall, changes in prices are not likely to have a significant effect on searching activity. Another change that may have some effect on searching activity is a proportional increase in prices and wages. If p, w_c, and $\mathbf{w}_c^+$ increase by the same proportion, the utility from the current job remains fixed, but the returns from search may increase because of the increase in the spread of the wage distribution. Thus searching activity may be stimulated. If the individual is 'very' risk averse the effect may be in the opposite direction. Finally, minor changes in search activity may be caused by a proportional increase in all wage offers with prices remaining fixed. In this case searching activity may increase because of the increase in the spread of the wage distribution, but also because when wealth increases the individual becomes more tolerant to small risks, and so the expected returns from search may increase further, over and above the increase in the current utility level.

The most important changes in searching activity, however, arise when the position of the own wage rate *vis-à-vis* other wage rates changes – what we may loosely call changes in the individual's *relative* wage. If one or more wage rates, other than the one currently received by the individual, increase, then V_0 rises, so D falls. Thus, when other wages rise with the own wage rate remaining fixed, searching activity is stimulated, in that the individual may find it optimal to join the pool of active searchers and try and discover the higher wage rates. Clearly, when other wage rates rise with the own wage rate remaining fixed the individual's relative wage falls.

The relative wage will also fall, with the result that searching activity will be stimulated, when the own wage rate falls and all other wage rates remain fixed. Thus, when w_c falls and $\mathbf{w}_c^+$ remains fixed D necessarily falls, so searching activity is stimulated: although the expected returns from search will also suffer from a wage cut (since the current job is one of the possible job situations that searching may uncover and, if the individual is searching on-the-job with the option of remaining at the current job if he does not find a better one, not an unlikely one), the utility from remaining at the current job suffers a lot more.

It follows that the factor most likely to encourage searching for a new job is a wage cut at the job currently held. Wage increases in other jobs will also encourage searching, but they will not have the same effect on searching activity as the wage cut, unless *all* other wages rise in the same proportion except the own wage. In other words, when the relative wage falls the individual may choose to search for a new job. The own wage rate affects the relative wage to a much greater extent than any other wage rate taken in isolation.

Suppose now we are in an uncertain world where workers are only imperfectly informed of other firms' wage rates, and where wages are not fixed across firms and over time. This, of course, will be the world of our flexwage firms when there is no central coordination of their action. If then prices rise by a certain proportion, the individual receives a cut in his real wage rate, but the difference between the utility from his current job and the expected returns from search remains fixed, since the individual knows with certainty that when prices rise the real wage rate of *all* firms falls in exactly the same proportion.

But if the fall in an individual's real income is due to a fall in his money wages there is a number of possibilities, depending on the way in which expectations are formed and revised over time. At one extreme the individual may suppose that sooner or later all other wage rates will follow suit, so search is neither encouraged nor discouraged, i.e. the effects of the wage cut are the same as the effects of the price increase. At the other extreme he may suppose that there is no reason for similar changes in other wages, so the returns from search stay the same and, with the utility from the own job falling, search is encouraged. In the intermediate case, which is likely to be the most common, the individual revises his expectations for other job offers downwards, but not by the full extent of the wage cut. So V_0 falls as well, but not by as much as $U(\mathbf{J}_c)$. Wage expectations in this case are said to be inelastic.

Search then is encouraged, but in a world where the individual is uncertain about the changes in other jobs, he is unlikely to give up his job at the first wage cut to search for another. Rather, he is likely to want to collect more information about the market before taking a final decision, and this may be done by on-the-job search, or waiting to see whether general unemployment is rising, or whether the economy is booming. In any case, he is better off if he resists the wage cut whatever the changes in the market as a whole. Becoming unemployed to search involves too many uncertainties and immediate psychic costs, so he is unlikely to give up his job to search for another without resisting the wage cut in the first place. However, the potential existence of search acts both as a threat to employers and as a force on which the worker can resist the wage cut, since if the relative position of a job lags behind for a long time, more and more workers will be giving up the job to search for another, or join another one which they found after on-the-job search, and fewer (new) searchers will be willing to accept it even if offered it.

It follows that if a worker's expectations are inelastic it is not illogical for him to resist a money-wage cut more strongly than a price increase, because, although they both lead to a fall in real wages, the former makes searching for a new job more attractive and the worker feels his bargaining position improved.[19]

[19] This is a proposition used by Alchian (1970) and Leijonhufvud (1968, pp. 75–81) to rationalize the existence of money-wage rigidity in Keynes's system. See below, p. 236, for criticism.

PART III

Market Interaction

13

Short-run Equilibrium and Long-run Extensions

It is time we paused and looked back, to see where our theory is leading us, and to ensure that the behaviour we have been attributing to the two parties in the exchange, firms and households, is indeed consistent with the market structure and trading rules originally assumed. This question is extremely important, and the fact that it is neglected by the majority of existing models does not render it any easier – it simply warns of the difficulty involved in answering it. At a different plane of analysis, admittedly not so important as the first, we would like to know what happens in the long run – how does the firm choose its capital and how does the worker choose his skill, and how do these affect the short-run behaviour we have already described? This chapter will attempt to give answers to these questions.

The persistence of wage variability

The novel feature of our model is the absence of a central organization in the labour market, such as the Walrasian auctioneer, which can convey full information about potential buyers and sellers of labour services and conduct exchange. Exchange in the labour market has to take place directly between firm and worker, and the terms agreed between any pair of transactors need not be the same as the terms agreed between any other pair. We called this market decentralized, and considered in detail the behaviour of the two parties in the transaction, both in this and the other markets in the system. All markets apart from the labour market are completely centralized (Walrasian) markets, which are in supply-and-demand equilibrium at every point of time.

The trading arrangement in the labour market is fairly general, and stems directly from the sequential model of job search. At every point of time each firm that wishes to buy labour services offers a wage rate for every hour of work supplied. It is then contacted by an individual who wishes to sell labour services, and who considers whether to accept to sell at the offered wage or not; and if yes, how much to sell. If they both agree to the exchange it takes place; if not, the worker turns to another firm and the firm makes an offer for a second time. The worker will look at the wage rate in relation to that offered by other firms before deciding whether to accept or reject the offer. The firm will look at the worker's efficiency in relation to its wage offer and the efficiency of others in the market before deciding whether to agree to buy the quantity offered by the worker or not. The special features of labour services as commodities[1] give the analysis the special character which it has taken, simplify it by enabling it to concentrate on one particular problem which has received considerable scrutiny in the past from different viewpoints, and introduce empirical content into the analysis. Although the empirical side has often taken second place to the theoretical, in the few instances where we did digress into the outside world we found a very satisfactory confirmation of our theoretical expectations.

But despite the various restrictions which the special features of labour made possible, the underlying model remains one of a decentralized market upon which an explicit trading arrangement is imposed. Theoretical interest therefore extends beyond the confines of a labour market, and it goes deep into post-Samuelsonian adjustment theory and post-Patinkin monetary theory. In this chapter we close the system by considering the market mechanism which results from the individual models which we considered – in particular whether the trading arrangement is 'robust': will optimal individual behaviour in the light of the assumed trading arrangement undermine the arrangement, or will it result in perpetual reconfirmation?

The problem may be put differently. We have seen that when firms' wages differ, workers may find it optimal to walk into a firm, find out how much it is willing to offer them, and walk out again to search another firm. When workers walk away from firms, however,

[1] These include: labour is attached to the human agent so it cannot be resold; firms need labour to produce and sell for profit, whereas households offer labour services to get the income necessary to buy commodities; if two parties agree to an exchange then that exchange must be repeated for a few periods at the very least (there is an employment contract); each worker can only work for one firm at a time; human capital does not depreciate and it can only be improved through a time-consuming educational process (i.e. it is fixed in the short run).

the firm realizes that it has some monopsony power – the higher the wage it offers the less workers will walk away. Since workers try to find as high a wage as possible, they will try to take advantage of wage variability and search a number of firms before accepting an offer. Similarly, since firms try to maximize profits they will try to exploit their monopsony power to their advantage. Will wage variability persist when workers and firms take advantage of this power they have? If it does not, our trading arrangement will collapse under the pressure of the forces which it set up in the first place.

Fortunately wage variability will not disappear in the short run when the participants observe the trading rules, however hard they try to exploit their respective powers. There is a large number of factors which ensure that wage variability will persist, some of which are consistent with our model but have not been mentioned explicitly because they were not central to the analysis, but also some others which were of crucial importance and were discussed extensively in previous chapters. For our purposes it suffices to show, in a flexwage world, that (1) given a distribution of reservation wages, optimal entrepreneurial behaviour under the postulated trading arrangement leads to a distribution of wage offers, and (2) given a distribution of wage offers, optimal worker behaviour leads to a distribution of reservation wages. In a fixwage world we need to show that there will be a distribution of minimum acceptable coefficient levels, i.e. that firms' recruitment standards will be different.[2]

The most important factors outside our trading arrangement that ensure that firms will offer different wages for the same type of labour are the existence of alternative policies of recruitment, ranging from the fixwage extreme to the flexwage, the existence of differences in the technological arrangements of firms which ensure that some workers are more efficient with some firms than with others, and the existence of differences in the non-pecuniary characteristics of jobs.

In our analysis of optimal firm behaviour we considered behaviour under the fixwage and flexwage systems without saying what factors may induce a firm to follow one system rather than the other. In practice the firm is free to choose the extent of wage flexibility which

[2] Showing this does not necessarily imply that there will be a stationary equilibrium distribution of wages. However, this question does not concern us here. For some analysis of the (static) behaviour of markets when there is a stationary distribution of wages see Lucas and Prescott (1974) and Stiglitz (1974).

it should allow in its optimal policy, so it is free to choose to operate in a fixwage or flexwage environment, or in any position between the two. In general the firm will choose that system which yields highest expected profits, so firms will choose different wage policies if there is not a unique degree of wage flexibility that maximizes profits. But if the extent of wage flexibility does not influence the flow of labour to a firm, then the two instruments of firm policy – the wage offer and the recruitment standard – enter the determination of expected profits symmetrically,[3] so the firm may vary one or the other to achieve maximum returns. If not all firms allow the same degree of wage flexibility in their optimal policy, wage offers will differ, and since the same profit may be obtained from different policies there is no reason why firms should follow the same policy. In the long run new factors may induce all firms to reduce wage flexibility, but the uniqueness of desired flexibility will not necessarily be ensured.[4]

Secondly, firms may choose to offer different wages because of the existence of different technological arrangements within firms, which imply that a worker is not necessarily equally efficient in all firms. Thus even if all firms paid the same wage rate per unit of labour efficiency supplied, they will not be paying the same wage rate per unit of man-hour offered. The technology chosen by the firm is part of the long-run decision, so firms may not choose the same technology. Like the choice of wage flexibility the firm may again be shown to have 'too many' control variables at its disposal which lead to the non-uniqueness of the optimal technology. Thus, suppose that the firm has the option of choosing between a technology which can be operated by skills which are available in the market, and a better technology which requires some training expenditure on new labour. If the firm chooses the second type of technology it will be producing more per man-hour employed, but it will also have to pay a training cost if one of its own employees quits and is replaced by a new recruit. Thus labour turnover is more costly for the firm which chooses the second type of technology than for the firm which chooses the first. Therefore the firm may choose one of the following three possibilities: a technology of the first type; a technology of the second type, offer the same wage rate as in the first case and spend the profit from the additional production on training new labour;

[3] See chapter 3.

[4] See below, pp. 236–7.

a technology of the second type and spend the profit from the additional production on higher wage offers to reduce labour turnover. In general it is not possible to say which alternative will be preferred by the firm, since the only difference between the three alternatives lies in the distribution of expenditure: in the first case the firm foregoes some production by choosing the first technology, in the second it spends more on labour turnover, and in the third it spends more on wages. Since profit-maximizing firms are indifferent about the distribution of their expenditure some firms may choose one alternative and others another. If there is a continuum of possible technologies the possibilities for variations in the policies of different firms increase.[5]

The final source of wage variability which is independent of our trading arrangement, but consistent with the general framework of the model, is the existence of non-pecuniary characteristics of jobs. Since workers' preferences among non-pecuniary characteristics are likely to differ, there is no unique wage rate that can compensate for the non-pecuniary features of a job. Thus, only if all workers valued all non-pecuniary characteristics equally would it be possible for each job to have the same 'net advantage' to all workers. Since jobs have characteristics which are subjective to the holder of the job, such as the personality of colleagues or the holder's aversion to the likelihood of future dismissal or wage reduction, an objectively measured characteristic such as the wage rate cannot compensate all workers equally. Thus, even if all jobs have the same net advantage for one worker, they are not likely to have it for another.

The trading arrangement which we have assumed is, of course, independent of these sources of wage variability, so an alternative arrangement may be used and still ensure that wage variability persists.[6] But there are also some other sources of wage variability which are peculiar to our trading arrangement and so may not arise under different arrangements. We may refer to the most important of these as *history*. History will affect the wage offers of different firms because if some workers are willing to accept a given offer whereas some others not (i.e. if there is a distribution of reservation wages),

[5] Models which make this their most important source of wage variability were explored by Salop (1973*b*) and Stiglitz (1974).

[6] Like our arrangement, this alternative arrangement should also be shown to preserve the variability created by these outside forces, i.e. it should contain nothing which would tend to cancel the operation of these forces.

the experience of firms in the labour market will diverge. If a firm is lucky enough it may find a worker in the first period, if it is not it may have to wait a few periods before recruiting someone. Since there is a probability between zero and one that a vacancy will be filled in any period, the experience of firms, in the sense of how many periods they have had their vacancies standing idle, will diverge. In our model of optimal firm behaviour we have seen that the number of periods the vacancy has been standing idle is an important factor in the determination of the wage offer, in that the 'reasonable' firm will be increasing its offer over time as workers search it and walk out again without taking the job. Since the experience of firms will diverge in a random fashion, as to whether the firm is lucky enough to be searched quickly by a worker with a low reservation wage, their wage offers will also diverge.

A second source of wage variability which is peculiar to our trading arrangement is the length of the short run (T elementary periods). If the length of the run is different for different firms then their wage offers are also likely to differ, because, as we have shown in chapter 3, the length of the run specifies the terminal condition of the dynamic sequence that determines the optimal wage policy, and so is an important determinant of that policy.

The length of the short run depends partly on the nature of the firm's business, e.g. whether it produces goods which require very durable capital or goods which may also be produced with a small amount of capital, and partly on firm policy both before and after the installation of capital. The policy before the installation of capital affects the length of the short run by determining the technique of production and the amount and durability of capital, whereas the policy after the installation of capital affects the length of the run by determining the optimal replacement time, given the actual course of events. For instance, if the firm uses the profits accumulated during the short run to finance the purchase of capital for the next T elementary periods, an (*ex post*) exceptionally profitable beginning to the short run may induce quicker replacement of the capital than originally planned. However, variations in the number of periods comprising the short run are likely to be small after the installation of capital, and will only take place if events turn out to be very different from those predicted.

A more controversial assumption about the length of the short run is that the length of the run is independent of the number of periods that the capital has been standing idle, i.e. the firm's capital depreciates even if there are some idle vacancies. This assumption, however, may be justified by the fact that capital replacement is mainly the result of economic obsolescence and not physical depreciation. In the model of the firm developed in chapter 3 we adopted the assumption of fixed coefficients in the short run but free substitutability between factors in the long run, as a more realistic description of the environment faced by the firm in its choice of short-run recruitment policy. Under these conditions technological progress is embodied in new machines, so the firm which installs some machines in period t should expect technological progress to render them absolete in some future period $t + T$, independently of the utilization rate of these machines.[7]

Thirdly, firms' wage offers will differ because their information about the market differs. We have argued above that even if firms start from the same initial wage, their wage offers will soon diverge because of the different experience they will have during trading. In general, however, they will not start from the same wage, because when there is no central market organization to convey full information about the market they will be imperfectly informed about the future flow of labour to themselves, given a wage offer. So different firms will conceive of their optimal starting wage offer differently. Since during bilateral exchange the firm will never be able to collect full information about the market, differences in information between firms will persist.[8]

Thus in a flexwage market the wage offers of firms will differ if workers' reservation wages differ. But it can also be shown that reservation wages will differ if wage offers differ. The factors that produce variations in reservation wages are similar to those that produce variations in wage offers, something which is not surprising given that both firms and workers follow a sequential maximization procedure in the same environment. Thus the most important factor within our trading arrangement giving rise to variations in reservation wages is again history, i.e. the experience of the worker during search. When firms' wage offers differ there is a probability between zero and one that a worker will find an acceptable job offer at a firm which he picks either at random or because he has some information about it (but he does not know its wage offer). Thus

7 See, for instance, Salter (1960) and Johansen (1972), and above, p. 31, for the assumption of a fixed T.

8 Rothschild and Yaari, in work reported in Rothschild (1974*a*), have developed a model for commodity markets with recurrent selling where it does not even pay firms to be curious and collect full information about the market.

there is also a probability between zero and one that the worker will continue searching after visiting one firm. Since when a worker walks into a firm and finds its offer too low to be acceptable he will continue searching with a lower reservation wage, the experience of the worker during search, in the sense of the number of periods he has already spent searching, will be an important determinant of his reservation wage. In general, the longer one has spent searching the lower the reservation wage one will have. Since workers' experiences during search diverge in a random fashion their reservation wages will also diverge, even if every worker chose the same reservation wage when he first started the search.

Thus the sequential nature of search and the existence of a distribution of wage offers implies that workers' reservation wages will not be the same at any given point of time. These two factors are sufficient to generate the distribution of reservation wages required for the workings of our decentralized system, but there are other factors within the model which will lead to further differences in reservation wages. These additional factors will affect reservation wages mainly by influencing the value of the wage chosen when the individual starts his search, i.e. they are factors which lead workers to adopt a different reservation wage from the outset of search. They will not influence to any appreciable extent the revision of the reservation wage over time, so this revision will lead to additional differences across workers.

First, searching is a process which takes place in an uncertain environment, so individuals' risk attitudes are an important influence on decision-making.[9] Risk averters, as we have seen, will choose a lower reservation wage to avoid the risk of remaining idle for long time periods, whereas risk lovers will aim for the few very highly-paid jobs available by choosing a higher reservation wage. Thus risk averters will normally choose a lower reservation wage than risk lovers. A firm will in general be better off if it lives in a society dominated by risk averters.

Second, the length of the individual's horizon is also an important determinant of his optimal searching policy, since it completely specifies the terminal condition of the dynamic sequence which gives the optimal reservation utility levels. As we argued in chapter 6 it is what we called the 'search horizon' that plays the crucial role, i.e. the time

[9] See above, pp. 142–3.

of periods that the individual plans to be searching before becoming discouraged and dropping out of the pool of searchers. The search horizon is partly a matter of policy, so individuals' search horizons will be different for the same reasons that reservation wages are different – with the exception of the first reason given above, the searcher's experience in the market. But the search horizon also depends on the individual's age, since it can never extend beyond the age of retirement, so the age of the worker is an additional factor giving rise to variations in search horizons, and through them to variations in reservation wages. *Ceteris paribus*, a higher search horizon implies a higher reservation wage, so the firm may find that older searchers are more willing to accept its offer than younger ones.

Finally, reservation wages will be different because the information that each worker has about the market is different. Like the firm, the searcher in a decentralized market is imperfectly informed about the policy of other searchers and firms, and so he is not aware of all the opportunities available in the market. When there is no central market organization to convey full information about available opportunities no worker will search all firms and learn about their policy before accepting an offer, partly because no worker would be willing to spend as much time searching as is required to search all firms, but more importantly because information will be outdated soon after it is collected if many workers search firms just for information-gathering. The latter will arise because when workers search firms to gather information about their wage offers they will walk into firms, enquire about their job offers and walk out again, and firms will respond to this by changing their wage offers, mostly upwards. Thus the mere act of information-gathering by searchers will cause changes in wage offers, and so it will lead to the outdating of information as it is being collected. But even without this self-defeating mechanism, the optimal searching policy implies that workers will be willing to accept an offer on less than perfect information, so no worker will ever attempt to obtain full information about the market before choosing a reservation wage and accepting a job.

The reason no worker will find it optimal to search all firms before accepting a job offer is the existence of a positive cost of search. This cost is partly the direct monetary cost that has to be paid in order to sample a firm, and partly the indirect time cost, i.e. the income foregone during search. If the individual is employed during search, and searches for another job when he is not at work, then the time cost is the foregone leisure suffered during search. Now, the individual will put a positive value on time costs if the total amount of time available is limited, or if he exhibits a positive rate of time preference. In the case where the time costs take the form of foregone earnings time is limited only when the horizon is finite, since when there is a perfect capital market, money can be transferred freely between periods. But even if the horizon is infinite the existence of a positive rate of time preference or a positive rate of interest will also lead the worker to treat foregone earnings as a cost of search. In the case where the time cost is the cost of foregone leisure, time is limited by its very nature, since leisure-time cannot be transferred from one period to the next. The existence of a finite lifetime or a positive rate of time preference adds to the cost of foregone leisure.

Thus even if the monetary cost of search is equal to zero the individual will still find search a costly activity because of the time cost. It will therefore not pay him to search all firms before accepting a job offer. In our model, however, the horizon was explicitly taken to consist of a finite number of periods, and we argued that this is an important feature of the model, since it explains the phenomenon of variations in participation and discouragement. The replacement of existing employees by new ones which is implied by this phenomenon is a source of ignorance in the market, since when a worker leaves the market he does not pass on to a new entrant the information about job opportunities which he has already collected. This is an additional source of information imperfections, and hence of variations in reservation wages, which results from the finiteness of the horizon.

Thus in the flexwage system there is a distribution of wage offers interacting with a distribution of reservation jobs, and optimal firm and worker behaviour implies that none of the distributions will collapse to a single point. In the fixwage system the distribution of wage offers gives place to a distribution of recruitment standards, whereas the distribution of reservation wages remains the same as before. The same factors that support a distribution of wage offers in the flexwage system support a distribution of recruitment standards in the fixwage system, and given variations in workers' reservation wages and their efficiency, the variations in recruitment standards will persist. Wages, of course, are largely historically given in the fixwage system, so there is no reason why they should be the same across firms. However, variations in recruitment standards are not conditional upon variations in wages. Although it is true that a firm which offers a higher wage will also have a more stringent recruitment standard, wages may be equal across firms and yet recruitment standards differ. Given the wage offer, recruitment standards will vary across firms because, as the wage offer in the flexwage system, they depend on the firm's chosen technology, on its experience in the market, on the length of the planning horizon, and the information that each firm has about the market. However, when the wage rate is equal in all firms, any worker who wishes to participate in the labour market must, by necessity, find that wage rate acceptable, so no firm will experience rejections of its offer by a searcher. Rather, searchers will walk into firms, reveal their efficiency level, and either be offered the job or turned down. Since recruitment standards differ across firms when efficiency levels differ, the worker who is turned down need not 'discourage' himself immediately. A different firm may be willing to recruit him at the same wage rate as the first firm.

Unemployment in the fixwage system where the wage rate is equal across firms is therefore a purely involuntary phenomenon. Workers search firms until they find one which is willing to recruit them. As long as workers' efficiency levels differ, there will be variations between firms' recruitment standards, and so there will be involuntary unemployment and search. However, wage rates are not absolutely fixed in what we have called the fixwage system. They are merely more rigid than prices, i.e. they do not change every time a change in the recruitment policy is required, but they only change under continuous pressure in the same direction for a fairly large number of periods, day-to-day changes in policy being implemented by variations in the recruitment standard. Thus there will be variations of wage rates across firms, and so there will be a fairly rigid distribution of wage offers interacting with a flexible distribution of reservation wages, alongside a flexible distribution of recruitment standards interacting with a rigid distribution of efficiency levels. The result of the first interaction will determine the path of wages and frictional unemployment, whereas the latter interaction will largely be reflected in changes in the level of involuntary unemployment.[10]

[10] This issue is raised again in the next chapter.

Long-run extensions

Thus optimal individual behaviour in the short run implies that a distribution of wage rates will persist over time, and that if the firm is operating in a fixwage system it will take advantage of the heterogeneity of the labour force by fixing a recruitment standard which need not be equal to that of other firms. This conclusion is sufficient for the examination of the short-run behaviour of the market over time, which, as we argued in the Introduction, is the *raison d'être* of the economic analysis of individual behaviour. Nevertheless, we shall make a digression in this section and consider the long-run decision of the two parties in the exchange, workers and firms, and show how this is related to the sequential decision-making that takes place in the short run.

Workers. The worker plans for a lifetime – he only looks for a permanent job and he will rarely retrain into another skill, after he has completed his first training. Thus we may view the labour market as consisting of a number of independent skill markets, each one of which is the market where the buyers and sellers of a particular skill meet. By 'skill' we mean the broad skill which is acquired through time-consuming educational and practical training, so each worker is assumed to possess only one skill, although he may be capable of performing a number of different jobs within his broad occupational group.

The worker's long-run decision with respect to choice of job is the choice of broad occupational group. This problem, which is the typical problem considered by the literature on investment in human capital,[11] is equivalent to the choice of skill market. Every worker has to make this choice before entering the job market for the first time, but some may revise the choice of skill market and move into another market at a later stage. This inter-market movement, however, will continue to be regarded as a long-run decision, since the acquisition of a new skill requires training which normally extends over many time periods and is very costly in terms of direct monetary costs and foregone earnings. Even if a firm is willing to bear the costs of training of some of its employees, not many workers will desire to make the change during their lifetime and those that do

[11] For a collection of representative readings see Blaug (1968).

make it will not make it more than once. Most reallocation of workers between skill markets still takes place gradually, as old workers leave the job market and juveniles are directed to those markets which are in greatest need of workers.

Once the individual has chosen which skill market to enter, he has restricted himself to a particular set of job offers. His problem then, is to choose a job out of the particular skill market which he has entered. When exchange is decentralized his problem is one of job searching. Job searching is a process that takes place in the short run. First, in terms of calendar time, the length of time one devotes to searching for a job is very short when compared with the length of time one plans to spend in a job. Second, in capital-theoretic terms, searching is a short-run investment which is capable of altering to *some* extent the returns from one's human capital, but it is not capable of altering the more 'durable' capital invested during schooling and on-the-job training. Thus once in a skill market, the individual can search firms which make offers to participants in that market. He may change his condition by choosing to search more or less, but he is only able to move within the broader limits set by the long-run decision. It is only when these broader limits do not allow the hope of a good situation which the search process may reveal that he will reconsider the choice of skill market. As long as his skill market is not very slack for a long time, compared with other markets, he will stay there, and if he is not satisfied with his current job he will try to improve it by searching for another.

The net cost which has to be suffered to acquire a new skill, including the direct monetary cost and foregone income and the non-pecuniary features of education and other training, may be viewed as a fee which has to be paid in order to enter some skill market. Once in the skill market, the individual can search firms which make offers to participants in that market, but if he desires to leave that market and enter another one he must incur the cost of entry into the new market, an allowance being made for the fact that the entrant has already acquired a skill so he may not have to go through the whole process again.

The need for search after entry into a skill market, and the persistence of a distribution of job offers, has at least one important implication for the long-run decision – that when choosing how much to invest in himself the individual should take into account the fact that he is choosing a particular *distribution* of job offers which he will search, and not that he is choosing a particular job. Conversely, the need to choose a particular skill market before search carries the important implication that the distribution of job offers is not identical for all searchers and, since the distribution which each individual searches was chosen by him at some earlier point, the search–acceptance decision may not be independent of the human-capital decision. These interdependencies, in their turn, carry important implications for aggregate analysis which have been neglected both by the human-capital literature, which has largely neglected the existence of search, and the search literature, which has largely neglected the existence of occupational choice.[12]

It is not our aim here to develop the aggregate implications of the interdependence between occupational choice and job search. However, as it happens, this interdependence has little effect on the nature of the short-run dynamic process implied by the model of job search, although it does have important implications for the relationship between risk attitudes and the distribution of income.[13] Also, the individual choice model of chapters 6–12 is unaffected, since it describes behaviour in a particular skill market, but strictly speaking it is relevant only if there is no movement of workers between markets, since then the sequence of the distributions of job offers will not be fixed and the definition of the lifetime job will have to be changed to take account of the change in the occupational group. As pointed out above, there is ample empirical evidence which suggests that such movement is very limited, provided we define the occupational groups broadly.

Thus from the point of view of individual choice behaviour the optimal search policy is of the same nature whatever the choice of occupational group, whereas the choice of occupational group is partly influenced by the existence of search. The essentials of the long-run choice problem, and how it is related to search, may be described in the following simple manner.

Suppose that in the combined choice of occupational group and job, the individual attempts to maximize a utility function, which is additive between the utility of the lifetime job obtained via the

[12] However, the pioneers of the literature in human capital did note that job search was a particular problem within the more general problem of investment in human capital. See Becker (1964, pp. 31–3).

[13] See Pissarides (1974) for some analysis of this problem.

search process which takes place after training, and the utility of the cost of that training. Now the former utility is, clearly, the maximum expected returns from search V_0, when both the search horizon and acceptance policy are optimal, since at the time the individual has to choose his skill, job search in the particular skill market chosen is the only alternative open. So the individual should choose that occupational group for which the difference between the expected returns from optimal search and the cost of training is a maximum. Given that imperfect information and search do not influence the cost of training for an occupational group, the effects of imperfect information and search on occupational choice may be analysed via their effects on the expected returns from search V_0.

Let the cost of training for two occupations be equal. Then the individual will choose that occupation for which the expected returns from search are highest. Let V^i_0 be the expected returns from search in one of these occupations and V^j_0 in the other. Occupation i will be chosen if V^i_0 exceeds V^j_0, so, once again we are led into the problems of stochastic-dominance criteria. In the case of occupational choice it is not possible to simplify the dominance conditions, as it was with choice of search horizon, so it is not possible to obtain strong results about the chosen occupation without restricting either the utility function, or distribution over the termination periods, or both. Thus all results about the effects of job search on occupational choice must be conditional on a particular utility function or distribution of offers.

One such restriction is implicit in Adam Smith's assertion that the 'liberal professions' attract a large number of men, despite the fact that the chance of success in them is very small, and that overall they are very unfair lotteries. Adam Smith (1776, pp. 118–22) attributes this to the 'desire of the reputation which attends upon superior excellence in any of them', and to the 'natural confidence which every man has more or less, not only in his own abilities, but in his own good fortune'. The first factor is equivalent to arguing that the utility from the good jobs in the profession is so high that it outweighs the small chance of obtaining such good jobs, whereas the second means that the subjective probability distribution over the jobs calculated by each individual is more favourable than warranted on the aggregate. These factors imply a preference for right skewness in a distribution of offers, which is consistent with risk aversion in the small and can explain the phenomenon even if on average individuals are risk averse. There is some evidence that risk averters do exhibit a preference for right skewness.[14]

Changes in the information network of each occupation, and hence changes in the variability of the distribution of job offers and the riskiness attached to each occupation, are conveniently analysed via shifts in the distribution of job offers, along the lines of the analysis of chapter 10. It appears that if the information network of a particular skill market improves and the distribution of job offers shrinks, those individuals who are willing to accept the average job offered in that skill market are attracted by that change, whereas those who aim for something better than average are repelled. Conversely, if the distribution of offers spreads out, the latter group are attracted and the former repelled.

It is apparent that knowledge of the search policy of a group of individuals may enable the derivation of strong results about occupational choice. Although such knowledge can only help if it is accompanied by a restriction on the utility function, some reasonably mild restrictions are capable of yielding strong results.

Firms. The problem facing the firm in the long run is that of choice of capital and technique of production. Thus in the model of entrepreneurial behaviour we viewed the firm as choosing its capital and technique of production at every T elementary periods, and recruiting labour and producing with fixed capital between the planning dates. So the capital installed at some period t imposes an upper limit on the output of the firm in periods $t + 1, \ldots, t + T$. Actual output, however, may fall short of maximum output because of failure (or unwillingness) to recruit labour immediately in all vacancies. The firm's optimal recruitment policy, and its expectations about the flow supply of labour, determine expected output and profit given the capital equipment installed. Capital influences output and expected profit by setting the upper limit on output and the number of vacancies. In equilibrium the firm should choose that capital to install which, given its rental price, the firm's current labour force, and an

[14] See Alderfer and Bierman (1970) for experimental evidence. See also Tsiang (1972). Knight (1921, pp. 367–8), following up Adam Smith's assertions, talks of preference for skewness on the one hand, and risk preference 'on the average' on the other, as equivalent statements. This, of course, is not in general correct.

optimal recruitment policy in the future, maximizes expected profit.

Suppose the firm plans to install capital which will open up a total of n jobs, but it is currently employing only m men. Then if it does install the capital it will open up $n-m$ new vacancies. Let Z_i be the profit that the firm expects to have from its ith employee if he stays with the firm throughout the short run. Since the efficiency of each one of its employees is known to the firm, it also knows Z_i precisely for all its employees $i = 1, \ldots, m$. However, suppose the firm attaches probability c_i to its ith employee quitting at the time of the purchase of its new capital equipment.[15] Then, if the employee does not quit, the returns from that position will be Z_i, whereas if he does quit the firm will offer the job to the market following an optimal recruitment policy, so its expected returns will be V_0. Thus, the expected returns from the position held now by the ith employee may be written as

$$V'_{0i} = (1 - c_i)Z_i + c_i V_0 \quad (i = 1, \ldots, m). \tag{1}$$

It follows that the firm's total expected profit from the positions which are currently filled is equal to $V'_0 = \sum_{i=1}^{m} V'_{0i}$.

Consider now the expected profit from any new vacancies. If the workers who are taken on in the short run are not expected to quit before the end of the short run, the expected profit of the firm from each one of its vacancies is equal to the expected returns from an optimal recruitment policy, V_0. Since the production function exhibits fixed coefficients in the short run, the total expected profit from all the vacancies is equal to the sum of the returns from each individual vacancy.

However, since searchers do not in general know how many vacancies exist in each firm, the supply of labour to the firm is largely independent of the number of vacancies opened up by the firm. Thus the supply of labour *to each vacancy* is a declining function of the number of vacancies opened up by the firm. If, for instance, a firm has only one vacancy and it is searched by s men within a specified period of time, the supply of labour to that vacancy will be s men within that period of time, whereas if it has two vacancies it will be $s/2$ men to each vacancy, and so on. But the expected returns from

[15] The probability of quitting after the installation of capital is ignored, to simplify the exposition. As it will become obvious, it can easily be taken into account without qualitative difference to the results.

each vacancy, V_0, fall when the supply of labour to the firm falls,[16] so if we write V_{0j} for the expected returns from the jth vacancy, the fact that workers search firms (and not individual vacancies) implies that V_{0j} falls as j rises, i.e. $V_{0j} > V_{0j+1}$ for all $j = 1, \ldots, n - m$. The total returns from all the vacancies of the firm are therefore equal to $V_0'' = \sum_{j=1}^{n-m} V_{0j}$.

It follows that the total return from a capital investment which will open up n job positions when the firm's labour force is equal to m men is equal to $V_0' + V_0''$, where V_0' stands for the total expected returns from the currently filled positions, and V_0'' for the expected returns from new recruits. If $n < m$, i.e. if the firm plans to reduce its labour force, then clearly $V_0'' = 0$ and

$$V_0' = \sum_{i=1}^{n} \left[(1 - c_i) Z_i + c_i V_0 \right],$$

whereas a total of $m - n$ men are either laid off or they quit.[17]

The firm will employ capital up to the point where the addition of sufficient capital to open up one more vacancy adds at least as much to revenue as it adds to costs. Let p_{Kj} be the price that has to be paid to increase capital such that the firm has j job positions instead of $j - 1$. p_{Kj} may be called the marginal cost of capital at employment level j, and it may be either constant or increasing, although at small levels of employment and if there are indivisibilities it may fall. On the other hand the addition to revenue when capital expands such that the firm's job positions rise from $j - 1$ to j is equal to V_{0j}' when $j \leq m$ and V_{0j}'' when $j > m$. We may call this addition to revenue the value of the marginal product of capital at employment level j, and denote it by VMP_{Kj}. Clearly, the firm will buy capital until $p_{Kj} \geq VMP_{Kj}$. The first j that satisfies this condition is the firm's optimal labour force.

Since VMP_{Kj} varies with the size of the existing labour force the latter also influences the size of the optimal labour force. If the firm knew that no one of its workers would wish to quit, then the value of the marginal product of employee i would be equal to Z_i, which is independent of the size of the labour force. So if the marginal cost of capital p_{Kj} does not rise for $j \leq m$, the optimal size

[16] See chapter 5.

[17] There is a slight reinterpretation of the quit probability c_i here. Since $m - n$ men are separated from the firm, c_i is the probability that the ith man quits, *in addition* to a minimum of $m - n$ other quits. If less than $m - n$ men wish to quit the firm, the return from the firm's capital is $V_0' = \sum_{i=1}^{n} Z_i$.

of the labour force is definitely not less than the current labour force. However, in a dynamic system the firm will in general attach a positive probability of quitting to each one of its employees, so the expected returns from each one of the positions currently held by its labour force will also decline as the size of the firm rises. (In equation (1), V'_{oi} will be less than V'_{oi-1} because V_o declines as i rises, and $c_i \geq 0$, although Z_i is independent of i.) But since the probability of quitting, c_i, will in general be less than one, the expected returns from the currently filled positions fall less rapidly than the expected returns from the unfilled vacancies, V_{oj} for $j > m$. Thus the firm gains by having a labour force readily available, and this gain is reflected in a higher value of the marginal product of capital, VMP_{Kj}, for $j \leq m$ than $j > m$, and a discontinuity at $j = m$, which reflects the fact that any men beyond m will have to be acquired through a time-consuming job offer policy. This is shown in Fig. 13.1. The curve $ABCD$ gives the value of the marginal product of

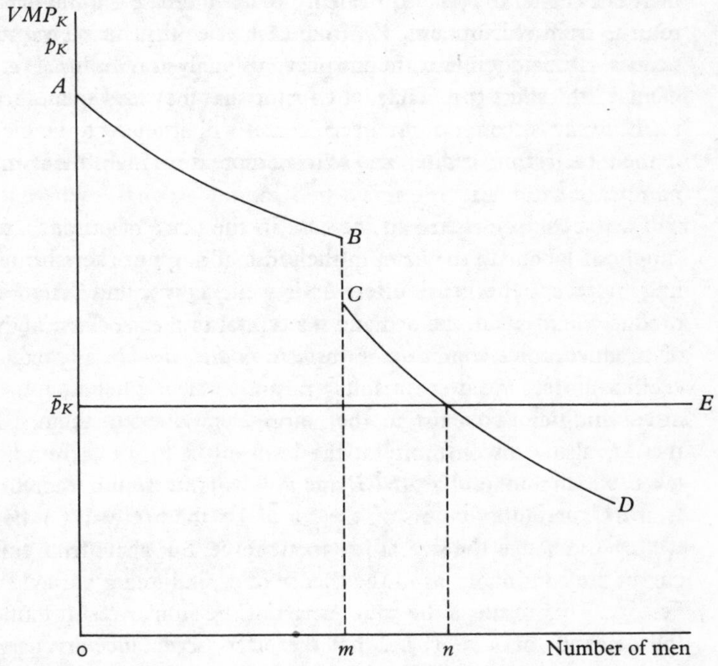

Fig. 13.1

labour as the size of the firm rises. The slope of AB and the distance between B and C will depend on the probability of quitting c_i, in that an increase in the probability of quitting will shift AB down and it will also make it steeper.

Suppose the marginal cost of capital p_{Kj} is constant at $\bar{p}_K$ for all j. Then the firm's optimal labour force is given by the intersection of $\bar{p}_K E$ and $ABCD$. (The same of course is true when p_{Kj} rises or falls with j.) In Fig. 13.1 the firm will have a minimum of $n - m$ vacancies, plus any additional vacancies that are created by quits of its currently employed men.

Any factor that shifts $ABCD$ up, or any factor that shifts $\bar{p}_K E$ down, leads to an increase in the optimal labour force, and hence to an increase in capital investment and the number of vacant positions in the market. The second factor, a fall in the cost of capital, is the more obvious cause of an increase in the demand for capital, but the least interesting one from our point of view, because it is independent of the trading process in the labour market. But the first factor, increases in VMP_K, is equivalent to an increase in the expected returns from recruitment, V_0, from each one of the firm's vacancies, so it is intimately related to our previous analysis of optimal recruitment in the short run. Thus, any factor that may lead to an increase in the returns from optimal recruitment will also lead to an increase in the returns from capital, and so to an increase in investment and the number of vacancies.

Two such factors are an increase in the price of output and the supply of labour to the firm, in the sense of more workers being willing to accept the firm's offer. As is well known, these factors also produce increases in the demand for capital in the neoclassical theory of production *when production coefficients are variable.* If production coefficients are fixed the results are not so clear-cut because of the discontinuities that exist in the marginal products of factors. Here there is also a discontinuity at the level of the firm's current labour force, which implies that $ABCD$ and $\bar{p}_K E$ will intersect more frequently at BC than other points on the curve, i.e. the firm will not be very willing to change the size of its labour force. But apart from this the curves are continuous as in the theory of capital under variable coefficients. This result is the counterpart of the similar result found for the demand for labour, i.e. that the offer–acceptance arrangement in the labour market implies that the fixed-coefficient model of production behaves more like the traditional variable-coefficient model than the fixed-coefficient one.[18]

Summary

In this chapter we examined the very important question of the internal consistency of our model, in particular whether the assumed trading rules preserve the wage variability which we found to be so important in our analysis of the offer–acceptance policies of firms and workers. We found that the model is inherently consistent, because the existence of varying market experiences and uncertainties about market opportunities, which are implied by the very nature of the trading arrangement, imply that there will be variations in wage offers and reservation wages. Thus wage variability will be preserved over time and the trading arrangement will never collapse by its own internal rules of behaviour.

In the second part of the chapter we examined the long-run decision facing the individual and the firm. We argued that by long-run decision we mean the choice of human capital by the individual and physical capital by the firm, and showed that both decisions depend on the expected returns from an optimal policy in the short-run. The human-capital decision depends on the individual's tastes and expectations about the returns from search, because he will choose that skill to specialize in which will give him maximum returns from searching, given the costs of training for that skill. The firm, on the other hand, will behave as it usually behaves in a neoclassical world when production coefficients are variable, although the fact that it can only acquire additional labour through a time-consuming offer–acceptance policy implies that there will be a bias towards choosing that capital which is just sufficient to employ the same labour force as it is currently employing.

[18] See above, chapter 5. The fixed- and variable-coefficient models are treated exhaustively in Ferguson (1969).

14

Towards a Short-run Macrodynamics

We began this study by arguing that the economic way of viewing the analysis of individual behaviour is as a preliminary to the study of the functioning of markets. This preliminary is an essential part of the analysis. With this in mind we set up a multi-market framework whose most distinguishing feature was the absence of perfect information about job opportunities and about the availability of labour to the firm, and the decentralization of exchange in the labour market. We then formulated a model of optimal household and firm behaviour under the postulated conditions, and examined its features in some detail. Thus, in a sense, the task taken up by this study is complete–the foundations for the study of the behaviour of markets over time when the labour market is out of Walrasian equilibrium have been laid on firm economic principles, and they exhibit a uniformity and consistency which should enable extension of the analysis to the interaction of household and firm behaviour and the study of the dynamic path of the market as a whole.

However, finishing the work at this point leaves a gap ahead. Some may doubt whether the individual models may be put at the foundation of the dynamic functioning of markets; others may doubt whether the model has something new to offer; and others still may doubt whether there is any connection between the model and what we normally call adjustment economics. Full demonstration that none of these doubts is justified would require another volume, perhaps longer and, at any rate, technically more difficult than the present one. For this reason we shall settle, in this chapter, for a less ambitious solution. By using the individual models of the foregoing chapters we shall demonstrate that alternative assumptions about individual behaviour give us the two most common models employed in the literature to analyse macrodynamic processes in the short run, namely the 'neoclassical' models which employ some variant of the Phillips curve and the 'Keynesian' models which deal with the multiplier. In the final chapter we shall take up the question of the relationship of the model with the economics of adjustment in general, and the general conclusion that our analysis leads to.

Flexwage dynamics: the Phillips curve

In the last chapter we saw that when firms follow a pure flexwage policy the trading arrangement in the labour market implies that there will be a distribution of wage offers over time. Each firm will offer that wage rate which maximizes expected profits, given the supply of labour to itself, so variations in the supply of labour to each firm produce variations in the firm's wage rate. The Phillips curve may be shown to be the outcome of the dependence of the firm's wage offer on the supply of labour to itself and the interdependency that exists between the wage offers of different firms, given that firms compete for the acquisition of part of a limited stock of workers[1].

The supply of labour to the firm depends on (1) the availability of labour in the market as a whole, and (2) the availability of labour to this firm *vis-à-vis* other firms. By availability of labour in the market as a whole we mean the stock of active searchers in relation to the stock of vacancies, since if the stock of searchers increases, each and every firm will be searched by more potential employees as the additional searchers are allocated among the various firms; and if the stock of vacancies falls, searchers will find it more difficult to find a job, so their searching will be prolonged and each firm will feel the repercussions by observing a greater flow of labour to itself. Since the higher the stock of searchers, or the lower the stock of vacancies, the greater the supply of labour to the firm, the firm will respond, *ceteris paribus*, to an increase in the stock of searchers or a fall in the stock of vacancies, by lowering its wage offer.

The availability of labour to a particular firm *vis-à-vis* other firms is determined by this firm's wage in relation to that of other firms. A searcher, as we have seen, decides whether to accept an observed wage offer w by considering the relative position of w on the distribution of wage offers. Thus, if a firm raises its wage offer, the probability that a searcher will find another firm's wage offer acceptable declines, whereas if it lowers it the probability increases.

[1] See above, chapter 5.

It follows that the stock of searchers, the stock of vacancies, and all other firms' wage offers are shift parameters in a firm's supply-of-labour function, so they influence the firm's optimal wage-offer policy.[2]

The mechanism which links the optimal wage offer of a firm to the various exogenous variables which enter the decision was developed in the main part of the book, and it may now be used to describe the interaction of firms over time. In particular, it is now possible to use the results obtained to simplify the mechanism which links the wage offers of the various firms in the system, and so describe more simply the dynamic behaviour of the system. Consider the wage-offer decision of firm i. The main exogenous variables that interest us here are the price of this firm's output, which may be taken as an indication of the pressure of demand, the stock of searchers, the stock of vacancies, and all other firms' wage offers. The last three variables describe the supply of labour to the firm. Writing $\mathbf{w}(i)$ for the vector of the wage offers of all firms other than i, p for output price, s for the stock of searchers, and v for the stock of vacancies, the optimal wage offer of firm i may be written as

$$w_i^* = \phi_i(\mathbf{w}(i), p, s, v).$$

ϕ_i is the *reaction function* of firm i; it is increasing in $\mathbf{w}(i)$ and p, decreasing in s, and increasing in v.

Each firm in the system is characterized by a different reaction function which reflects its experience during recruitment, its information about the market and its technology. Firms will change their wage rates as long as their actual wage deviates from their desired, and they will stop changing them when the actual and desired coincide. Thus if there are n firms in the system, the conditions for static (but stochastic) wage equilibrium are the n equations

$$w_i^* = w_i \quad (i = 1, \ldots, n).$$

Substituting the equilibrium conditions in the reaction functions we obtain

$$w_i = \phi_i(\mathbf{w}(i), p, s, v) \quad (i = 1, \ldots, n). \tag{1}$$

[2] Neglecting these in the analysis of individual firm behaviour does not undermine that analysis since, as we have seen in chapter 5, changes in shift parameters can easily be incorporated into the model.

This describes a system of n equations in the n unknown wage offers $w_1, \ldots, w_n$. If there are any values of p, s and v which imply that the system can be solved for all w_i, then there is static equilibrium, otherwise wage offers will never rest even in the absence of exogenous shocks.[3]

The restrictions on individual behaviour which we derived in the first two parts of the book do not guarantee that the system of equations in (1) has a solution. However, the literature on the Phillips curve does not necessarily depend on the absence of a solution to (1) for its main result. In contrast, it does accept that there may be values of the triple (p, s, v) which imply that (1) has a solution, so, if those values are reached, money wages will come to rest.[4] But it denies that all possible combinations of p, s, and v are consistent with static equilibrium; and argues that the levels of unemployment which are consistent with those values of the triple (p, s, v), which imply the existence of a static equilibrium, are too high, given the levels we have been experiencing since the war, and certainly too high to be acceptable to policy-makers. Thus for practical purposes we should be concerned with values of the triple (p, s, v) which do not imply the existence of a solution to the equations in (1). In particular we should be concerned with values which imply that unemployment is below the level consistent with static equilibrium.[5]

In a pure flexwage world the level of employment is determined by workers, given the structure of wage offers, since firms are willing to recruit anyone who finds their wage offer acceptable. Unemployment is a purely voluntary phenomenon, and it consists of those people who prefer to be unemployed during search than be temporarily employed at an inferior job. Thus, to obtain a stock of unemployed we must assume that at least some searchers prefer to be unemployed during search[6]. The level of unemployment, then, is some proportion of the stock of searchers, so the argument that we must be

[3] The existence of equilibrium does not guarantee stability, i.e. the system may have a solution and yet never approach it. The analogy of this problem with the one in non-cooperative oligopoly is obvious. For recent work in this area see James Friedman (1971, 1973).

[4] In terms of the fitted Phillips curve the point of rest corresponds to the point of intersection of the curve with the horizontal axis.

[5] Phillips' (1958) original estimate was that there will be static equilibrium at a 5.5 per cent unemployment rate.

[6] See chapter 11 for the implications of this assumption, and the last section of this chapter where the assumption is relaxed.

concerned with levels of unemployment below those consistent with a solution to (1) implies that we should be concerned with levels of s below those consistent with a solution. Since the reaction functions are decreasing in s, a lowering of the value of s would lead to an increase in the value of the desired wage offer above the actual value of the offer. Thus, at those values of s, firms will be increasing their offers in their attempt to reach their desired offer. The result will be a continuous upward revision of wage offers, which will stop only if the inflationary process produces any feedback effects on the exogenous variables (p, s, v) which result in static equilibrium. Such feedback effects, if they existed, would have to come from the reactions of workers, since it is the workers who choose the level of unemployment and aggregate spending in the economy.

The Phillips curve may be shown to be the outcome of these feedback effects from the money-wage inflation rate to the level of unemployment chosen by workers[7]. Let $\dot{w}_i$ be the rate of change of the wage offer of firm i. Since all firms will try to adjust their actual wage offer to their desired we may write, as an approximation,

$$\dot{w}_i = \lambda_i(w_i^* - w_i),$$

where λ_i is a positive constant which measures the speed by which firm i adjusts its actual wage to the desired wage offer. The average inflation rate $\dot{\overline{w}}$ may then be approximated by

$$\dot{\overline{w}} = \lambda(\overline{w}^* - \overline{w}), \tag{2}$$

where $\overline{w}^* = \phi(\overline{w}, p, s, v)$ satisfies the same properties as the 'average' reaction function, and $\overline{w}$ is the average wage offer. Dividing both parts of (2) by $\overline{w}$ we obtain for the proportional rate of change of money-wage rates

$$\frac{\dot{\overline{w}}}{\overline{w}} = \lambda\left(\frac{\overline{w}^*}{\overline{w}} - 1\right). \tag{2'}$$

Equation (2′) gives the proportional rate of money-wage inflation

[7] We are using the term 'Phillips curve' here in place of the more cumbersome 'the negatively-sloped path which the economic system traces in an inflation–unemployment plane'. We do not wish to imply that this is indeed what Phillips (1958) had in mind, and indeed further below we shall argue that there is a clear break in this formulation from the more traditional one of Lipsey (1960).

as an increasing function of the level of demand for output[8] and the stock of vacancies, and a decreasing function of the stock of searchers. Since empirically the level of unemployment may serve as a good proxy for the stock of vacancies and the stock of searches[9] this equation looks very much like a generalized Phillips curve, i.e. a theoretical justification for the observed inverse relationship between $\dot{\overline{w}}/\overline{w}$ and the unemployment rate. However, interpreting (2) or (2′) as a Phillips curve neglects the supply side of the labour market, which is primarily responsible for choosing the level of employment. Before we can say how the market as a whole behaves over time we need to describe the interaction of both sides of the market. Equation (2) may be taken as a summary statement of the behaviour of firms, given the choice of employment by workers. If the choice of employment is such that $\overline{w}^* = \overline{w}$ there will be money-wage stability, but if not there will be either inflation or deflation, depending on whether employment is higher or lower than the level consistent with stability.[10]

The mechanism by which searchers choose their employment is as complex as the one which firms use in their wage-setting policy, but as with the latter the model of optimal behaviour is powerful enough to enable an unambiguous simplification which may be used alongside equation (2) to analyse the dynamic behaviour of the market as a whole. We have seen in our development of the model of job search that the main factor which induces a worker to accept or reject an observed wage offer is the relationship between that wage offer and the offers that the worker expects to find in the future if he continues the search. The first simplifying assumption which we make is that the searcher does not expect the shape of the distribution of job offers to

[8] In a model where the equations in (1) give an inflationary solution it may be more appropriate to write the rate of price inflation as a proxy for the pressure of demand. The appropriate representation of demand will be neglected here because it is of no direct interest to the argument.

[9] See Thirwall (1969) and Gujarati (1972) for evidence of an inverse relationship between the vacancy and unemployment rates in Britain.

[10] In a sense inflation or deflation in this system is a result of the breakdown of coordination between firms in their wage-setting policies. If firms cooperated in setting their wage offers they would realize that it is futile to try and reach their desired levels, given all other wage offers, since all other wage offers are determined by their own collective action. However, the fact that there is no such cooperation between firms is one of the fundamental assumptions of a competitive market, and it is natural that it should be maintained in an atomistic market like the one which arises when the institutions which generate perfect information in the competitive world are removed.

change over time, so when we consider changes in the distribution of offers over time we need only consider changes in the mean wage offer $\bar{w}$. Secondly, we assume that the searcher revises his reservation wage rate over time in proportion to the change in the average wage offer, i.e. the searcher keeps the position of his reservation wage on the distribution of wage offers fixed over time, although wage offers in general may be inflating or deflating.[11] Now the chance of finding an acceptable job in any period depends on the position of the reservation wage on the distribution of wage offers, so it is independent of the rate of money-wage inflation *if the searcher knows that inflation rate*. But we must also allow for the case where the rate is not known. Suppose the worker thinks the inflation rate is equal to $\dot{\bar{w}}^e$, and that this is below the true rate $\dot{\bar{w}}$.† Then he will be adjusting his reservation wage according to $\dot{\bar{w}}^e$, whereas wage offers will be inflating at $\dot{\bar{w}}$. Since $\dot{\bar{w}}^e < \dot{\bar{w}}$ the searcher's reservation wage will be moving down the scale of wage offers over time, and so his chances of finding an acceptable job will be increasing. Conversely, if $\dot{\bar{w}}^e$ is above $\dot{\bar{w}}$ the searcher's reservation wage will be moving up the scale of wage offers, so the chance of finding an acceptable job will be diminishing.

The stock of active searchers depends inversely on the probability that the typical searcher will find an acceptable job and directly on the probability that the typical employed worker will find his job unacceptable and search for another. The probability of finding an acceptable job depends, as we have seen, on the difference between $\dot{\bar{w}}^e$ and $\dot{\bar{w}}$, diminishing over time when the difference is positive, increasing when it is negative, and remaining constant when it is equal to zero. But the probability of finding one's job unsatisfactory also depends on the same difference: when relative wages remain fixed a worker will find his job unsatisfactory only if his reservation wage moves up the scale of wage offers, i.e. when $\dot{\bar{w}}^e$ is greater than $\dot{\bar{w}}$. Hence we can approximate the rate of change of unemployment by

$$\dot{u} = k(\dot{\bar{w}}^e - \dot{\bar{w}}), \tag{3}$$

where k is a constant showing the speed of the searchers' response to

[11] In chapter 2 we showed that in a two-period model the second assumption follows immediately from the first. In the multi-period framework this is approximately correct, since the reservation wage is revised downwards during unsuccessful search independently of any changes that may be taking place in the distribution of wage offers.

† For notational convenience, from now on a dot over a variable will denote the proportional rate of change of the variable.

the discrepancy between expected and actual wage inflation and the speed by which they find a new job or quit their own when the actual and expected rates deviate.

Equation (3) describes the behaviour of the supply side of the market given the money-wage inflation rate determined by firms, so it may be analysed alongside (2′) to give the dynamic path of the system as a whole. The possible paths that the economy may follow in an inflation–unemployment plane are shown in Fig. 14.1. Curve *RR* is equation (2′) with unemployment taken as a proxy for the stock of searchers, so the point of intersection of *RR* with the horizontal axis corresponds to the point of static equilibrium obtained by solving (1). Suppose we are at point *A*, and at that point $\dot{\bar{w}}^e = \dot{\bar{w}}$. Then from (3) $\dot{u} = 0$, so unemployment is constant. The system is in inflationary equilibrium, in the sense that firms will never move from *A* in the absence of exogenous shocks. Now suppose demand increases because of an exogenous injection of money into the system. This change will lead to an increase in the rate of price inflation, so the desired wage offer of firms, given by their reaction functions, will increase. Thus

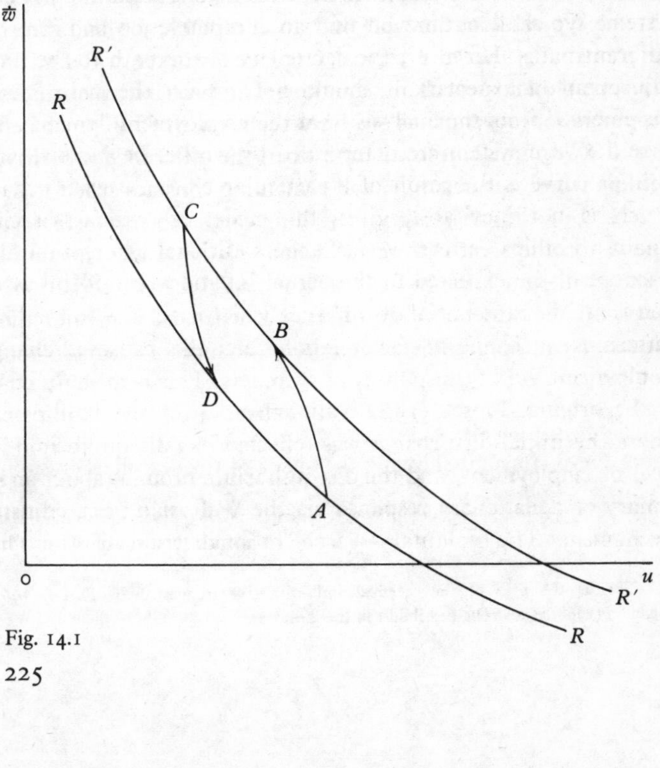

Fig. 14.1

RR will shift to some new position $R'R'$, and point A will start moving upwards towards $R'R'$ as firms adjust to the new conditions. But as A moves upwards $\dot{\bar{w}}$ will increase, and this may or may not disturb the worker equilibrium given by (3), depending on the response of $\dot{\bar{w}}^e$ to the change. If worker expectations are such that $\dot{\bar{w}}^e = \dot{\bar{w}}$ at all times, then whatever the changes taking place in firm policy, unemployment will remain constant and firms will be moving up and down a vertical line through A.[12] But if the expected inflation rate is slow to respond to the actual rate, when $\dot{\bar{w}}$ starts increasing the difference $\dot{\bar{w}}^e - \dot{\bar{w}}$ becomes negative, so unemployment begins falling. The economy will then travel from A to some point B on $R'R'$, and then along $R'R'$ in a leftward direction until $\dot{\bar{w}}^e$ rises to the level of $\dot{\bar{w}}$. The exact position of B depends on the speed of adjustment of wages by firms, λ, and the speed with which searchers find new jobs, k. The position of B, however, is not crucial to the theory. What *is* crucial is how far can the system move to the left of A without expectations catching up with the actual inflation rate, and this depends on the speed of adjustment of expectations to the actual rate.

One can explore several alternative assumptions about the formation of expectations and how these assumptions affect the path of the system. We shall outline below two alternatives, which imply very different paths. However, the sensitivity of the path to the speed of adjustment of expectations should not obscure the main issue that has emerged from the analysis: that the employment dynamics in the pure flexwage system are determined by worker behaviour, and the Phillips curve is the result of a particular type of worker behaviour which is not inevitable, given the model of optimal search. To obtain a Phillips pattern we need the additional assumption of slow response of the expected to the actual inflation rate. If this assumption is satisfied the initial disturbance which gives rise to the Phillips pattern is a change in the inflation rate; this causes a change in employment via the responses of searchers. This is in sharp contrast to the original Lipsey (1960) rationalization of the Phillips curve, where the initial disturbance was reflected in a disequilibrium in the level of employment, and the disequilibrium brought about an inflationary or deflationary response via the Walrasian price-adjustment mechanism. The voluntary-search rationalization of the Phillips

[12] This is the case of the 'vertical Phillips curve' suggested by Phelps (1967) and Friedman (1968) as a strong possibility in the long run.

curve reverses the original Lipsey line of causation and shifts the responsibility for the downward sloping curve from an anonymous auctioneer groping for the equilibrium wage rate to misinformed workers searching for a new job.

It remains to illustrate some of the paths of the economy that alternative assumptions about workers' expectations can give us. We first consider the most common assumption employed in the literature, Cagan's (1956) adaptive expectations mechanism. According to this hypothesis the individual corrects his expectations in proportion to the difference between the actual and expected rate of inflation. Thus this hypothesis has the important implication that when the actual inflation rate is rising, the expected rate is always below the actual, whereas when the actual rate is falling, the expected rate is always above the actual. The actual and expected rates will be equal only if the actual rate remains constant for a sufficiently long period of time. Using this in our employment adjustment equation we obtain that unemployment will be falling as long as the actual inflation rate is rising, and rise only when the actual rate begins falling. Thus, when the system gets to point *B* in Fig. 14.1, it starts travelling along *R'R'* in a leftward direction and, since this implies a continuous increase in the rate of inflation, unemployment will never stop falling in the absence of a further exogenous shock. So if left by itself the initial expansionary shock that raised *RR* to *R'R'* results in a self-sustaining movement up and to the left without a resting point.

Now suppose that when the system gets to some point *C* there is a contractionary shock in the form of a fall in demand. From the wage adjustment equation (2) the relationship between $\dot{\bar{w}}$ and u shifts down to a position such as *RR*, so the rate of change of money wages falls, inducing a downturn in the path of the economy along *CD*. But, as $\dot{\bar{w}}$ falls, the expected rate $\dot{\bar{w}}^e$ remains at a relatively high level, and as long as $\dot{\bar{w}}$ continues to fall $\dot{\bar{w}}^e$ will exceed $\dot{\bar{w}}$. Thus, unemployment will start rising as workers find it more difficult to find new jobs, so the system will move to some point *D* on *RR* and then start moving along *RR* to the right of *D*. As with the upward movement there is nothing in the adjustment equations to induce a reversal of the path. As long as the rate of inflation falls the system will move down alongside *RR*, and it will stop only when there is an exogenous expansionary shock. In the latter case there will be an upturn such as *AB* and the cycle will be repeated.

The conclusion to emerge from this illustration is that an adaptive mechanism in the formation of expectations implies that the economic system will travel along a cyclical anti-clockwise path over the business cycle. The system is inherently unstable in that it will never be able to reach a resting point in the absence of exogenous changes. But the existence of alternating expansionary and contractionary shocks checks the instability of the system by ensuring that the path of the economy will not extend for many periods in the same direction.[13]

The clockwise path around a vertical line which characterizes the state of employment equilibrium, which, as Brechling (1968) first noted, is implied by the Phelps–Friedman hypothesis, appears to depend on two additional restrictions on the expectation-formation mechanism. First, the mechanism must be such that after being wrong for some time, workers adjust their expectations fully to the actual rate of inflation, although the latter may be moving monotonically up or down. This implies that once we get to some point C the path stops, even in the absence of exogenous shocks. Second, those workers who found themselves in employment because of the lag in the adaptation of expectations, now realize that the reason they are employed was an error in their expectations. So they try to correct the error by quitting their jobs and becoming unemployed. Put differently, we began the discussion by arguing that the worker will wish to keep his reservation wage at the same point on the wage-offer scale, independently of the inflation rate. Because of wrong expectations he now finds himself at a different point on the scale, so, when he finally finds out about it, he moves his reservation wage back to its original position. This assumption implies that once at C the system turns up and to the right, so it traces the clockwise path implied by the Phelps–Friedman hypothesis.

Thus the path that the economy travels in an inflation–unemployment plane depends crucially on the way workers form their expectations. The expectation-formation mechanism is independent of the model of optimal behaviour developed in the second part of this volume, so it may be considered disturbing that the conclusion to

[13] This finding is consistent with the observations of Phillips and Lipsey but does not seem to conform to the findings of those who used an adaptive expectations mechanism in a similar environment; e.g. Mortensen (1970*a*, pp. 201–2) claims that if expectations are adaptive the path will turn up and to the right at some point C until it reaches a point exactly above A, where it will rest.

emerge from this preliminary and very brief analysis of the workings of the market is that the model of this volume implies that the economy may behave in any manner, depending on how expectations are formed. However, this is by no means our main result. The main result to emerge from the analysis of this section may be put as follows: *if* wage rates were as flexible as prices, both over workers with different efficiencies and over time, then the burden for the adjustment of wages falls on firms, and the burden for the adjustment of employment on workers. There is no place for layoffs and involuntary unemployment in this model, and the employment dynamics depend to a large extent on whether workers prefer to be unemployed during search or not. If no worker chooses to be unemployed during search there will always be full employment, so there will be no employment dynamics. This may not be considered a satisfactory state of affairs. The analysis that follows suggests why it may not be reasonable to take this as the state of affairs in general, although there may be cases where it is indeed reasonable to do so.

Fixwage dynamics: the multiplier

Suppose that wage rates are fixed at the same value for all firms, so no worker will participate unless he finds that wage rate acceptable, and no worker will find it optimal to reject an observed offer. In this system, which we may call 'pure' fixwage, each firm will choose a recruitment standard on the basis of the efficiency of potential employees and its experience in the market, and workers will search firms until they find one whose recruitment standard is low enough for them to qualify. It follows that there will be no on-the-job search, and no quitting to search, in this system. A worker will be indifferent between the jobs offered by each firm in the system, so he will only search for another job when he is laid off by his current employer. Unemployment in the pure fixwage system is an entirely involuntary phenomenon, and the stock of searchers is exactly equal to the stock of unemployed workers.

If workers are always able to sell the desired number of hours of work at the going wage rate, as under flexwage, the constraint on consumption decisions will be a price constraint. The world will be one of voluntary exchange, albeit under imperfect information about job offers and reservation wages. The dynamics of this world will be those of the Phillips curve, the quantity dynamics amounting to little more than small changes in the quantity of frictional unemployment (and even those will only be temporary under the Phelps–Friedman expectations hypothesis), whereas at low unemployment rates the price dynamics will amount to a continuous inflation of money wages and prices.

The dynamics of the fixwage system are completely reversed. Unlike those of the flexwage system, which could be obtained from the analysis of the labour market in isolation, the fixwage dynamics depend on the interaction between the labour market and the commodity markets, in particular on what we called in chapter 1 the 'spillovers' between markets. We shall again present a simplified picture of the model of the previous pages, which nevertheless captures the essence of the dynamic process.

Consider an individual who visits a firm and observes a wage rate w, which he finds acceptable. In the terminology of Clower (1965) his 'notional' (desired) supply of hours of work will be some positive number y^*, and his income will be equal to the product wy^*. If the firm recruits the individual, the latter's demand for commodities will be the 'notional' demand $\mathbf{x}(w)$, which is a function of the wage rate. But if the individual is turned down (if he is involuntarily made unemployed) he will have no alternative but continue the search. His 'effective' supply of labour services will be zero, his current income will be either zero, or positive if there is unemployment insurance, whereas his lifetime income will be uncertain, there being a distribution of possible future incomes which he can earn at the job which he will eventually find. Let the current income under involuntary unemployment be denoted by m_0 and the distribution over future incomes by π. The *effective* demand for commodities will then be some function $\mathbf{x}(m_o, \pi)$. The important result for macrodynamics is that the value of the notional vector $\mathbf{x}(w)$ evaluated at market prices $\mathbf{p}$, $\mathbf{p}'\mathbf{x}(w)$, will be greater than the value of the effective demand, evaluated at the same prices, $\mathbf{p}'\mathbf{x}(m_o, \pi)$, since the former is associated with termination of search whereas the latter with continuation.[14] The difference between the value of notional and effective demand, $\mathbf{p}'[\mathbf{x}(w) - \mathbf{x}(m_o, \pi)]$, is what Clower calls 'involuntary underconsumption', and it is the counterpart of the involuntary unemployment which exists in the labour market.

[14] See above, chapters 7 and 8. If capital markets are imperfect and the individual is constrained by liquidity the difference between the notional and effective demand will be even greater.

Thus we now have a precise measure of the spillover between the labour and commodity markets. The spillover from the disequilibrium in the labour market to the market for commodity j is the difference between the notional and effective demand for j, evaluated at the prevailing price, $p_j[x_j(w) - x_j(m_o, \pi)]$. Since the spillover is due to involuntary unemployment, the income effect will result in a fall in the demand for the good, unless the good is inferior, but the substitutability–complementarity effects between commodities and leisure may push its demand in any direction. However, the aggregate spillover will be negative.

This spillover will have repercussions in commodity markets, which will in turn feed back into the labour market. When commodity prices are flexible and change to bring the supply and demand for each commodity into equality with each other, as in our system, the repercussions will be felt wholly on prices, i.e. the spillover will result in changes in the prices of commodities which would not have taken place had there been no involuntary unemployment. The change in prices will in turn have effects on the labour market, since firms read prices when choosing how much to produce and how many men to employ. So the effects of the involuntary unemployment eventually feed back into the labour market via commodity prices and produce additional effects.

The multiplier may be shown to be the outcome of the interaction of the spillovers and feedbacks between the commodity and labour markets – it is the chain reaction which follows an initial disturbance in the labour or commodity markets. Suppose we are in a booming fixwage world and the state of entrepreneurial confidence falls. This may be translated to mean a fall in expected prices. But if expected prices fall, entrepreneurs will increase their recruitment standard, dismissing the less efficient of their employees and refusing to employ workers who would otherwise have been acceptable. Thus involuntary unemployment sets in, and through the fall in the demand of those made involuntarily unemployed the current and expected prices of commodities fall further. Entrepreneurs respond to the new setback by raising their recruitment standard again, and so increasing the number of those involuntarily unemployed. The latter, in their turn, reduce their effective demand for commodities, so the process, which started in the first place by the fall in entrepreneurial expectations, gathers momentum. The Keynesian multiplier is the factor by which the initial disturbance is multiplied in a specified period of time.

Exactly the opposite process is generated when we are in a depressing fixwage world and the state of entrepreneurial confidence rises. The multiplier works in both directions and it is the natural outcome of the optimal responses of firms and households to initial disturbances in a fixwage world. Just as inflation was the result of the breakdown of cooperation between firms in a flexwage world, the multiplier is the result of the breakdown of cooperation between firms and households in a fixwage world. Because, just as workers depend on firms for their income, firms also depend on the same workers, in their role as consumers, for their income, so if a firm cuts its payment to workers by dismissing some of its less efficient employees, it is at the same time reducing the income of all firms taken together by forcing those employees to reduce their expenditure. Had firms agreed between themselves not to reduce their wage bills, and had households assured firms that they will continue spending as much as before if they are not laid off from their jobs, there would be no spillovers and feedbacks between markets, and no multiplier. Once again an atomistic decentralized labour market results in the breakdown of the coordination of activities between participants. This time the dynamics are those of the multiplier.

Short-run neoclassical and Keynesian dynamics: a synthesis

It is evident from the analysis of the neoclassical and Keynesian dynamic systems that the crucial factor for short-run dynamic analysis is whether firms follow a fixwage or a flexwage policy in their recruitment of labour. If firms follow a *pure* fixwage policy the dynamics of the system will be solely those of the multiplier, whereas if they follow a pure flexwage policy the dynamics will be those of the Phillips curve. In the former the short-run dynamic process is dominated by changes in the level of employment which are determined by the actions of firms. Households play a passive role in the process, acting merely as the link between the money that firms pay out as wages and that which they receive as sales. In the latter the short-run dynamic process is dominated by money-wage dynamics, which are also determined by the actions of firms, but now households have a more active role to play. In particular, households, in their role as workers, choose the level of employment by deciding whether to accept an observed wage offer or reject it to search for another, so the employment dynamics of the pure flexwage system are largely determined by worker behaviour. Thus the two dynamic processes have very different implications, not only for the behaviour of the system as a whole, but also for the role of firms and households in the functioning of the economic system.

As two alternative logical possibilities the dynamic processes which we described are, of course, internally consistent. But a theory which can do nothing other than list logical possibilities can hardly qualify as theory. In the very least we would expect a theory to indicate which process is likely to arise in practice given its rules of optimal behaviour; and whether the two processes can coexist under similar environments.

To answer these questions we have to go back to the model of firm behaviour and pose a different question from the one we posed there. Now the question would not be *how* firms behave given a flexwage or a fixwage world, but *what* might give rise to a flexwage or fixwage world given the way firms and households behave. Firms are, in general, free to choose either a fixwage or a flexwage policy, so they will adopt that policy which will maximize their profits in the short and the long run. In general, there are two different dimensions to the wage flexibility problem. First there is the problem of wage flexibility over time, and second the problem of flexibility across workers with different efficiencies. The two extreme systems which we have been analysing refer to perfect flexibility along both dimensions on the one hand (flexwage) and perfect rigidity along the same dimensions on the other (fixwage). We showed, however, that the crucial rigidity for fixwage is the one across workers, because it is only when different workers have different contributions to the firm's profit that a firm will find it at all meaningful to employ a recruitment standard.

Now the possibility of maintaining some rigidity across workers with different efficiencies depends partly on firm policy, but also on worker response to this rigidity. If each worker's efficiency was the same in all firms then workers could force, through their searching activity, the mean wage of more efficient employees to rise above that of less efficient ones. If the mean wage differentials increased to the level of the efficiency differentials firms would be indifferent between the employment of different workers, because all workers would contribute the same amount to the firm's profit. A necessary condition for such a situation, however, is that workers be equally efficient in all firms, since if they were not they would find that the firms which could employ them more efficiently could offer them higher wages and still maintain some rigidity across workers. Thus the existence of firm-specific efficiencies and the conduct of trade through a process of search imply that firms could follow a policy of discriminatory recruiting, as they do in what we have called the fixwage system. But even the absence of firm-specific efficiencies does not exclude the possibility of wage rigidity across workers. In a search market, workers have no means of *forcing* firms to offer wages which are proportional to their efficiencies. A firm will offer such a differential only if it finds it impossible to recruit more efficient workers at the wages which attract less efficient ones, and this will happen only if firms as a whole offer wages which are proportional to efficiencies. It is not clear, however, how a process of search can bring about the initial state where at least the majority of firms offer wages proportional to efficiencies.

Thus the existence of wage rigidities across workers is a strong possibility in a market which relies on a process of search for the allocation of labour to firms. In such an environment firms can use a recruitment-standard policy alongside, or as an alternative to, a wage-offer policy. Clearly the firm which takes advantage of this and uses both tools for recruiting workers will have more flexibility in its policy and so will be able to raise expected profits above those obtained by relying solely on one of the policies. So firms will be encouraged to maintain some rigidity across workers. For purposes of the dynamic behaviour of the economy as a whole, however, the crucial rigidity is not the one across workers but the one over time. If wages are as flexible as prices over time, the dynamics of the system will still be dominated by money-wage dynamics, even if there is some rigidity across workers[15], whereas if wages are fairly rigid over time, the dynamics will be dominated by changes in employment, even if wages are flexible across workers.

In a system where wages are rigid across workers firms will be making a higher profit on their more efficient employees than on their less efficient ones. Consider a typical firm in such a system when the demand for its product falls. The firm can rely on the wage offer as a recruiting tool and reduce its offer until the required

[15] However, the employment dynamics will now be partly determined by firms as the latter adjust their recruitment standard to changing conditions.

number of workers quit; or it can maintain wages fixed and raise its recruitment standard, until a sufficient number of men disqualify and are laid off. In the former case there is an equal probability that any one of the firm's employees will quit, so there is a positive probability that both highly efficient and inefficient workers will quit. In the latter case, however, the firm will lay off only inefficient workers, whereas its efficient workers will remain with the firm and work for the same wage rate. Since each worker's contribution to profit varies positively with his efficiency, the firm will be better off if it maintains wages fixed (or rigid) and relies on a policy of layoffs. Hence the wage rigidity across workers implies that during depressions the firm will keep wages rigid over time as well. It will only reduce them when the probability of losing employees after a wage cut declines, so the gains from the fall in wage payments outweigh the costs from the loss of efficient employees.

During expansions there will also be a preference for wage rigidity when the boom first sets in, but in general there will be more reliance on both increases in wages and reductions in the recruitment standard. By raising its wage offer the firm ensures that its own workers do not quit to join another firm, and it also raises the probability that searchers will find the offer acceptable. But at the same time it also reduces the profit that it makes on each one of its employees.[16] The firm could also arrive at a similar situation, where it employs more men but the average worker's contribution to profit is lower, by maintaining wages fixed and reducing its recruitment standard. In the latter case if the firm could maintain its labour force and recruit new workers at the old wage offer it would benefit from the wage rigidity, because own employees would continue having the same contribution to profit whereas only new ones will have a lower contribution. Thus during expansions the wage rigidity across workers implies that the firm will prefer to maintain wages rigid as long as it can recruit new workers at the old wage offer without losing its own employees. When the possibility of expanding the labour force on the basis of recruitment-standard reductions alone ceases, the firm will raise wages.

It follows from this that the existence of wage rigidities across workers with different efficiencies induces the firm to maintain wages

[16] Contributions to profit are evaluated at old prices. If prices increase during the expansion, contributions to profit could increase even when the wage offer is raised.

rigid over time as well, at least for some time after the onset of booms and depressions. But even if wages are flexible across workers and the workers' contribution to profit is independent of their efficiency, there may be grounds for arguing that a policy of wage rigidity will be preferred. An argument to this extent was put forward by Hicks in an illuminating but sadly neglected part of the *Theory of Wages.*[17] We shall present a brief summary of his argument here.

When each worker contributes an identical amount to the firm's profit the firm is indifferent about which workers in particular it employs. Thus in the short run there is nothing to induce the firm to abandon the wage offer as its main recruiting tool and rely on a policy of layoffs. But in the long run workers learn of the recruitment practices of the various firms, so they search by starting from those firms whose policy system they like more. So a firm will adopt that system which leads to a better flow of labour to itself in the long run, in the sense of more workers searching it and willing to work for it at the offered wage. Hicks devoted two chapters of his book to explaining that although on short-term grounds the firm may be indifferent between a fixwage and a flexwage policy, long-term arguments will induce it to adopt a policy of infrequent changes in wages in both the short and the long run. Hicks's argument rests largely on the assertion that workers are averse to fluctuations in wages, in that a job which offers the same mean wage over the long run, but which allows greater fluctuation around this mean than another, will be less attractive than the other. So a firm which changes its wages less frequently than another will have an advantage over the latter, and so it will attract more workers.[18] It should be emphasized, however, that the reason workers are averse to fluctuations in wages is that they are averse to wage cuts, so a firm will hesitate before raising its wage rate only when it expects the optimal wage offer to fall again. If it expects the optimal offer to rise permanently it will not hesitate to raise its wage rates.[19]

[17] See Hicks (1932, chs. 3–4).

[18] In his own words (pp. 49–50) 'A firm which maintained wages steady would have a definite advantage over one which was always changing the wages it offered . . . for a long time. . . . If a firm varies its rates that means that the terms it offers to permanent employees are, on a long view, rather less attractive; and it may find that as a consequence it gets less good workmen than it would get if it paid the same average rate regularly throughout the year.'

[19] Usually the argument that wages are more rigid than prices is attributed to Keynes (1936, esp. ch. 2). However, Keynes relies on an *ad hoc* justification why workers may resist

For these reasons a firm may be reluctant to change its wage rates at the onset of booms and depressions. But if aggregate demand changes in the same direction period after period, the firm cannot survive if it remains indifferent. If a boom is extending over many periods the firm which does not grant a rise in wages will find that its employees are gradually drifting away and fewer good workmen are searching it. The process will speed up when other, more adventurous firms begin raising their wages. It only takes a few optimistic entrepreneurs to set the whole system of wages into motion in an upward direction. If the boom extends over many periods the optimists will sooner or later appear.

Similarly if a depression does not reverse itself after a few periods firms will find that they cannot sustain the high wages with the prices they are receiving from their sales. The pessimists will be the first ones to attempt and force a wage cut, but others will soon follow. As unemployment rises at the first stages of a depression workers will be less likely than before to resist a proposed wage cut. But a wage cut will always be resisted more strongly by the workers than a wage increase by the employers during a boom. There is likely to be an asymmetry in wage changes, with employers offering wage increases almost without reluctance when they do not expect to have to put them down again within a short period of time, and workers resisting a wage cut at all times, but less so during prolonged depressions.

The unwillingness of firms to change their wages as frequently as prices, and their inability to maintain them entirely fixed during prolonged booms and depressions, have certain important implications for the dynamic path of aggregate variables. In particular it is now possible to abandon the two most troublesome assumptions of the pure flexwage system, namely that workers are mainly responsible for choosing the level of employment and that at least some workers prefer to be unemployed during search, and still obtain a dynamic path which has features of both a multiplier and a Phillips process. Thus, suppose that workers always prefer to be employed during

wage cuts, which bears no relation to his 'revolutionary' idea of reformulating the neoclassical budget constraint and considering a model of quantity adjustment. Nor have Alchian (1970) and Leijonhufvud (1968, pp. 75–81), who sought to rationalize Keynes's assertions about wage rigidity by using the voluntary-search model, faced up to the problem that the latter model is incapable of rationalizing the multiplier at the same time. Keynes's analysis is clearly superior in the derivation of the aggregate process of adjustment in a multi-market framework *given* that wages are more rigid than prices. But Hicks's analysis of the reasons for the wage rigidity is unequalled in any part of Keynes's book.

search, so they will search on-the-job if they are employed and want to change their job. All unemployment in this system is involuntary, so it consists of workers who have been laid off by their employers and of new entrants in the labour market who have not yet succeeded in finding a job.

We shall trace the movement of the system over time by starting from a point where there is extensive unemployment but entrepreneurial expectations change for the better (or alternatively aggregate effective demand rises, e.g. through an increase in government expenditure, the supply of money, etc.). The first response to such a change will be the lowering of the recruitment standard by firms. When the boom first sets in employers will be reluctant to grant a wage increase and workers will not demand it. The willingness of those involuntarily unemployed to accept the ruling wage rate will be a major factor encouraging the stability of the wage rate. Thus a multiplier process will be set in motion – those newly employed will increase their demand for commodities, firms will lower their recruitment standard further, and so on. During this process prices may be rising, but not by very much, since output will also be increasing as employment rises and money wages are fixed. But as those involuntarily unemployed are being taken on, firms will find that they cannot attract new employees at the ruling wage as easily as before. If the boom results in the order of new capital equipment with new vacancies opening up, the problem will be more acute, so the more optimistic firms and those whose demand is expanding more rapidly will gradually start offering higher wages. The increase in the wage offer will not take place simultaneously in all firms, but a few firms in the more rapidly expanding sectors will take the lead, with others following sooner or later. Once some firms grant wage increases, and the information becomes known, other firms will find it difficult to maintain their labour force intact, and still expect to be searched by a constant flow of employees, unless they put their wages up too. Thus increases in wages will begin to appear when the more adventurous firms decide to grant them and, if the boom in the trade does not show signs of decline, wages will rise throughout the market.[20]

It may take a considerable time to observe a wage increase in all firms, but if the boom persists, the wage rate, rather than showing signs of decline, will be rising further, as firms try to maintain a steady

[20] See Hicks (1932, pp. 71–4).

flow of employees by maintaining a fixed wage offer *relative* to the average in the market. Further increases in demand will be met by successive increases in wage rates with firms trying, unsuccessfully, to attract new employees and speed up production. Alongside the wage increase, prices, which were more or less stable before, will rise as demand continues to increase with the general rise in incomes, but output and employment fail to keep in line with their rate of expansion.

Thus if the boom is not short-lived there will be a change in the dynamics of the system occurring at the point where firms begin to grant their first wage increases. Before this point the dynamics of the system will be dominated by changes in employment and output, after that it will be dominated by changes in money wages and prices. The point at which firms put their wage offers up for the first time is therefore crucial for dynamic analysis.

Firms will be willing to increase their wage offer either when they are unable to recruit new employees at their ruling wage, or when they are unable to keep their own labour force intact. The former will occur when involuntary unemployment has fallen to such a low level, that the only searchers remaining who are willing to accept the ruling wage are so inefficient as to make their employment problematic even at the best of times. These are the 'unemployables', and their existence is, at best, of secondary importance. When the recruitment standard of firms has fallen to a very low level we may assume that the point of full employment, in the sense of zero *involuntary* unemployment, has been reached. Beyond this point a firm can change the flow of employees if it puts its wage rate up, since those searching are either employed by firms whose wage rate they find unsatisfactory or they are new entrants who have not found the offers of those firms which they have already searched acceptable.

The reaction of own employees to the boom will depend on this firm's policy compared with the policy of other firms. If no firm puts its wage rate up own employees will not quit, because from their point of view nothing has changed in the system. But when other firms begin putting their wages up a firm will find it difficult to maintain its labour force intact without following suit. Thus the pressure from a firm's employees for a wage increase will come when other firms put their wages up. But for the latter to do so, the market must be at a point near full employment, when the pressure for a wage increase acting from outside the firm will also be rising. So both factors acting for an increase in the wage offer will come into play at the same time – the time when involuntary unemployment has fallen to a minimum and the system has moved as close to full-employment equilibrium as the existence of imperfect information about job offers will permit.

The analysis of the upward movement of the economic system from a depressed state with involuntary unemployment to a booming state with a continuous inflation of money wages and prices is essentially that of Keynes in chapter 21 of the *General Theory* (esp. pp. 295–304). It remains to check whether the dynamics of the Phillips curve will still be observed when full employment has been established; and whether the same dynamics will be observed when the movement is in the opposite direction, i.e. in the downswing.

The dynamics of the Phillips curve require that the system travel in a north-western direction in an inflation–unemployment plane during expansion. The path that the system is likely to follow when there is involuntary unemployment and there is an increase in demand is shown in Fig. 14.2. Suppose at the origin there is zero involuntary unemployment, and that at present we are at point *A*,

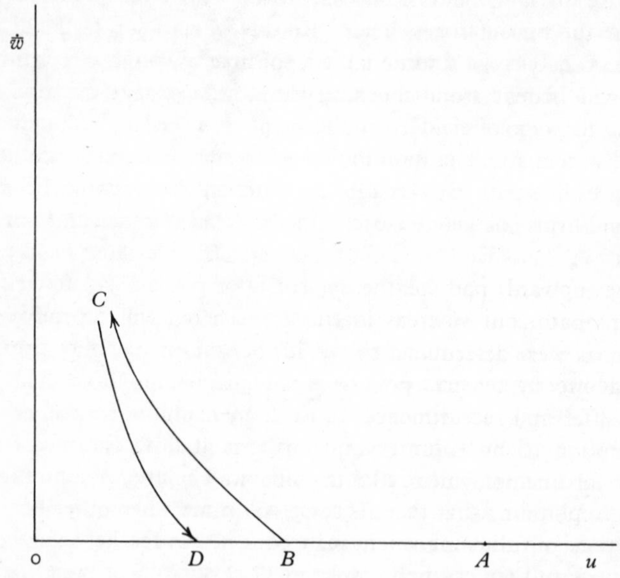

Fig. 14.2

so there is involuntary unemployment equal to o*A*. At a point like *A* firms are able to increase their labour force simply by reducing their recruitment standard, so when demand rises the system will move to the left of *A* alongside the horizontal axis. But when the system reaches a point such as *B* firms will begin to find it more difficult to recruit labour without raising their wage offers. Most searchers will now be employed, so a firm will be able to attract labour mainly by raising its wage offer and so inducing searchers to leave their jobs and join it. Once some firms put up their wage offers the structure of relative wages will be disturbed, with the result that labour flows between firms change. It is at this point that firms will begin showing concern about their relative wage offer, just as they do in a pure flexwage system, so it is at this point that money-wage inflation will set in, as firms are unsuccessfully trying to maintain their relative wage offer at the higher level required to attract new workers. The exact position of point *B* will depend on the probability of finding a new man that firms are willing to tolerate before they raise their wage offer. At point *A* that probability was assumed to be high so no firm would try to increase it by raising its wage offer; at the origin it is zero since there are no unemployed searchers, so the firms that wish to expand will have to increase their wage offer. In moving from *A* to the origin the firm is made successively worse off by the decrease in the probability of finding a man, so there is a point after which the firm will benefit from checking the decline in the probability by raising its wage offer. This is the point we called *B*. The movement of the system after that point will be in a north-western direction, as shown by the path *BC*, as the few remaining unemployed find new jobs and firms compete for each other's workers by raising their wage offers.

The (upward) path of the system after point *B* is similar to the Phillips path, but whereas in the flexwage system the employment dynamics were determined by worker behaviour now they are determined directly by firm policy, as firms adjust simultaneously their wage offer and recruitment standard. We could, of course, relax the assumption of no voluntary unemployment, and obtain a path of frictional unemployment like the one we obtained in the flexwage system. Assuming that there is some voluntary unemployment under conditions of full employment may, in fact, be reasonable, as workers discover that they can find employment easily so they do not hesitate to take advantage of the conditions and quit to search more efficiently.

In this case there will be additional employment dynamics determined by worker expectations and behaviour during search, but whereas in the pure flexwage system permanent equality between the expected and actual wage inflation gave a vertical path, in this system such equality yields the path *BC*. Thus in the present system the Phillips pattern does not depend entirely on a particular expectations-formation mechanism, but it is the outcome of firm and worker behaviour in a full-employment situation, with both contributing to a leftward rising path when worker expectations are slow to adjust to the actual inflation rate. Even with correct expectations, however, the path will move in a north-western direction.

Now, consider the case where we have reached full employment but aggregate demand (or entrepreneurial expectations for the future) fall. Firms will respond to the onset of depression by raising their recruitment standard. Some 'marginal' employees may be dismissed and those firms which were in line for a wage increase will not now grant it. If expectations and aggregate demand fail to recover, the fall in the effective demand due to the onset of involuntary unemployment will result in further dismissals and raising of the recruitment standard, and so to further increases in involuntary unemployment. Prices will also fall, to some extent, so there will be a point after which firms will be running the risk of bankruptcy if they do not lower wages. At this point the more pessimistic and least solvent firms will put their wages down, and once some firms take the lead others will find it easier to follow. But a wage cut will not be allowed to take place as easily as a wage increase. Firms prefer the fixwage system because they fear the effect of wage cuts on the supply of labour in the long run, and in the current period workers will resist a wage cut even if they know conditions to be unfavourable. It will usually take a very severe depression for general wage cuts to be allowed to take place, and even then some other means will also be found which will minimize the extent of the wage cuts. If commodity prices do not fall by very much, hardly any wage cuts will be observed whatever the level of (involuntary) unemployment, so the most obvious policy that will be favoured to avoid extensive wage cuts will be one of price stability.[21] The rigidity of wages itself will act as a stabilizer on prices in the downward direction, as well as the upward. Thus, although we may

[21] See Keynes (1936, p. 307).

observe wage cuts in severe depressions we are unlikely to observe anything like the Phillips pattern in periods of high unemployment.

Considering again the path in terms of Fig. 14.2, suppose that the fall in entrepreneurial expectations takes place when the system is at point *C*. Then the almost immediate cessation of wage increases as a first response to this change implies that the path of the economy will drop towards the horizontal axis almost vertically once at *C*. If, however, not all firms stop granting wage increases at once, e.g. because some firms were in line for a wage increase which they cannot now withhold, the system will follow a steep but downward sloping path such as *CD* before it starts moving towards *A*. Thus this system may generate a cyclical path moving in an anti-clockwise direction independently of wage expectations.

Thus, the dynamics of the system below full employment will be primarily those of the multiplier, with some wage cuts taking place in depressions and some wage increases in the upswing. But once full employment has been reached the Phillips curve will emerge as the predominant dynamic relationship.[22] This coexistence of Keynesian and neoclassical dynamics does not depend on alternative assumptions about household and firm behaviour in and out of full-employment equilibrium. The same optimizing assumptions guide behaviour in both states, but the special features of each state, in particular the existence of *involuntary* unemployment in disequilibrium, make the optimal behaviour different in equilibrium from that in disequilibrium. The outcome of this difference in behaviour is the difference in the dynamic pattern observed in each state. The fundamental assumption guiding behaviour is that firms favour a policy of infrequent wage changes, and that within that system wage increases during a boom take place with less friction than wage cuts during a depression.

That it is optimal to change wages infrequently was argued by both Hicks in the *Theory of Wages* and Keynes in the *General Theory*. But

[22] There are at least two findings in the empirical literature on the Phillips curve which support the views expressed here. First, the rate of change of wage rates is estimated using data from five consecutive quarters in the quarterly data series (Lipsey–Parkin, 1970), and three years in annual data series (Phillips, 1958; Lipsey, 1960), so a policy of infrequent changes in wages may also reveal the pattern if there is low unemployment. Second, the high convexity of the curve to the origin becoming almost horizontal at high unemployment rates, with the rate of change of money wages close to zero, supports the view that the relationship is essentially a feature of full employment, disappearing almost completely at high (involuntary) unemployment levels.

only Keynes developed the short-run dynamic implications of the (fixwage) analysis.[23] It is not surprising therefore that our analysis and Keynes's (in particular chapter 21 of the *General Theory*) have so much in common. Although what has come to be known as the 'Keynesian system', the multiplier process in particular, is peculiar to a less-than-full employment equilibrium, Keynes explicitly recognized that 'if our central controls succeed in establishing an aggregate volume of output corresponding to full employment as nearly as is practicable, the classical theory comes into its own again from this point onwards'.[24] The analysis of this chapter has shown that this claim can be extended beyond the static analysis of value and distribution, to the dynamic analysis of changes in employment, wages and prices.

[23] Hicks also made a beginning (see the second edition of the *Theory of Wages*, 1963) which was to lead to *Value and Capital.* In the event, the dynamic model turned out to be different from that to which the first part of the *Theory of Wages* was leading.

[24] Keynes (1936, p. 378).

15 Conclusion

The economic system is dynamic – one moment ago is history that cannot be undone, and one moment from now is future ridden with uncertainty. This undisputed fact has been, and will always be, common knowledge.

It is precisely because this is so obvious that the abstraction of static and certain economics is so important. Even conceiving of a system where there is no time and no uncertainty, but which is capable of providing solutions for a great variety of problems which arise in a dynamic and uncertain world, is a considerable advance. That that system should reach the degree of elaboration that it has done in the hands of Hicks, Samuelson, Arrow and Debreu is evidence of its significance as the starting point of every major work in economics, critical or otherwise.

The static[1] and certain model of general economic equilibrium is our only major example of what Thomas Kuhn (1962) calls 'paradigm', and the elaborations, extensions and criticisms of that model, as well as the derivation of policy implications and inferences about actual behaviour, is the 'normal-scientific' practice of economics. The most fundamental assumptions of that model are (1) the behaviour of the system depends on the behaviour of the individuals that make up the system, (2) individuals maximize subject to constraint, and (3) prices are always at their full equilibrium value. The most important finding of the model is, ironically, that these assumptions are consistent, i.e. the maximization of utility by households and profit by firms implies that there is a set of prices which, *if attained*, will not be changed again from factors within the system, because at these

[1] Under 'static' we are also including 'metastatic', i.e. the analysis of dynamic problems by assuming that time is one of the characteristics of goods with no further distinguishing features, so the techniques and results of statics apply, with the only difference that the number of 'commodities' is extended. The standard reference is Debreu (1959).

prices every participant in the system will be able to carry out all his desired actions.

Neoclassical economic theory took this finding to imply that we can analyse our economic system by assuming that prices are at their equilibrium value, i.e. that if for any reason actual prices deviate from their equilibrium values they will move quickly back towards equilibrium. Many well-known neoclassical economists, however, have expressed uneasiness about this assumption, whereas some Keynesians have never quite accepted it.[2] In the words of Frank Hahn (1970, p. 12) 'the most intellectually exciting question of our subject remains: is it true that the pursuit of private interest produces not chaos but coherence, and if so, how is it done?' This book was about this 'most intellectually exciting question'.

The problem, of course, has a long history in economics. Clower and Leijonhufvud have convincingly argued that the essence of Keynesian economics is a negative answer to this question. The equilibrium analysis of markets as exercised by neoclassical theory requires an affirmative answer, or at least it needs to show that if the answer is not exactly 'yes' at all times, its results are not too sensitive to small deviations between actual and equilibrium prices. In our analysis of optimizing individual behaviour out of equilibrium we made an attempt to lay the foundations for a more convincing answer to this question, since it is now clear that most of the controversy about it has been carried out on the wrong premises. What we should ask is not 'What type of restrictions on excess demand functions imply that some dynamic process converges to neoclassical equilibrium?' as Samuelson and his followers have done, but: Does reasonable economic behaviour by individuals when prices are out of equilibrium imply that the system will converge to equilibrium? To what equilibrium will it converge? How fast will it converge? And finally, a question which is often neglected but which this study has brought to the forefront: Is it really important that the system does converge to some equilibrium?

It is desirable to know whether optimizing behaviour can lead to the type of equilibrium we normally analyse in economics simply because it is desirable to know whether the type of behaviour we assume in equilibrium *can* lead to that equilibrium. But if we can

[2] See, for instance, Joan Robinson (1971) and Kaldor (1972), and for some recent skepticism in the neoclassical literature see Arrow (1959), Hicks (1965, Part I) and Hahn (1970).

devise an economic model where prices may not be at their equilibrium values, where participants optimize, and which is *capable of giving us the results that we normally get from an equilibrium model*, then the question of the convergence of that model is obsolete, or at best of secondary importance. If we can show that the model is not inherently inconsistent, i.e. that the behaviour of individuals we assume does not lead to the collapse of the model by contradicting the standards of consistency imposed on transactions, then we need not concern ourselves with convergence.

The neoclassical model has shown that if equilibrium is attained it is consistent, i.e. there are no inherent forces which will lead to its destruction. The question of convergence has proved an incurable headache – we do not know whether optimizing individual behaviour can lead the system to equilibrium. The model of this volume has shown that the whole question of convergence (and with it the assumption of full Walrasian equilibrium) may be by-passed. Since, if we assume the absence of equilibrium and analyse individual behaviour along the principles set out by equilibrium economics, we get an inherently consistent dynamic system which is capable of answering the most important questions asked within the equilibrium framework, there is no reason why we should concern ourselves with convergence to equilibrium.[3] And since the new model is capable of giving answers to many questions not asked within the equilibrium framework, there is good reason why we should concern ourselves with the analysis of economic problems within the new framework, rather than devote most of our efforts to mathematical proofs of convergence.

This conclusion, of course, is hardly surprising to anyone familiar with the 'magnificent dynamics' of the trade cycle,[4] although it may seem surprising that we should recommend a return to a methodology which has been attracting more attention from economic historians than theorists for over two decades. Nevertheless, it appears that the difference between a short-run dynamic system such as the one we developed here, and a longer-run one such as the Hicksian or Goodwin

[3] There is, however, at least one question that is left unanswered, and so may justify the concern with neoclassical stability. The neoclassical equilibrium state is the only known system which satisfies the conditions for Pareto optimality, so in cases where policy recommendations rely on the notion of Pareto optimality the proof of convergence of the system becomes fundamental.

[4] See Matthews (1959) for a comprehensive analysis.

cycle models, arises because in the former capital is fixed, whereas in the latter it plays the crucial role in determining the lower and upper turning points.[5] This is also the crucial difference between the short run and the long run in static economics. It appears ironic that we should devote most of our efforts in analysing the short run in static economics, and switch to the long run when we move into dynamics, neglecting completely the short-run questions which take up almost the whole of statical analysis.

The economist who comes into dynamics via the Keynes–Hicks route may think it natural that we should come to the conclusion that the short-run dynamic problems are best analysed within the framework of an optimizing model which has its origins in neoclassical economics, but which makes use of the essential features of the short run and dynamic economics in general – that capital is fixed and that trading takes place sequentially, that the past cannot be undone and the future is uncertain. But one who is bred in the Samuelsonian tradition may still ask, after he is forced to admit that the behaviour of individuals does matter: 'What type of individual behaviour leads to the kind of equilibrium we have been analysing for nearly two centuries?'

The latter question is clearly more important and more faithful to normal-scientific economics than the Samuelsonian 'What types of restrictions on excess-demand functions ensure stability?'[6] But the most important question to emerge from the present analysis is: How does a short-run dynamic system behave when individuals optimize irrespective of whether the market is in or out of equilibrium? This last question is the one that should attract most of future research in this area. In this book we made a beginning, although it was a beginning more at asking the right questions than at providing the answers. Asking the right question is often more important than answering it, or at least it is logically prior to it. The Hicksian and Keynesian dynamic analyses have gone some way towards asking the right question, but the Samuelsonian analysis which overrode them has, unfortunately, asked the wrong question.

[5] The methodology of the von Neumann growth model is also similar with that of the cycle models, although there has been considerable shift of emphasis in the types of problems analysed. On this see Hicks (1965) and Morishima (1968).

[6] Recently there has been some work on the former question and it has produced some interesting results. See the survey by Rothschild (1973) and footnote 3 of chapter 1 for more references.

References

Abbreviations:

AER	American Economic Review
EJ	Economic Journal
Ec	Economica
Em	Econometrica
IER	International Economic Review
JPE	Journal of Political Economy
JET	Journal of Economic Theory
QJE	Quarterly Journal of Economics
RES	Review of Economic Studies

Alchian, A. A. 1950, 'Uncertainty, Evolution, and Economic Theory', *JPE*, **58**, pp. 211–21.

1970, 'Information Costs, Pricing, and Resource Unemployment', in E. S. Phelps *et al.*, *Microeconomic Foundations of Employment and Inflation Theory*, New York: Norton.

Alderfer, C. P. and Bierman, H. 1970, 'Choices with Risk: Beyond the Mean and Variance', *Journal of Business*, **43**, pp. 341–53.

Allingham, M. G. and Morishima, M. 1973, 'Veblen Effects and Portfolio Selection', in M. Morishima and others, *Theory of Demand: Real and Monetary*, Oxford: Clarendon.

Arrow, K. J. 1953, 'Le Rôle des Valeurs Boursières pour la Répartition la Meilleur des Risques', *Econométrie*, Paris, Centre National de la Recherche Scientifique, pp. 41–8 (or see the translation, 'The Role of Securities in the Optimal Allocation of Risk Bearing', *RES*, **31**, 1964, pp. 91–6).

1959, 'Toward a Theory of Price Adjustment', in M. Abramovitz *et al.*, *The Allocation of Economic Resources*, Stanford, Cal.: Stanford University Press.

1965, 'The Theory of Risk Aversion', in K. J. Arrow, *Aspects of the Theory of Risk-Bearing*, Helsinki: Yrjo Jahnssoninsaatio.

Arrow, K. J. and Hahn, F. H. 1971, *General Competitive Analysis*, San Francisco: Holden–Day.

Barro, R. J. and Grossman, H. I. 1971, 'A General Disequilibrium Model of Income and Employment', *AER*, **61**, pp. 82–93.

Barzel, Y. and McDonald, R. J. 1973, 'Assets, Subsistence, and the Supply Curve of Labor', *AER*, **63**, pp. 621–33.

Becker, G. S. 1964, *Human Capital*, New York: NBER, Columbia Univ. Press.

1965, 'A Theory of the Allocation of Time', *EJ*, **75**, pp. 493–517.

References

Bellman, R. E. 1957, *Dynamic Programming*, Princeton, N.J.: Princeton Univ. Press.

Blaug, M. 1968, *Economics of Education 1*, London: Penguin Books.

Borch, K. 1968, 'Economic Equilibrium under Uncertainty', *IER*, **9**, pp. 339–47.

Bowen, W. G. and Finegan, T. A. 1969, *The Economics of Labor Force Participation*, Princeton, N.J.: Princeton Univ. Press.

Bowers, J. 1970, 'The Anatomy of Regional Activity Rates', in NIESR, Regional Papers I, Cambridge Univ. Press.

Brechling, F. P. R., 1965, 'The Relationship between Output and Employment in British Manufacturing Industries', *RES*, **32**, pp. 187–216.

1968, 'The Trade-Off between Inflation and Unemployment', *JPE*, **76**, pp. 712–37.

Cagan, P. H. 1956, 'The Monetary Dynamics of Hyperinflation', in M. Friedman, ed., *Studies in the Quantity Theory of Money*, Chicago: Chicago Univ. Press.

Chapman, S. J. 1909, 'Hours of Labour', *EJ*, **19**, pp. 353–73.

Clower, R. W. 1965, 'The Keynesian Counter-Revolution: A Theoretical Appraisal', in F. H. Hahn and F. P. R. Brechling, eds., *The Theory of Interest Rates*, IEA, London: Macmillan.

1967, 'A Reconsideration of the Microfoundations of Monetary Theory', *Western Economic Journal*, **6**, pp. 1–9.

Corina, J. 1972, *Labour Market Economics*, London: Heinemann.

Corry, B. A. and Roberts, J. A. 1970, 'Activity Rates and Unemployment: The Experience of the United Kingdom 1951–1966', *Applied Economics*, **2**, pp. 179–201.

Craine, R. 1973, 'On the Service Flow from Labour', *RES*, **40**, pp. 39–46.

Cripps, T. F. and Tarling, R. J. 1974, 'An Analysis of the Duration of Male Unemployment in the U.K., 1932–73', *EJ*, **84**, pp. 289–316.

Cyert, R. M. and March, J. G. 1963, *A Behavioral Theory of the Firm*, Englewood Cliffs, N.J.: Prentice-Hall.

Debreu, G. 1959, *Theory of Value*, New York: Wiley.

Diamond, P. A. 1971, 'A Model of Price Adjustment', *JET*, **3**, pp. 156–68.

Feldstein, M. S. 1967, 'Specification of the Labour Input in the Aggregate Production Function', *RES*, **34**, pp. 375–86.

Ferguson, C. E. 1969, *The Neoclassical Theory of Production and Distribution*, Cambridge: Cambridge Univ. Press.

Fisher, F. M. 1970, 'Quasi-competitive Price Adjustment by Individual Firms: A Preliminary Paper', *JET*, **2**, pp. 195–206.

1972, 'On Price Adjustment without an Auctioneer', *RES*, **39**, pp. 1–15.

1973, 'Stability and Competitive Equilibrium in Two Models of Search and Individual Price Adjustment', *JET*, **6**, pp. 446–69.

Fisher, M. R. 1969, *The Economic Analysis of Labour*, London: Weidenfeld and Nicolson.

Fowler, R. F. 1968, *Duration of Unemployment on the Register of Wholly Unemployed*, Studies in Official Statistics, Research Series No. 1, London: HMSO.

Friedman, J. W. 1971, 'A Non-cooperative View of Oligopoly', *IER*, **12**, pp. 106–22.

1973, 'On Reaction Function Equilibria', *IER*, **14**, pp. 721–34.

Friedman, M. 1957, *A Theory of the Consumption Function*, Princeton, N.J.: Princeton Univ. Press.

1968, 'The Role of Monetary Policy', *AER*, **58**, pp. 1–17.

Gronau, R. 1971, 'Information and Frictional Unemployment', *AER*, **61**, pp. 290–301.

Gujarati, D. 1972, 'The Behaviour of Unemployment and Unfilled Vacancies: Great Britain, 1958–1971', *EJ*, **82**, pp. 195–204.
Hadar, J. and Russell, W. R. 1969, 'Rules for Ordering Uncertain Prospects', *AER*, **59**, pp. 25–34.
Hahn, F. H. 1965, 'On Some Problems of Proving the Existence of an Equilibrium in a Monetary Economy', in F. H. Hahn and F. P. R. Brechling, eds., *The Theory of Interest Rates, IEA*, London: Macmillan.
1970, 'Some Adjustment Problems', *Em*, **38**, pp. 1–17.
Hahn, F. H. and Brechling, F. P. R. 1965, *The Theory of Interest Rates, IEA*, London: Macmillan.
Hakansson, N. H. 1970, 'Optimal Investment and Consumption Strategies under Risk for a Class of Utility Functions', *Em*, **38**, pp. 587–607.
Hanoch, G. and Levy, H. 1969, 'The Efficiency Analysis of Choices Involving Risk', *RES*, **36**, pp. 335–46.
Hayek, F. A. 1937, 'Economics and Knowledge', *Ec*, **4**, pp. 33–54.
Hicks, J. R. 1932, *Theory of Wages*, London: Macmillan (Reprinted in 2nd ed., 1963).
1946, *Value and Capital*, 2nd ed., Oxford: Clarendon.
1965, *Capital and Growth*, Oxford: Clarendon.
Holt, C. C. 1970, 'Job Search, Phillips' Wage Relation, and Union Influence: Theory and Evidence', in E. S. Phelps *et al.*, *Microeconomic Foundations of Employment and Inflation Theory*, New York: Norton.
Howitt, P. W. 1974, 'Stability and the Quantity Theory', *JPE*, **82**, pp. 133–51.
Hutt, W. H. 1939, *The Theory of Idle Resources*, London: Jonathan Cape.
Johansen, L. 1972, *Production Functions*, Amsterdam: North-Holland.
Kaldor, N. 1972, 'The Irrelevance of Equilibrium Economics', *EJ*, **82**, pp. 1237–55.
Karlin, S. 1962, 'Stochastic Models and Optimal Policy for Selling an Asset', in K. J. Arrow, S. Karlin and H. Scarf, eds., *Studies in Applied Probability and Management Science*, Stanford, Cal.: Stanford Univ. Press.
Kasper, H. 1967, 'The Asking Price of Labor and the Duration of Unemployment', *Review of Economics and Statistics*, **49**, pp. 165–72.
Keynes, J. M. 1930, *A Treatise on Money*, London: Macmillan.
1936, *The General Theory of Employment, Interest and Money*, London: Macmillan.
Knight, F. H. 1921, *Risk, Uncertainty and Profit*, Boston: Houghton Mifflin.
Kohn, M. G. and Shavell, S. 1974, 'The Theory of Search', *JET*, **9**, pp. 93–123.
Koopmans, T. C. 1957, *Three Essays on the State of Economic Science*, New York: McGraw-Hill.
Kuhn, T. S. 1962, *The Structure of Scientific Revolutions*, Chicago: Chicago Univ. Press.
Lancaster, K. J. 1966, 'A New Approach to Consumer Theory', *JPE*, **74**, pp. 132–57.
Leijonhufvud, A. 1968, *On Keynesian Economics and the Economics of Keynes*, New York: Oxford Univ. Press.
Leland, H. 1968, 'Savings and Uncertainty: The Precautionary Demand for Saving', *QJE*, **82**, pp. 465–75.
Lipsey, R. G. 1960, 'The Relation between Unemployment and the Rate of Change of Money Wages in the United Kingdom, 1862–1957: A Further Analysis', *Ec*, **27**, pp. 1–31.
Lipsey, R. G. and Parkin, J. M. 1970, 'Incomes Policy: A Reappraisal', *Ec*, **37**, pp. 115–38.

Lluch, C. and Morishima, M. 1973, 'Demand for Commodities under Uncertain Expectations', in M. Morishima and others, *Theory of Demand: Real and Monetary*, Oxford: Clarendon.

Lucas, R. E. and Prescott, E. C. 1974, 'Equilibrium Search and Unemployment', *JET*, **7**, pp. 188–209.

McCall, J. J. 1970, 'Economics of Information and Job Search', *QJE*, **84**, pp. 113–26.

MacKay, D. I. 1972*a* 'After the "Shake-Out"', *Oxford Economic Papers*, **24**, pp. 89–110.

1972*b*, 'Redundancy and Re-engagement: A Study of Car Workers', *Manchester School*, **40**, pp. 295–312.

MacKay, D. I. and Reid, G. L. 1972, 'Redundancy, Unemployment and Manpower Policy', *EJ*, **82**, pp. 1256–72.

Markowitz, H. M. 1959, *Portfolio Selection*, New York: Wiley.

Marschak, J. and Radner, R. 1972, *Economic Theory of Teams*, Cowles Foundation Monograph 22, Yale Univ. Press.

Marshall, A. 1920, *Principles of Economics*, 8th ed. London: Macmillan (page references from post-1949 reprints).

Matthews, R. C. O. 1959, *The Trade Cycle*, Cambridge: Cambridge Univ. Press.

Mayer, T. 1972, *Permanent Income, Wealth and Consumption: A Critique of the Permanent Income Theory, the Life-Cycle Hypothesis, and Related Theories*, Berkeley and Los Angeles: University of California Press.

Mincer, J. 1965, 'Labor-Force Participation and Unemployment: A Review of Recent Evidence', in R. A. Gordon and M. S. Gordon, eds., *Prosperity and Unemployment*, New York: Wiley.

Modigliani, F. and Brumberg, R. 1954, 'Utility Analysis and the Consumption Function: An Interpretation of Cross-Section Data', in K. Kurihara, ed., *Post Keynesian Economics*, New Brunswick, N.J.

Morishima, M. 1968, *Theory of Economic Growth*, Oxford: Clarendon.

Mortensen, D. T. 1970*a*, 'A Theory of Wage and Employment Dynamics', in E. S. Phelps *et al.*, *Microeconomic Foundations of Employment and Inflation Theory*, New York: Norton.

1970*b*, 'Job Search, the Duration of Unemployment, and the Phillips Curve', *AER*, **60**, pp. 847–62.

Mossin, J. 1969, 'A Note on Uncertainty and Preferences in a Temporal Context', *AER*, **59**, pp. 172–74.

Negishi, T. 1962, 'The Stability of a Competitive Economy: A Survey Article', *Em*, **30**, pp. 635–69.

1965, 'Market Clearing Processes in a Monetary Economy' in F. H. Hahn and F. P. R. Brechling, eds., *The Theory of Interest Rates*, IEA, London: Macmillan.

Oi, W. 1962, 'Labor as a Quasi-fixed Factor', *JPE*, **70**, pp. 538–55.

Ostroy, J. M. 1973, 'The Informational Efficiency of Monetary Exchange', *AER*, **63**, pp. 597–610.

Papandreou, A. G. 1952, 'Some Basic Problems in the Theory of the Firm', in B. F. Haley, ed., *A Survey of Contemporary Economics*, Homewood, Ill: Irwin.

Parsons, D. O. 1973, 'Quit Rates Over Time: A Search and Information Approach', *AER*, **63**, pp. 390–401.

Patinkin, D. 1965, *Money, Interest and Prices*, 2nd ed., New York: Harper and Row.

Phelps, E. S. 1962, 'The Accumulation of Risky Capital: A Sequential Utility Analysis', *Em*, **30**, pp. 729–43.

1967, 'Phillips Curves, Expectations of Inflation and Optimal Unemployment Over Time', *Ec*, **34**, pp. 254–81.

1969, 'The New Microeconomics of Inflation and Employment Theory', *AER*, *Pap. Proc.* **59**, pp. 147–60.

1970, 'Money Wage Dynamics and Labor Market Equilibrium', in E. S. Phelps *et al.*, *Microeconomic Foundations of Employment and Inflation Theory*, New York: Norton.

Phelps, E. S. *et al.*, 1970, *Microeconomic Foundations of Employment and Inflation Theory*, New York: Norton.

Phelps-Brown, E. H., 1962, *The Economics of Labor*, New Haven: Yale Univ. Press.

Phillips, A. W. 1958, 'The Relation between Unemployment and the Rate of Change of Money Wage Rates in the U.K. 1861–1957', *Ec*, **25**, pp. 283–99.

Pissarides, C. A. 1974, 'Risk, Job Search, and Income Distribution', *JPE*, **82**, pp. 1255–67.

Pratt, J. W. 1964, 'Risk Aversion in the Small and in the Large', *Em*, **32**, pp. 122–36.

Radner, R. 1968, 'Competitive Equilibrium under Uncertainty', *Em*, **36**, pp. 31–58.

1970, 'Problems in the Theory of Markets under Uncertainty', *AER*, *Pap. Proc.*, **60**, pp. 454–60.

Reddy, B. 1971, 'Choice of Assets under Uncertainty: A Generalised Approach', Univ. of Essex Discussion Paper No. 33.

Reder, M. W. 1955, 'The Theory of Occupational Wage Differentials', *AER*, **45**, pp. 833–52.

1969, 'The Theory of Frictional Unemployment', *Ec*, **36**, pp. 1–28.

Rees, A. E. 1966, 'Information Networks in Labor Markets', *AER*, *Pap. Proc.*, **56**, pp. 560–66.

Reid, G. L. 1972, 'Job Search and the Effectiveness of Job-Finding Methods', *Industrial and Labor Relations Review*, **25**, pp. 479–95.

Reynolds, L. G. 1948, 'Toward a Short-Run Theory of Wages', *AER*, **38**, pp. 289–308.

Robbins, L. 1930, 'On the Elasticity of Demand for Income in Terms of Effort', *Ec* (old series), **29**, pp. 123–29.

Robinson, J. 1971, *Economic Heresies: Some Old-Fashioned Questions in Economic Theory*, New York: Basic Books.

Rothschild, M. 1973, 'Models of Market Organization with Imperfect Information: A Survey', *JPE*, **81**, pp. 1283–1308.

1974*a*, 'A Two-Armed Bandit Theory of Market Pricing', *JET*, **9**, pp. 185–202.

1974*b*, 'Searching for the Lowest Price When the Distribution of Prices is Unknown', *JPE*, **82**, pp. 689–711.

Rothschild, M. and Stiglitz, J. E. 1970, 'Increasing Risk: I. A Definition', *JET*, **2**, pp. 225–43.

1971, 'Increasing Risk II: Its Economic Consequences, *JET*, **3**, pp. 66–84.

Salop, S. C. 1973*a*, 'Systematic Job Search and Unemployment', *RES*, **40**, pp. 191–201.

1973*b*, 'Wage Differentials in a Dynamic Theory of the Firm', *JET*, **6**, pp. 321–44.

Salter, W. E. G. 1960, *Production and Technical Change*, London: Cambridge Univ. Press.

Samuelson, P. A. 1947, *Foundations of Economic Analysis*, Cambridge, Mass: Harvard Univ. Press.

Sandmo, A. 1969, 'Capital Risk, Consumption, and Portfolio Choice', *Em*, **37**, pp. 586–99.

1970, 'The Effect of Uncertainty on Saving Decisions', *RES*, **37**, pp. 353–60.

Simon, H. A. 1959, 'Theories of Decision-Making in Economics and Behavioral Science', *AER*, **49**, pp. 253–83.

Smith, A. 1776, *An Inquiry into the Nature and Causes of the Wealth of Nations* (page references from the 6th ed. by E. Cannan, London: Methuen, 1950).

Smolinski, L. 1973, 'Karl Marx and Mathematical Economics', *JPE*, **81**, pp. 1189–204.

Spence, M. 1973, 'Job Market Signaling', *QJE*, **87**, pp. 355–74.

Spence, M. and Zeckhauser, R. 1972. 'The Effect of the Timing of Consumption Decisions and the Resolution of Lotteries on the Choice of Lotteries', *Em*, **40**, pp. 401–3.

Stein, R. L. 1960, 'Unemployment and Job Mobility', *Monthly Labour Review*, **83**, pp. 350–8.

Stigler, G. J. 1961, 'The Economics of Information', *JPE*, **69**, pp. 213–25.

1962, 'Information in the Labor Market', *JPE*, **70**, pp. 94–105.

Stiglitz, J. E. 1974, 'Equilibrium Wage Distributions', Cowles Foundation Discussion Paper No. 375.

Thirwall, A. P. 1969, 'Types of Unemployment: With Special Reference to 'Non Demand-Deficient' Unemployment in Great Britain', *Scottish JPE*, **16**, pp. 20–49.

Tobin, J. 1972, 'Inflation and Unemployment', *AER*, **62**, pp. 1–18.

Tsiang, S. C. 1972, 'The Rationale of the Mean-Standard Deviation Analysis, Skewness Preference, and the Demand for Money', *AER*, **62**, pp. 354–71.

Whipple, D. 1973, 'A Generalized Theory of Job Search', *JPE*, **81**, pp. 1170–88.

Williamson, O. E. 1967, *The Economics of Discretionary Behavior: Managerial Objectives in a Theory of the Firm*, Englewood Cliffs, N.J.: Prentice-Hall.

Winter, S. G. 1971, 'Satisficing, Selection, and the Innovating Remnant', *QJE*, **85**, pp. 237–61.

Index

Index

Index